Slavery, Capitalism, and
Women's Literature

Gender and Slavery

SERIES EDITORS

Daina Ramey Berry, *University of Texas at Austin*
Jennifer L. Morgan, *New York University*

ADVISORY BOARD

Edward E. Baptist, *Cornell University*
Kristen Block, *University of Tennessee, Knoxville*
Sherwin Bryant, *Northwestern University*
Camillia Cowling, *University of Warwick*
Aisha Finch, *University of California, Los Angeles*
Marisa J. Fuentes, *Rutgers University*
Leslie M. Harris, *Northwestern University*
Tera Hunter, *Princeton University*
Wilma King, *University of Missouri*
Barbara Krauthamer, *University of Massachusetts, Amherst*
Tiya Miles, *Harvard University*
Melanie Newton, *University of Toronto*
Rachel O'Toole, *University of California, Irvine*
Diana Paton, *Newcastle University*
Adam Rothman, *Georgetown University*
Brenda E. Stevenson, *University of California, Los Angeles*

Slavery, Capitalism, and Women's Literature

ECONOMIC INSIGHTS OF
AMERICAN WOMEN WRITERS,
1852–1869

Kristin Allukian

The University of Georgia Press
ATHENS

© 2023 by the University of Georgia Press
Athens, Georgia 30602
www.ugapress.org
All rights reserved
Designed by Kaelin Chappell Broaddus
Set in 10.5/13.5 Garamond Premier Pro Regular
by Kaelin Chappell Broaddus

Most University of Georgia Press titles are
available from popular e-book vendors.

Printed digitally

Library of Congress Cataloging-in-Publication Data

Names: Allukian, Kristin, author.
Title: Slavery, capitalism, and women's literature : economic insights of American women writers, 1852–1869 / Kristin Allukian.
Description: Athens : The University of Georgia Press, [2023] | Series: Gender and slavery | Includes bibliographical references and index. |
Identifiers: LCCN 2022058138 (print) | LCCN 2022058139 (ebook) | ISBN 9780820364605 (hardback) | ISBN 9780820364599 (paperback) | ISBN 9780820364612 (epub) | ISBN 9780820364629 (pdf)
Subjects: LCSH: Stowe, Harriet Beecher, 1811–1896. Uncle Tom's cabin. | Larcom, Lucy, 1824–1893. Weaving. | Jacobs, Harriet A. (Harriet Ann) Incidents in the life of a slave girl. | Harper, Frances Ellen Watkins, 1825–1911. Minnie's sacrifice. | Slavery in literature. | Capitalism in literature. | LCGFT: Literary criticism.
Classification: LCC PS2954.U6 A45 2023 (print) | LCC PS2954.U6 (ebook) | DDC 810.9/3553—dc23/eng/20230411
LC record available at https://lccn.loc.gov/2022058138
LC ebook record available at https://lccn.loc.gov/2022058139

To my mother

CONTENTS

ACKNOWLEDGMENTS

xi

INTRODUCTION
Nineteenth-Century Women Writers
and the Slavery and Capitalism Debates

1

CHAPTER 1
Accounting for Harriet Beecher Stowe's
Uncle Tom's Cabin

21

CHAPTER 2
Slavery's Cotton Market in Lucy Larcom's "Weaving"

57

CHAPTER 3
Property Knowledge in Harriet Jacobs's
Incidents in the Life of a Slave Girl

85

CHAPTER 4
Reconstruction's Inheritance in
Frances Ellen Watkins Harper's *Minnie's Sacrifice*

117

EPILOGUE

149

NOTES
161

BIBLIOGRAPHY
183

INDEX
201

ACKNOWLEDGMENTS

FIRST AND FOREMOST, my deepest appreciation goes to my mother, Ruth Allukian, who offered me unconditional love, encouragement, and support. Her faith in me sustained me throughout the lifetime of this project. Without her, this book would not exist.

One of the best parts of writing this book was the wonderful colleagues I was able to think and work with along the way. I was incredibly fortunate to be part of a supportive writing group with Faith Barter, R. J. Boutelle, Monica Mercado, and Alice Rutkowski. I am grateful for their individual and collective wisdom and their many readings of my drafts. They challenged me and cheered for me, and they made me a better thinker and writer. I extend heartfelt thanks to Eric Gardner for conferencing with me several times to discuss Frances Harper and her novel *Minnie's Sacrifice*. I'm very appreciative of his knowledge and expertise and willingness to share both. Many, many thanks to Robin Muller for her sharp intellectual and philosophical insights and her illuminating conversations. Every exchange with Robin, no matter how big or small, helped refine my own thoughts and push my arguments and my project forward. My sincere thanks to Ed White. I met Ed as a graduate student and ever since have benefited from his deep literary, historical, and theoretical knowledge and his support of my career, no matter distance or time. This book is better because of him. Small group meetings with Shirley Samuels and Brigitte Fielder helped me think through future directions for the book, and our conversations played in my mind as the project progressed. I was fortunate to workshop my book with them both at a crucial moment in the project. LuElla D'Amico, R. J. Ellis, Faye Halpern, and James Huston read sections and chapters at varying stages. They asked questions, offered feedback, and engaged me in dialogue that moved my writing forward.

My most sincere appreciation and gratitude goes to Nathaniel Holly, my editor at the University of Georgia Press. A first-time book author could not ask for a better editor. I have so much to thank him for. He saw the potential of my project early on and supported my project fully throughout the entire process, guiding me through each step with extraordinary graciousness and professionalism. Sincere thanks also to the three anonymous reviewers who read on behalf of the University of Georgia Press; their detailed attention and valuable feedback helped move my project forward to completion.

I extend appreciation to all my colleagues in the English Department at the University of South Florida (USF) for giving me a departmental and institutional home. I'm thankful to my chair, Lisa Melonçon, for her guidance and support, especially through the difficult and uncertain period of the COVID-19 pandemic. Debra Garcia, the academic services administrator for the Department of English, was a tremendous help to me throughout this project, and I'm grateful for her administrative support. I'm especially thankful for my USF colleagues who offered friendship and support: Ylce Irizarry, Meredith Johnson, Nate Johnson, Jarod Roselló, and Heather Sellers. The USF library staff, especially Cynthia Brown and LeEtta James, helped me access much-needed books and other resources in a timely manner. I was fortunate to receive financial support for this project in the form of two summer research grants from the USF Humanities Institute, headed by Liz Kicak, and a McKnight Junior Faculty Development Fellowship from the Florida Education Fund.

The Society for the Study of American Women Writers (SSAWW) is an organization that has truly given me an academic home. I am so grateful for the support of colleagues I've met through SSAWW, including LuElla D'Amico, Brianne Jaquette, Kristin Jacobson, Greg Spector, Ana Stevenson, Arielle Zibrak, and the many others I have met at conferences, regional meetings, and online.

I am grateful for friends who were by my side from the very beginning of this project. No person was more at the beginning than Mauro Carassai, who I met the first day of graduate school—every laugh and conversation we have shared since then has been a special one. Tamar Ditzian's friendship has buoyed me over the course of my career, since our graduate school days and beyond. At USF, I was incredibly fortunate to have a friend and colleague in Ylce Irizarry. I am appreciative of her sage advice, fierce intellect, and generosity of spirit. Sincere thanks to R. J. Ellis who has supported, encouraged, and motivated me over the course of my career. Many thanks to Emily Murphy for her generous advice and encouragement at every turn.

My final acknowledgments go to my family. I am especially appreciative of my sisters and brothers for being daily sources of inspiration, support, love, and laughter. My deepest love and gratitude goes to my grandmother, M. Louise

Losco: her words of encouragement were the final push that convinced me to pursue a PhD, though she passed away before I was able to tell her that. Her spirit stays with me always. Most of all, I am eternally thankful to my parents, Myron and Ruth, for teaching me the importance of perseverance. This book is for them.

Slavery, Capitalism, and
Women's Literature

INTRODUCTION

Nineteenth-Century Women Writers and the Slavery and Capitalism Debates

SCHOLARS HAVE LONG DEBATED the relationship between slavery and capitalism. But, from the beginning of the slavery and capitalism debates to their most recent iteration, nineteenth-century women's literature is rarely referenced. When it is, it is typically referenced as the popular novel or poetry of the day, or by way of the author's abolitionism or reform activism. Rarely, however, is women's literature, as such, cited because it specifically holds a woman's perspective on the economic debate. Yet economic concerns about slavery and capitalism permeate women's writing. The questions then arise: Where does nineteenth-century women's literature fit into the scholarly conversation about slavery and capitalism? What gets lost when we overlook women's voices as part of this conversation? And what is the contribution, moreover, of women's literature in particular? This book answers these questions.

Slavery, Capitalism, and Women's Literature: Economic Insights of American Women Writers, 1852–1869 explores the intersections between slavery, capitalism, and women's literature, expanding the existing canon of slavery and capitalism scholarship by adding the voices of some of the nineteenth-century's best-known women writers. The significance of the study is, however, not intended to be merely additive. Women's literature, I argue, offers previously unconsidered economic insights into the relationship between slavery and capitalism and about the developing nineteenth-century capitalist economy in the United States. In their own time, these writers' insights were prescient, political, and persuasive. And the stories through which they narrated their insights are crucial to the story we tell today about the relationship between slavery and capitalism. Without them, our national narrative is incomplete.

This book examines literary works by Harriet Beecher Stowe, Lucy Larcom, Harriet Jacobs, and Frances Ellen Watkins Harper. These four authors understood that making sense of the nation's evolving economy, politics, and culture, and woman's place in those arenas, called for gendered accounts of the relationship between slavery and capitalism. Writing from their various subject positions, as middle- or working-class white women and enslaved or free Black women, the question for each of these writers was not *whether* slavery and capitalism were linked, as the question would later become, but rather *how*. They published written accounts, often eyewitness, of the very continuities that twenty-first-century scholars are currently documenting: between language and activism, sentimentalism and accounting, labor and manufacturing technology, race and property, and inheritance and reparations. Their texts challenge assumptions about capitalism as a purely public enterprise—and nineteenth-century economic discourse, critique, and theory in American literature as the domain of men or even male-defined—and show how slavery and capitalism appeared in the intimate spaces of women's everyday lives.

In their own time, women's literature created forums that documented data, stimulated debate, generated resistance, and imagined alternatives to what historians Sven Beckert and Seth Rockman today call "slavery's capitalism," a term that foregrounds slavery as the engine of nineteenth-century U.S. capitalist development. Because "slavery's capitalism" is central to my book, I spend a moment here explaining to what end I use the term. According to Beckert and Rockman, the phrase emphasizes how "slavery became central to and perhaps even constitutive of a particular moment in the history of capitalism" (10). In this way, the term is useful to my study because, in its construction, it serves as an effective reminder that understandings of U.S. slavery and U.S. capitalism must always be in conjunction with one another, and that slavery's capitalism, as a singular concept, uniquely contributed to U.S. economic development. It must be noted, with these understandings in mind, that when I discuss the "relationship between slavery and capitalism" in women's literature, I do so not to suggest slavery and capitalism as two discrete entities that have a relationship with one another. Rather, I do so to tease out the particular ways in which women writers already understood and were then documenting and responding to slavery as central to and constitutive of the mid-nineteenth century's evolving capitalist system. To this end, when I use Beckert and Rockman's term "slavery's capitalism" in my own analysis of women's economic critique, I refer to all that their explanation encompasses, including, for example, slavery's fundamental role in the advancement of arenas such as finance, accounting, management, and technology. In this sense, I use the term to illuminate the continuities between slavery and capitalism that nineteenth-century women writers documented in their fiction and nonfiction.

But I also expand its functionality beyond its original implications. Because slavery's capitalism was an incredibly pervasive system that seeped into every aspect of nineteenth-century life and culture, I extend the term to include the way it appears in the everyday lives of women, as taken up in women's literature. More specifically, I understand the term as one that is intimately intertwined with gender, domesticity, and sentimentality, both as sites from which women writers theorized and critiqued slavery's capitalism and as concepts that were co-constituted alongside slavery's capitalism.

To theorize the appearance of slavery's capitalism in women's lives and literature and to critique the logics of its economics, nineteenth-century abolitionist women writers, I argue, took a developing language of capitalist critique and insightfully saw its relevance for critiquing slavery. By understanding women's writing in this way, my study reverses the traditional analytic that critics have used to explore nineteenth-century rhetoric around slavery and capitalism. That is, previous critics have documented the ways in which nineteenth-century writers, especially in the second half of the century, used the language of slavery to critique industrial capitalism. Alternatively, this book, through close readings of four key texts—Stowe's *Uncle Tom's Cabin* (1852), Larcom's "Weaving" (1868), Jacobs's *Incidents in the Life of a Slave Girl* (1861), and Harper's *Minnie's Sacrifice* (1869)—documents how women writers used a developing language of capitalism to critique slavery. Recognizing this, my aim is not, therefore, just to situate women as participants in the economic discourse around slavery's capitalism but rather to reinstate them as writers who contributed to that discourse all along.

LYDIA MARIA CHILD'S PATHBREAKING *APPEAL*

Although this book focuses on some of the best-known nineteenth-century women writers and texts, all of which were published in the middle decades of the nineteenth-century, abolitionist women writers offered economic observations and critiques of slavery's capitalism much earlier in the century. An emblematic example is Lydia Maria Child and her 1833 *An Appeal in Favor of That Class of Americans Called Africans*. Across 230 pages and eight methodically laid out and thoroughly researched chapters, Child attacks the institution of slavery from all angles—historical, economic, political, and social—and calls for the immediate emancipation and full inclusion of African Americans in all aspects of American life. "Organized with flawless logic," as Child's biographer Carolyn L. Karcher describes it, "the book moves from past to present, from history to political economy, from fact to argument, from problem to solution" (184).

The moment in which Child was writing *An Appeal* was a crucial one for the abolitionist movement. According to historian Paul Goodman, it was in the early 1830s that the movement began to gain momentum and took one of its most decisive turns; spurred primarily by the free Black community as well as increasing religious factions and women's activism (xiii–xvi), the Garrisonian-led movement converted to the more radically antiracist mission of immediate abolitionism. Economic discourse and critique was an important part of this momentum, as Goodman notes: "a critical view of the market revolution was central to the rise of the antislavery movement" (xvi). Lydia Maria Child's *Appeal*, with its extensive economic critique of slavery, became "one of the founding texts of the movement" (57). Karcher also marks *An Appeal* as a monumental achievement of historical scholarship at the time it was published, writing that it "provided the abolitionist movement with its first full-scale analysis of the slavery question. Indeed, so comprehensive was its scope that no other antislavery writer ever attempted to duplicate Child's achievement" (183). Writing in the crucial early years of the 1830s, right before the height of the movement in the middle and later part of that decade, Child's *Appeal*, then, was on the cusp of a major U.S. cultural transformation—and central to it. Given this broader historical context, it is worth underlining at least three striking features of Child's work as an early example of women's writing that participated in the slavery and capitalism conversations of its day.

First, the philosophy behind Child's attempt to offer a broad and sweeping overview is exceptionally comprehensive and deeply nuanced. She begins the text with a history of American slavery as far back as 1442 and offers a comparative analysis of slavery across different time periods and nations. Having situated U.S. slavery in a global context, she moves to contemporary U.S. political and economic arguments against slavery in the third and fourth chapters. She then turns more acutely to an analysis of the debates around gradual versus immediate emancipation, and finally, across the last three chapters, ends *An Appeal* by confronting racist myths around the "intellect" (140) and "moral character" (168) of people of African descent and calling on a "union of individual influence" (206) among the reading public to redirect its efforts, "produce an entire revolution of public feeling" (206), and abolish slavery. Arguably, Child's *Appeal* is the first scholarly American history of U.S. slavery, one that also speaks directly to slavery's economic dimensions. The kind of detailed attention Child gives to all aspects of slavery—and especially its economics—and her insistence on situating U.S. slavery in a global context anticipates the studies conducted by historians of slavery in the twentieth and twenty-first centuries. One might argue, in fact, that today's historians are returning to the kind of comprehensive format that Child laid out in 1833. Yet Child herself is rarely cited in these histories, and *An Appeal* even less so—its disappearance from the canon of slavery and capitalism literature best understood as a consequence of the nineteenth- and twentieth-century masculinization of the history and economics fields.[1]

Second, Child is an early example of an author who took a developing language of capitalist critique and, with striking clarity, applied it to her critique of slavery. Throughout *An Appeal*, Child's scholarly history of slavery is contoured by economic discourse that foregrounds the continuities between U.S. slavery and U.S. capitalism. This is especially clear in chapters 3 and 4, respectively titled "Free Labor and Slave Labor—Possibility of Safe Emancipation" and "Influence of Slavery on the Politics of the United States." In these chapters, Child offers similar critiques to those made more recently by historians of slavery and capitalism. For example, she references slavery's "overseers" as a kind of middle management (114). She discusses the influence of slavery's economics on the government's application of direct taxes, duties, and national debt (99–102, 110–13). She notes that the "great proportion of [southerners'] plantations are deeply mortgaged in New-York and Philadelphia" (105) and theorizes how underwriters adjusted their rates of insurance (108). She compares the profitability of agricultural capitalism with mercantile capitalism and includes the manufacturing and maritime industries in her analysis (107). And she cites books and speeches by others who indict "merchants, capitalists, bankers, and all other people not planters, as so many robbers, who live by plundering the slave-owner, apparently forgetting by what plunder they themselves live" (114). In addition to documenting economic insights of slavery's capitalism gleaned from her own study of it, Child's *Appeal* also engaged in theoretical economic discourse to make sense of slavery's economic logics. Child draws, for example, from Adam Smith and his conception of capitalism's foundation, the self-interest of the entrepreneur, and alludes to what would later become known as Karl Marx's theory of estranged labor. In her discussion of enslaved versus waged labor she argues for "high" wages according to socialist thought, running parallel to socialist forerunners like Charles Fourier, and his theory of "harmonious order," and Pierre-Joseph Proudhon, who demonstrated that even equality of wages would not solve the problem of the worker. This is to say, Child's histories, analyses, and denouncements of slavery were profoundly engaged with economic discourse and capitalist critique.[2]

What makes Child's scholarly history so worthy of attention to today's slavery-capitalism debates is the extent to which her critique of slavery was contoured by economic (capitalist) discourse, across all sections of *An Appeal*. Referencing the remarkably detailed, wide-ranging, and innovative format of

Child's study, Karcher notes that none "of Child's predecessors had sought to weave the diverse strands of antislavery thought into a single panoramic tapestry. Nor had anyone sought to combine them with the economic and political analysis she offered" (187). In this sense, Child's economic prescience was remarkable both in her own time and in ours. It is this through line of economic analysis persisting in women's writing that this book aims to foreground, leading me to the third and final feature of Child's *Appeal* I want to underline here.

Lastly, though my study does not aim to evince literary or intertextual influence, it is difficult to deny the influence of Lydia Maria Child in activist and literary networks, within which all the authors discussed here participated. *An Appeal* was widely read and circulated in these circles. It was part of the American Anti-Slavery Society's first library, meaning that the society disseminated *An Appeal* as part of every subsequent library set that was added to the first library as its abolitionist literature collection grew (Goddu 25). Abolitionists immediately recognized the academic and political heft of Child's groundbreaking text. For example, a reviewer for the *Unionist* lauded the "extensive research which characterizes the work," found the text "rich in important facts [...] and forcible, conclusive reasoning," and summed up *An Appeal* as "one of the most valuable publications which have for a long time fallen under our eye" (quoted in Karcher 192–93). Similar reviews were found across abolitionist outlets of the period (Karcher 193). Men and women alike credited *An Appeal* and Child's influence with their renewed or newfound commitment to the abolitionist movement (193–94). This influence also played out in the abolitionist literature of the time. In this regard, I consider her text, a persuasive scholarly historical work of nonfiction, as a touchstone for the more imaginative and creative women's writing that came after it, including the novels, poetry, and narratives explored in this book.

Angelina Emily Grimké, Sarah Moore Grimké, and Theodore Dwight Weld attested to this influence in their own study of slavery and its economics. Six years after *An Appeal*, in *American Slavery as It Is: Testimony of a Thousand Witnesses* (1839), the authors cite Lydia Maria Child's earlier work and refer to correspondence between themselves and Child (90). Like Child, they take a methodical and systematic approach in their study, piecing together their understanding of the institution by covering a range of different aspects, including the economic. As the title reflects, their call for "witnesses" and firsthand accounts advertised their desire to collect "facts and testimony respecting the condition of slaves, in all respects" (iv). In the text, the call goes on to outline the kind of detailed information they are looking for: "their food, (kinds, quality, and quantity), clothing, lodging, ... hours of labor and rest, kinds of labor, with the mode of exaction, supervision, &c.... the number and time of meals each day, ... and in detail, their intellectual and moral condition" (iv). As in *An Appeal*, the focus on the inner workings of slavery as a capitalist labor system is set by Weld and the Grimkés right from the beginning. Intent on understanding the intricacies of slavery as a labor system, Weld and the Grimkés drew on enslavers' testimonies and abolitionist fragments of information to piece together a bigger economic picture of the institution. From their compilation of numbers, testimonies, and observations, they generated a kind of database that indexed their findings according to five categories:

1. The Food of the Slaves, the Kinds, Quality and Quantity, also, the Number and Time of Meals each Day, &C.
2. Their Hours of Labor and Rest.
3. Their Clothing.
4. Their Dwellings.
5. Their Privations and Inflictions (10)

The format of *American Slavery as It Is* does not mirror the neat ledger lines of an enslaver's account book, the central capitalist instrument featured in the present book's discussion of *Uncle Tom's Cabin*, but the text created its own kind of balance sheet to tally the information it held within its pages. Using the same data that enslavers used in their accounting systems—indeed much of their information for the above categories came from enslavers' testimonies—the authors created a counter account, in both the narrative sense and in the accounting sense, that used numbers and calculations to explain the system of slavery. The Grimké sisters and Weld, like Lydia Maria Child before them, knew that understanding slavery meant understanding its accounting—its numbers and its narratives. As with Child and her *Appeal*, the authors of *American Slavery as It Is* did more than make a moral argument against slavery; they performed detailed calculations and analyses to piece together the rationale behind the ledger. This commitment to understanding slavery as a labor system was produced by writing that relied on capitalist rhetoric.

The literary influence of both texts is found throughout antebellum literature. Harriet Beecher Stowe, as is well known, drew inspiration from *An Appeal* and *American Slavery as It Is* to write *Uncle Tom's Cabin*. Her novel extends to the world of fiction what Child and Weld and the Grimkés began with their nonfiction accounts of enslavers' practices. These early texts influenced other writers as well. In *Selling Antislavery: Abolition and Mass Media in Antebellum America* (2020), Teresa A. Goddu explains the influence *American Slavery as It Is* had on subsequent slave narratives: "The narratives of Sojourner

Truth, Henry Box Brown, and Henry Watson include extracts of *Slavery as It Is* in their appendices. And still others, while not directly quoting Weld's tract, utilize its sources and methods" (79). Goddu notes, for example, that Harriet Jacobs employs the text's methodology and its "authoritative language of numeracy" (32) when she organizes her chapter titled "Sketches of Neighboring Slaveholding" by "cataloguing cruelties" (79).

When we look for it, capitalist economics' "authoritative language of numeracy" and women's responses to it are found throughout nineteenth-century women's literature. For, whether writing histories, novels, slave narratives, poetry, or essays, women writers were not able to write about slavery without also writing about capitalism. Such early women's economic discourse and critique is evident in Lydia Maria Child's early abolitionist text, which had a powerful and far-reaching activist and literary influence. In this way, the influence of Child and her *Appeal* are suggestive of the idea that the authors examined in the following chapters—Stowe, Larcom, Jacobs, and Harper—were part of a larger and ongoing women's literary conversation grounded in economic critique. When we put these authors and their texts side by side and hear them in conversation, we can better appreciate their unique economic voices.

AN OVERVIEW OF HISTORICAL AND ECONOMIC SCHOLARSHIP

The twentieth and twenty-first centuries have seen an enormous amount of scholarship on the relationship between slavery and capitalism. History and economics have generally been the domain of this work, and subfields in both disciplines have produced generations of scholarship on the topic. This scholarship has, for the most part, responded to two main questions: Was slavery capitalist? And, if so, in what ways and to what extent did slavery shape capitalism, then and now? It is difficult to overstate the extent to which scholarship has been consumed with answering these questions, with making sense of the overlaps between these two systems while also attending to their differences.[3] To cover all these studies is much too expansive a task for this introduction. However, in order to better situate my own study, I briefly outline some of the major turns in the scholarly conversation.

Mainstream accounts of these debates typically point to Eric Williams's groundbreaking research in *Capitalism and Slavery* (1944) as its starting point. Briefly put, Williams built on the work of C. L. R. James and argued that West Indian slavery played a central role in financing England's Industrial Revolution. The Williams thesis was limited in its use to U.S. scholars since it focused on Great Britain and not the United States. Around the middle of the twentieth century, scholars of U.S. history began turning to U.S. slavery and its relation to American capitalism.

But before the U.S. scholarship that followed Williams's text, African American economists, like W. E. B. Du Bois and Sadie Alexander, were already undertaking this work.[4] Du Bois's thinking on Black economic development in works like *The Philadelphia Negro* (1899) and *Black Reconstruction in America* (1935) moved from "an early racial culturalist framing to a systematic notion of racial capitalism" (Henry and Danns 267) and would influence Cedric Robinson's classic text *Black Marxism: The Making of the Black Radical Tradition* (1983) and Manning Marable's *How Capitalism Underdeveloped Black America: Problems in Race, Political Economy, and Society* (1983). And Sadie Alexander, who in 1921 became the first African American woman to earn a PhD in economics in the Unites States, looked at issues like the economic conditions of Black families that were moving from the South to Philadelphia as part of the Great Migration—issues other economists ignored.[5] Thus, it is worth explicitly noting that the origins of the twentieth-century slavery-capitalism conversations I mark here are transnational in scope, since slavery and capitalism are also transnational in scope, and originate in Black intellectual history with writers like those named above.

In the third quarter of the twentieth century, histories of slavery made their way into the mainstream, with works like Kenneth Stampp's *The Peculiar Institution: Slavery in the Ante-Bellum South* (1956), David Brion Davis's *The Problem of Slavery in Western Culture* (1966) and *The Problem of Slavery in the Age of Revolution 1770–1823* (1975), and Eugene D. Genovese's *Roll, Jordan, Roll: The World the Slaves Made* (1974). These histories took systematic, often Marxist approaches to understand slavery's inner workings. Following these histories, studies by economists and economic historians, like Robert William Fogel and Stanley L. Engerman's *Time on the Cross: The Economics of American Negro Slavery* (1974), Claudia Goldin's *Urban Slavery in the American South, 1820–1860: A Quantitative History* (1976), and Gavin Wright's *The Political Economy of the Cotton South: Households, Markets, and Wealth in the Nineteenth Century* (1978) employed statistical models and numerical data to conduct micro- and macro-economic analysis of enslavers' plantation economics and to determine the extent of slavery's profitability and efficiency as an economic system.[6] The debates of this period hinged significantly on one's definition of capitalism and one's interpretation of that definition within a particular economic theory, drawing from classical to neoclassical, from Marxist to Keynesian economic theories. And in many ways they still do. Across time, the debate over definition has been a large component of the scholarly conversations about slavery and capitalism, producing varying answers to the above two questions and, in turn, holding different political and economic implications for the nation's past.[7]

On the heels of these mainstream histories, crucial work by women's historians located gender and white and Black women as central to U.S. histories of capitalism. Scholarship in this field, such as Nancy F. Cott's *The Bonds of Womanhood: "Woman's Sphere" in New England, 1780–1835* (1977), Christine Stansell's *City of Women: Sex and Class in New York, 1789–1860* (1986), and Jeanne Boydston's *Home and Work: Housework, Wages, and the Ideology of Labor in the Early Republic* (1990), documented, respectively, women's culture as both responding and contributing to the post-Revolutionary period's rapid economic change, gender and women's labor as central to capitalism's tendency to transform, and the home as a key site for capitalist accumulation.[8] At the turn of the twenty-first century, women's historical scholarship on gender, slavery, and capitalism continued to make important contributions to the slavery-capitalism debates, examining with nuance the intersections of gender and race. For example, Amy Dru Stanley's *From Bondage to Contract: Wage Labor, Marriage, and the Market in the Age of Slave Emancipation* (1998) explored ideas of selfhood in relation to the problem of "contract," which she defined as a "worldview," a "transaction," and a "social relation" (x) that garners meaning against the backdrop of slavery, coverture, and the free market. Paradigm-shifting work like Adrienne D. Davis's "'Don't Let Nobody Bother Yo' Principle': The Sexual Economy of American Slavery" (2002) designated American slavery a "sexual political economy" (105) and made explicit the connections between its labor structure, markets, and violent practices of sexual exploitation. And Jennifer L. Morgan's groundbreaking work *Laboring Women: Reproduction and Gender in New World Slavery* (2004) centered African women in the development of slavery and examined the role of their labor and reproductive labor in colonial economic systems.

In the last few decades, scholars have been writing "histories of the present," locating, for example, the development of institutions (e.g., universities, banks, and corporations), financial tools and practices (e.g., credit and debt, taxation, management, and accounting), sectors and industries (e.g., finance, technology, politics, and law) within the linkages of slavery and capitalism. They often place these developments and others within transnational and global contexts of slavery and capitalism.[9] These more recent histories also center the lived experience of those people who lived and labored under slavery's capitalism. Such histories are interested in "the narratives created by the interplay of a broad variety of actors" (Beckert and Desan 11), featuring, for example, enslaved workers, sharecroppers, other non-waged workers, abolitionists, consumers, slave traders, New York financiers, Boston merchants, and Pittsburgh industrialists (11–12).

A crucial part of these recent histories continues to be told by women's historians and historians of slavery who center women as actors and focus on gender and race across a variety of subject positions. Scholars who move women to the center of these histories, including Daina Ramey Berry, Adrienne D. Davis, Alexandra J. Finley, Thavolia Glymph, Ellen Hartigan-O'Connor, Jessica Marie Johnson, Stephanie E. Jones-Rogers, Jennifer L. Morgan, Jessica Gordon Nembhard, and Alys Eve Weinbaum, have generated a remarkable and substantial body of scholarship on women's roles in eighteenth- and nineteenth-century economic histories and histories of slavery. Their research—on topics ranging from enslaved African women in the early English colonies and enslaved women's domestic, reproductive, and sexual labor, to white enslaving women and white women's consumer culture in early America—has reshaped the dual histories of U.S. slavery and U.S. economics.[10]

As highlighted by the above overview of economic and historical scholarship, the field of economics holds explanatory power to help make sense of the relationship between people, resources, and places. And the field of history helps bring the stories of those relationships to life. But if we want to continue moving in the direction of a more complete story of slavery's capitalism, we need to go beyond the current conceptions of economics and the recent histories of slavery. One way to do this is by looking to the field of nineteenth-century women's literary study.

WOMEN WRITERS AS ECONOMIC CRITICS AND THEORISTS

Slavery, Capitalism, and Women's Literature is unique in that it draws expressly from the two core fields of nineteenth-century women's literature and slavery and capitalism studies to situate women writers and their texts as participants in the slavery and capitalism debates, and it does so in distinctive ways. The value of my study is that while women writers understood economic discourse as a language of numeracy and often used it in their work, they did not only engage economic discourse in this way. Indeed, their literature more often pushes back against a view of economics as a discrete, numerical, or male-defined activity. Instead, it emphasizes, through imaginative and creative writing, the lived experiences of women and generates economic discourse and capitalist critique from the seemingly prosaic everydayness of women's lives. It is in this distinction that it is possible to access women's economic insights around the relationship between slavery and capitalism not elsewhere available. In this way, my study emphasizes the literary dimension of slavery's capitalism, not in the sense of literary production, markets, and consumption but as the structuring framework for women's writing. It emphasizes, in other words, the major problem of slavery's capitalism as the *setting* for nineteenth-century women's literature.

Scholars of nineteenth-century American women's literature, and scholars of nineteenth-century American literature more broadly, have consistently attended to the economic concerns and contexts found in women's writing.[11] They have done so through a range of issues including marriage, domesticity, motherhood, sexuality, suffrage, and work. To extend one example, scholars have explored this last theme, women's work, through the trope of the working woman, her unpaid or wage-earning work, her professional or domestic labor, and her contribution to economic and social culture. Research on women's labor in nineteenth-century literature has generated important and necessary scholarship of the working woman's moral, social, and political function: it helped disrupt separate sphere ideology, complicate ideas of womanhood, critique the range of occupations or quality of working conditions, and argue for a greater expansion of woman's rights.

My study builds on this previous scholarship by shifting focus away from, for example, the woman who works and toward the economic forces that shape her world. That is to say, before the Civil War, slavery's capitalism, as an economic, political, and social system was the central structuring force of the period, as was its codified aftermath in the postbellum period. Slavery's capitalism was also, then, the structuring force for the kind of labor undertaken and performed by literary representations of working women. Rather than reading for the ways in which women's work is depicted, then, this study reads for economic insights into the dynamics of slavery's capitalism that created that work.[12]

To undertake such readings, I deliberately chose some of the most well-read nineteenth-century women authors and texts. Each author and text examined here is commonly read, researched, and taught. For example, Harriet Beecher Stowe's *Uncle Tom's Cabin* holds iconic status in American literature and in the U.S. cultural imagination. Lucy Larcom is arguably one of the best-known and most prolific writers to come out of the Lowell mills. Harriet Jacobs's *Incidents* continues to be the most-read U.S. woman's slave narrative. And Frances Ellen Watkins Harper was the most popular and influential African American woman writer-activist of the nineteenth century. The canonicity of Stowe, Larcom, Jacobs, and Harper and their texts is useful in this regard. Privileging these influential literary figures as economic critics and theorists—and slavery's capitalism as the setting for their texts—lays the groundwork for future research that reconsiders their respective oeuvres. Such reconsideration of their oeuvres can then reposition other writers who are part of their literary and activist networks. This, in turn, allows new nineteenth-century intertextual conversations to emerge within the framework of women's economic critique.

The nineteenth-century U.S. economic system necessitated a wide spectrum of female disempowerment across racial, geographical, and class lines. And because these four writers come from a range of racialized, classed, and geographical backgrounds and write in a range of genres, the perspectives on slavery's capitalism that their texts bring to bear on the conversation, and the tensions created by them, are similarly wide-ranging. By placing in constellation Stowe's sentimental novel, Larcom's factory poetry, Jacobs's slave narrative, and Harper's Reconstruction novel, this book situates these writers as addressing the problem of slavery's capitalism and showcases women's texts as different yet unifying critiques of slavery's capitalism. So situated, all texts within this frame can be said to be speaking, if not directly to each other, then in general to a shared set of questions or perceived problems.

Additionally, these authors and their texts were addressing the same logics of slavery's capitalism from different subject positions *as* their differences in subject position were being structured by those logics. More than simply creating historical and material differences between Black and white women of differing classes, slavery's capitalism depended in part on its ability to reify differences among women as constructed in relation to one another across racialized formations and within those formations, across class formations.[13] For this reason, this book also reveals the ways women's critiques of slavery's capitalism influence, overlap, converse with, and depart from one another. In other words, the separate chapters and themes for each author stand as a reminder that while their texts are read as different nodes in the same constellation, they must be read with attention to the very different stakes embedded in each author's economic critique. By placing these writers and their texts in constellation with one another, we can begin to piece together the larger story of women writers' economic insights to the slavery-capitalism debates.

In addition to an exploration of the authors' explicit economic critiques, I explore economic insights that arise from their texts but are more implicit. More specifically, because the imaginative novels, poetry, and narrative I examine take the material-historical connection of slavery and capitalism as a starting point (established by the nonfiction of earlier writers like Child, Weld, and the Grimkés), they can be read for the more speculative extensions of that connection. Reading for such speculative extensions as a hermeneutical endeavor leads to insights about the relationship between slavery and capitalism that are not possible to discover on a material-historical level. In other words, these authors and texts disclose unique economic insights around slavery's capitalism in ways that are only possible through literary writing. In this regard, I use an expanded definition of "economic," one that understands the economic, and the economics of slavery's capitalism in particular, as a cultural category. Taken in this way, women's economic insights around slavery's capitalism appear in the dialogue between two characters, the description of a woman's bodily movement at work or her reach toward an object, or the way a plotline unfolds over time and space. Indeed, creative and imaginative literature makes visible economic insights that would not be—could not be—visible in other arenas.

The ultimate value of this study, however, may be found in the distinction between women writers as economic critics and women writers as economic theorists. As critics, abolitionist women writers who lived and wrote against the backdrop of slavery's capitalism, like Stowe, Larcom, Jacobs, and Harper, scrutinized, analyzed, and criticized the economic dynamics they observed. But as theorists, they generated new possibilities of economic meaning-making around key features and instruments of capitalism, outside of meanings slavery's capitalism attributes to those features and instruments.

This kind of meaning-making is different from that we typically find in economics and economic histories since economic theory, when nineteenth-century women practice it, sometimes appears as novels, poetry, and narratives.[14] Indeed, the literary form facilitates this process of creative and imaginative writing as economic theory: it allows, invites, and even demands different ways of thinking. For example, Stowe's *Uncle Tom's Cabin* reimagines the practices of plantation bookkeeping and theorizes capitalist accounting as a fictional practice itself. The rhythm of "Weaving," Larcom's poem about white, working-class New England mill girls, echoes the quickening pace of its speaker's recognition around her role as a worker in an industry that relies on the labor of enslaved women, and thus theorizes the gendered and racialized meaning of a worker's time under slavery's capitalism. Jacobs's *Incidents in the Life of a Slave Girl* participates in the meaning-making of property outside of those meanings attributed by slavery's capitalism and theorizes property, and her protagonist Linda's knowledge of property, as having liberatory properties. Through literary flashbacks to the Haitian Revolution and antebellum New Orleans, Harper's *Minnie's Sacrifice* rewrites the inheritance plot as a kind of reparative device and theorizes the economic meaning of money in postbellum Black citizenship practices. The meanings and values of numbers, women's labor, property, and inheritance that arise from these texts challenge common understandings of these seemingly static capitalist entities.

This book's exploration of economic meaning-making under slavery and capitalism arises from the nineteenth-century women's literature that emerged amid those systems and shows how women's theorization lends crucial new dimensions to how economic meaning-making can and did change over time and according to the person holding the pen. By rooting their imaginations in the "concrete reality" of slavery's capitalism and using its economic devices to imagine possibilities beyond that reality, these authors show economics as itself a kind of fiction.[15] *Slavery, Capitalism, and Women's Literature*, then, reminds us to read for women's economic theoretical voices to consider how the literary plays a role in creating, augmenting, challenging, and revising capitalism's own narratives.

Necessarily, the book has limitations. First, because this study is more interested in how women used their writing to challenge, resolve, reimagine, and survive the intersections of slavery and capitalism, rather than justify, reinforce, or benefit from them, I focus on antislavery and not proslavery women writers. Important literary economic insights can be gleaned from proslavery writers though I do not take them up here. However, in *Cavaliers and Economists: Global Capitalism and the Development of Southern Literature, 1820–1860* (2019), for example, literary scholar Katharine A. Burnett's analysis of proslavery women like Maria J. McIntosh can be read in conversation with the white women in my study, Stowe and Larcom, who similarly—but from the antislavery perspective—try to make sense of what it means to benefit from an economic system that they find morally repulsive.[16] Additionally, in *They Were Her Property: White Women as Slave Owners in the American South* (2019), historian Stephanie E. Jones-Rogers reads the private letters, legal contracts, and lawsuits of women enslavers for their economic engagement in both their plantation management practices and in their relationships with the domestic workers they enslaved. The real women in Jones-Rogers's study can be read in the enslaving women characters of Stowe, Jacobs, and Harper. For the purposes of this book, however, in the case of white, middle-class women writers, I am more interested in how these antislavery writers manage the tensions that arise when they acknowledge (or do not) how they benefit from the intersections of slavery and capitalism. In other words, it is precisely because these writers are antislavery and benefit from that system that their contradictions, complicities, frustrations, and resolutions make visible linkages between slavery and capitalism that we do not find in other texts.

Second, because my authors and texts operate largely within the historical U.S. Black-white binary of racial formation in labor and economic systems, and because my close readings arise from such operations, this study does not undertake an exploration of Indigenous, Latinx, or Asian American writers' contributions to the slavery-capitalism debates. However, it must be noted that nineteenth-century U.S. capitalism and its relationship to Black enslavement cannot be fully explained without also attending to Indigenous dispossession, Asian indentured servitude, and imperial expansion westward and into Mexican territories. Wider historical frameworks that reach beyond the ones offered by these four authors and texts could generate new readings. For example, in chapter 1, the account books of *Uncle Tom's Cabin* could be more accurately balanced by also accounting for the way in which the uptick in southern cotton production coincided with a decline in the deerskin trade (Usner 297–98). Discussion around Lucy Larcom's "Weaving", in chapter 2, could be extended to an even larger world of women to address a different kind of weaver than the one found on the floors of New England factories: Native Americans who "earned their livings in market activities such as weaving [and] spinning" (quoted in Harmon, O'Neill, and Rosier 712). In chapter 3, which takes up the theme of property, discussion could be extended to include land as property (both Flint's and Aunt Martha's) and the relationship of settler-colonialism to slavery. This could, in turn, offer a larger frame of analysis that would treat concentric circles of property including land, enslavement, and objects. And, although Harper does not weave it into her postbellum novel's historical framework, her book's publication coincided with the already unfolding history of Chinese immigrant men who, beginning in the early 1860s, were building the transcontinental railroad through Indigenous territories, which facilitated national and international trade. These are all components of the nineteenth-century story of slavery's capitalism, and these are just some of the different readings that the wide lens of slavery's capitalism might capture. Indeed, considering just how pervasive and inescapable the systems making up slavery's capitalism were, most, if not all, nineteenth-century women's literature can be read against at least some aspect of its wide-ranging backdrop.[17]

CHAPTER OVERVIEW

Four familiar lines of inquiry in women's literary scholarship—sentimentality, women's labor, materiality, and citizenship—shape the chapters of this book. The seemingly prosaic everydayness of women's lives out of which these lines of inquiry appear, this book argues, are crucial sites of knowledge about nineteenth-century women's economic (capitalist) critique and theory. To foreground their economic insights, I draw from the theoretical fields of critical accounting studies, phenomenology, intersectional feminist theory, and Black Marxism to newly frame these lines of inquiry as contoured by the various capitalist practices and instruments that the texts engage and the literary forms in which the authors write. Thus, sentimentality in *Uncle Tom's Cabin* is read through the language of slavery's capitalist accounting practices. The two middle chapters on "Weaving" and *Incidents in the Life of a Slave Girl*, which both demonstrate an insistence on the body and material objects, are read through the lens of feminist phenomenology. In *Minnie's Sacrifice*, Black citizenship practices are read, in the vein of Black Marxism, as a disruption to histories of capitalist inheritance practices. By focusing on these familiar spaces of inquiry in women's literary scholarship alongside the text's engagement with capitalist practices and instruments—sentimentality and accounting, factory labor and slavery's cotton market, material culture and property, and citizenship and inheritance—this book offers literary and theoretical analyses that foreground these four women writers' economic insights into the relationship between slavery and capitalism and the way it showed up in women's lives and literature.

The chapters proceed thematically, in a generally chronological fashion, and are framed by some of the broader nineteenth-century economic and political discourses of the time. The chapters that bookend this study, for example, center novels that respond to the historical events of 1850 and 1868, respectively. Stowe's *Uncle Tom's Cabin* famously responds to the Fugitive Slave Act of 1850, and Harper's *Minnie' Sacrifice* responds to the ratification of the Fourteenth Amendment in 1868. The middle chapters of the book, meanwhile, are situated within the contemporary economic and political discourse around slavery's cotton market and definitions of property, respectively, but are located in the more hidden corners of slavery's capitalism: in one's touch, reach, and bodily movements. All four of these writers and their texts very much participated in the current economic debates of the day. But their writing gives voice to what cannot be articulated through dominant economic rhetoric and discourse. Taken together, then, these four chapters comprise a critical record that registers different levels of women's economic intimacy with slavery's capitalism and documents women's literary participation in nineteenth-century economic discourse, critique, and theory.

Chapter 1 uses critical accounting studies to newly frame *Uncle Tom's Cabin*. If, in *An Appeal* and *American Slavery as It Is*, Lydia Maria Child and Weld and the Grimké sisters were using economic discourse to record their observations about slavery in their nonfiction, Stowe extends that discourse to its fictional and sentimental form. Expanding the ledger line and telling the sentimental story behind the numbers, *Uncle Tom's Cabin* offers an alternative narrative behind accounting's numbers, what the field of critical accounting studies calls a "shadow account" (Lehman 173, 176). Stowe's shadow account of her fictional enslavers' records attaches a narrative to the ledger line and tells a story that the ledger does not. In *Uncle Tom's Cabin*, then, sentimentalism does not just make an emotional or political argument. It also makes an economic one. Reading Stowe's shadow account through the shared logics of slavery, capitalism, and sentimentalism allows for a new understanding of her iconic and deeply problematic novel. To this end, chapter 1 considers how Stowe's novel, famous for its iconic status as a sentimental novel and for its equally enduring racist legacy, is perhaps our most emblematic demonstration of how sentimental accounting operates as an enabling mechanism of mainstream racism and economic injustice.

Chapter 2 moves from Stowe's fictional plantations of the South to the factories of the North and to a poem by Lucy Larcom, one of the best-known Lowell "mill girls." It focuses on Larcom's "Weaving," first published in 1868 but likely written during the early years of the Civil War, and analyzes the speaker's positioning as a white, working-class weaver on the factory floor and in the cotton market of slavery's capitalism. The chapter follows the cotton, so to speak, as it circles through the weaver's story, which pivots around that market. In this case, following the cotton through Larcom's poem rejects the fraught capitalist logic that would examine the development of raw material into a consumable commodity for sale in the market. Instead, my reading identifies a "world of women" who make up the cotton market to make visible the embodied process of cotton weaving, the tactile experience of cotton itself, and the racialized and gendered significance of cotton as it makes contact with the weaver's skin. This chapter foregrounds the author's textual focus on the body as apperceptive moments that reveal an awareness of her gendered and racialized embodied role in the cotton market and offers close readings of the speaker's lived experience, in a feminist phenomenological sense, as shaped by the dictates of the cotton market. Thus, the whiteness of the mill girl's laboring body in Larcom's poem is highlighted by slavery's cotton market. Foregrounding the sensory experiences that permeate the speaker's sense of subjectivity under slavery's capitalism allows us to read the poem for how whiteness—as a capitalist enterprise mediated by labor, gender, and the nineteenth-century cotton market—feels.

In chapter 3, cotton takes on a different meaning in *Incidents in the Life of a Slave Girl* as read through Harriet Jacobs's protagonist Linda and her experience with it. Here the focus on cotton is not in the typical sense—that is, through Linda's work with the staple fiber as a skilled seamstress. Rather, this chapter attends to understandings of property under slavery's capitalism by paying close attention to Linda's ownership of property, much of which was property in cotton fabric. It tracks Linda's account of her relation to objects, primarily fabric objects made from cotton and textiles, and explores what it means for her to touch, use, or own these objects, items that are imbued with racialized and sexualized meanings. In doing so, this chapter privileges a logic and language of property that originates in Linda's gendered and racialized counter-knowledge of material culture. It locates the meaning and definition of property in Linda's experience and knowledge, and it challenges views of property as existing solely in a private, white, and male domain. This chapter explores the function of property, as Linda would have it, and shows how Linda's engagement with property rather than as property undermines the very tenets on which property, according to the logics of slavery's capitalism, rests.

Finally, chapter 4 moves this study to the period immediately following the Civil War and reads Frances Ellen Watkins Harper's Reconstruction-era novel *Minnie's Sacrifice* as addressing the long shadow of slavery's capitalism. The chapter traces the economic dimensions of *Minnie's Sacrifice* to draw out Harper's exploration of economic meaning-making around two pivotal issues—inheritance and citizenship—that were shaped at a time of emerging postbellum capitalism. With attention to how meaning, rather than value, is attributed to money, chapter 4 follows the novel's insistence on the generational operations of inheritance. It historicizes Harper's narration of generational wealth accumulated in the slavery economy, beginning in St. Domingue before and during the Haitian Revolution through to antebellum New Orleans and the Northeast and then finally after the Civil War. Through this historical significance and monetary signification, Harper leverages Reconstruction's inheritance from slavery to advance individual and collective practices of Black economic citizenship during Reconstruction.

When the most recent wave of slavery and capitalism scholarship began to appear, I was certain that nineteenth-century women's literature had significant contributions to make. After all, as women's literary scholarship documents, nineteenth-century women writers have always engaged in economic discourse. It only made sense that these writers were also contending with the economics of slavery's capitalism even if the ways they contend with those economics are not always explicit or readily apparent. As this book attests, nineteenth-century women's literature offers significant contributions to slavery and capitalism scholarship. Specifically, the four women writers featured here—Harriet Beecher Stowe, Lucy Larcom, Harriet Jacobs, and Frances Ellen Watkins Harper—were critical and engaged participants in nineteenth-century economic discourse about the relationship between slavery and capitalism. They were, in other words, all along critiquing slavery and its codified aftermath as embedded in an overall capitalist system. Through the literary form, their economic thought, critiques, and theories appear in ways not otherwise accessible. The aim of this study, then, is to make their economic insights accessible through literary analysis and to emphasize that their contributions to the discourse of slavery's capitalism were significant, unique, and vital in the nineteenth century and continue to be so today.

CHAPTER 1

Accounting for Harriet Beecher Stowe's *Uncle Tom's Cabin*

> [Slavery] is like the account of a great battle, in which we learn, in round numbers, that ten thousand were killed and wounded, and throw the paper by without a thought.
>
> —HARRIET BEECHER STOWE,
> *A Key to Uncle Tom's Cabin* (1853)

HARRIET BEECHER STOWE'S 1852 novel *Uncle Tom's Cabin* opens by introducing Tom, the character from whom Stowe's novel takes its title, not as a person but as a line item in a financial transaction. Mr. Shelby, Tom's enslaver, and Mr. Haley, a slave trader, are found "sitting alone over their wine, in a well-furnished dining parlor," negotiating the sale of Tom (7). Shelby is a somewhat reluctant participant in the negotiations, but he had "speculated largely and quite loosely; had involved himself deeply" (15). And the consequent crushing debt left him no choice but to sell Tom to Haley, a man "alive to nothing but trade and profit" (40).

Capital, or rather the lack of it, is decisively foregrounded in the scene. "This small piece of information [about Shelby's speculative activities]," Stowe tells us, "is the key to the preceding conversation" (15). It is also the key to all the action following the conversation: the negative balance in Shelby's account book and the decisions he makes in service to his bottom line drive the rest of the novel. The storylines of every major character in Stowe's famous novel, from Tom to Eliza and her son Harry and from Little Eva to Simon Legree, are initially brought about by Shelby's need to square his debt. And though Tom himself does not appear fully in the first chapter, we already know his story. It is told through Shelby's account book.[1]

This chapter departs from previous discussions of *Uncle Tom's Cabin* that have interpreted the novel's financial subtext in a general or largely metaphorical way. Shifting attention to the novel's array of accounting systems, financial transactions, and bookkeepers, this chapter takes up the precision of Stowe's interest in accounting practices by centering Stowe's economic voice around bookkeeping in the discourse of slavery *as* capitalism. It takes seriously the role of slavery's accounting—the practice of recording financial transactions as developed by enslavers to account for the operations, management, and maintenance of the plantation—and reads *Uncle Tom's Cabin* through the lens of the ledger. Indeed, the centrality of accounting to the novel's storyline insists that we locate *Uncle Tom's Cabin* within the ever-growing archive of slavery's account books and argues that attempts to index slavery's accounting in its manifold textual expressions are incomplete without attention to its explicitly fictional representations.[2]

Uncle Tom's Cabin, the most frequently accessed item of that archive, is already well known for its sentimental depictions of the suffering inflicted by slavery. Focusing on the very real accounting practices subtending Stowe's plot thus extends the scholarly conversation concerning the novel's deployment of sentimentalism to the arena of capitalist accounting.[3] The intertwining of sentiment and economics was not, of course, new to nineteenth-century writers like Stowe since it was an integral part of sentimental writing from its outset. Throughout the eighteenth century, sentimental novels often used bookkeeping to clarify sentiment, specifically to calculate sentiment. Financial details, for example, are present throughout the work of Susanna Rowson, the most successful and significant early American sentimentalist. Adam Smith famously wrote two works suggestive of this connection: a study of the logic of sentiment in *The Theory of Moral Sentiments* (1759) and a study of the logic of capitalism in *The Wealth of Nations* (1776). Scholars who research the specific correlations of Smith's texts generally agree that these two studies, the first emphasizing sympathy for others and the second emphasizing one's economic self-interest are not antithetical but are, rather, undergirded by a shared logic of human motivation and behavior that optimizes for maximum exchange, whether social or market.[4]

Stowe, then, inherits this established connection between sentiment and accounting and in *Uncle Tom's Cabin* attempts to disrupt it by linking the shared logic of sentiment and economics to the world of slavery.[5] By extending the history of the sentimental accounting of capitalism (or the capitalist accounting of sentiment) to slavery, Stowe shows that sentimental feeling is not antithetical to slavery's capitalist accounting logic but, rather, fundamentally bound up with it. In this sense, her novel stands out among nineteenth-century abolitionist writing in that it assumes a radical foundation: that slavery and capitalism have a similar logic, one that also happens to be the logic of sentimentality.

Aware that "round numbers" do not tell a whole story, as evinced by the epigraph that opens this chapter, Stowe complicates the connection between sentiment, economics, and slavery for her readers. She uses the novel form to exploit the existing connection between sentimentalism and accounting—to attach a sentimental narrative to the ledger line—and thus create a "shadow account" of the enslaver's record, a critical secondary narrative that arises outside of the primary narrative intended by the accountant's documentation (Lehman 173, 176). Stowe's shadow account attempts to tell the sentimental story of the people behind the numbers, to narrate how the violence that took place on the plantation is translated into the numerical language of the ledger line, and to convince readers that the violence of these calculations informs their everyday lives. In other words, by framing slavery as a public accounting practice, her novel takes the public understanding of slavery quite literally into account, revealing how the widespread culture and practice of slavery's accounting implicates the nation as a whole.

The extent to which accounting is key to *Uncle Tom's Cabin* is evinced by its prominence in *A Key to Uncle Tom's Cabin* (1853), the subsequent book that Stowe wrote to defend her story as "a reality," a "mosaic of facts" (*Key* 5)—something that accounting seeks to establish. Published shortly after her novel, the full title of her defense reflects its accumulative nature: *A Key to Uncle Tom's Cabin: Presenting the Original Facts and Documents upon Which the Story Is Founded, Together with Corroborative Statements Verifying the Truth of the Work*. Concerned with understanding the intricacies of the system, Stowe, like others before her, pieced together the story of the individuals, laws, policies, and customs that created and sustained it. An important part of this story was slavery's accounting systems. Among *A Key*'s catalog of laws, policies, and customs related to the system of enslavement, one can find language similar to historical plantation records, such as descriptions of upkeep, value, productivity, and working and living conditions. For example, the chapter titled "Protective Acts with Regard to Food and Raiment, Labor, Etc" offers an extended analysis of the "market value" of an enslaver's "property" by assessing the "provisions" of "food" and "clothing" against the "exactions of excessive labor" (90). Thus, we can view Stowe's presentation of the collected documents within *A Key* as a kind of data set from which her sentimental novel, as a shadow account, arises.

In spite of her efforts, however, embedded in Stowe's shadow account is her problematic racial politics. Previously, scholars have explored Stowe's troubling racial sentimentalism as grounded in the liberalist tradition: it privileges bourgeois self-interest over the common good; it erases rather than bridges human difference; it upholds and promotes racist ideology; and it forecloses the possibility for her emotional or political arguments to generate real reform.[6] This chapter builds on and extends these explorations by demonstrating that Stowe's sentimentalism does not just make an emotional or political argument; it also makes an economic one. In other words, Stowe's deployment of sentimental rhetoric not only operates to evoke particular emotional (sympathetic) responses or to encourage political (abolitionist) action, it also operates to enforce economic ideology.

When read through the lens of slavery's capitalism, *Uncle Tom's Cabin* reveals how Stowe's liberal sentimentalism and her critique of capitalist economics—or slavery's accounting—are based in a similar logic of control. However, I do not use the word "control" here and throughout the chapter as it is typically understood within critiques of sentimental discourse as a method to influence emotion, nor do I use it in its colloquial sense as understood within the plantation economy as a form of domination. Instead, the sense of control I have in mind is drawn from the field of accounting, where it serves as the organizing logic of the accountant's ledger. Economist Richard Edwards defines accounting's control systems as those that manage the fundamental conflict between the worker's instinct to protect himself from exploitation and the capitalist's goal of accumulation, which demands exploitation of the worker (14–17).[7] Stowe's liberal sentimentalism, I argue, is a control system of just this sort: it manages the fundamental conflict she experiences as an author between her intention to offer or generate sympathy for the victims of slavery's capitalism and her own (and her white middle-class readership's) economic self-interest. Read in this way, the novel demonstrates that sentimentalism does not take the place of social or political action or act as a soothing balm, because it is not antithetical to the logic of the capitalist marketplace at all. Rather, sentimentalism can be read as its own economic framework, made up of transactions, calculations, and "controls"; it conjoins the economic framework of the marketplace, working hand in hand with it, both seeking to maximize the mutually constituted potential of sentimental and economic exchange. In *Uncle Tom's Cabin*, the control systems of Stowe's liberal sentimentalism thus map neatly onto the very control systems of slavery's accounting she critiques, appearing, ideologically and didactically, as interchangeable and complementary.

Because Stowe's novel assumes the shared logic of this triad—slavery, capitalism, and sentimentalism—it can readily recast the accounting practices of slavery and capitalism in a sentimental narrative form. Her novel thus contributes economic insights to nineteenth-century conversations around slavery as capitalism that rely on sentimental rhetoric: it emphasizes the shared accounting logics of southern slavery and northern industry, it analyzes the larger capitalist economic control systems that slavery is a part of (both partially, as a temporary part of a world-systems approach, and wholly, slavery as capitalism, in the classical economic sense), and it offers a platform for the critique of capitalism from both the proslavery and the white abolitionist perspectives of the day. Contrary to Ann Douglas's claim that sentimentalism tends to "obfuscate the visible dynamics of development" (13), sentimentalism in Stowe's novel makes visible the dynamics of capitalist accounting in both its proslavery and abolitionist forms. This chapter, then, reads the novel for its economic insights into the continuities between slavery and capitalism, and its contributions to the economic discourse of the day, by paying attention to the significance of their presentation in the sentimental and novelistic form.

But the more telling insights these continuities disclose are found in Stowe's problematic, sentimental racial and economic politics, which are all the more evident because she assumes this radical foundation yet cannot find a way, in the imaginary world that her own sentimental accounting creates (spurred by Tom's sale), to reach any liberatory solutions for racial economic justice.[8] The very existence of shadow accounts, after all, exposes the account book not as an objective depiction of events but as a series of decisions by its author. Accounting historian Jere Francis, for example, defines accounting as a discursive practice, one created by accountants "who author the discourse" and as a site for contested narrative where the stories behind the numbers can be created, contested, and re-created (5). It is, then, especially telling that Stowe herself does not produce, through her narrative, an inclusive, liberatory accounting. To the contrary, by the novel's conclusion she literally writes her enslaved characters out of the nation's bookkeeping entirely, ending the novel with a call for colonization and Black emigration to Liberia. It is with this "bottom line" of Stowe's own account book in mind, however short-lived in her activist work, that this chapter locates *Uncle Tom's Cabin's* greatest contributions to the slavery-capitalism debates: its novelistic narrations of both sentimentalism's economic logics and sentimentalism's economic role in slavery's capitalism. Ultimately, my reading of *Uncle Tom's Cabin* highlights the role of sentimentalism in securing the connection between mainstream racism, of which the novel itself is representative, and U.S. capitalist economics in the nation's account book. Stowe's sentimental shadow account illustrates this operation precisely inasmuch as it both critiques slavery's accounting while advancing the sentimental racism that subtends that accounting. In other words, the novel's accounting practices promote and uphold racial capitalism while engaging in emotional and political appeals on behalf of those racial capitalism violently oppresses. In its iconic status as a sentimental novel and for its equally enduring racist legacy, *Uncle Tom's*

Cabin therefore is perhaps our most emblematic demonstration of sentimental accounting as an enabling mechanism of mainstream racism.

If sentiment and economy are not antithetical but fundamentally bound up with one another—and if, as Shirley Samuels argues, "in nineteenth-century America sentimentality appears as a national project" and "is literally at the heart of nineteenth-century American culture" (3–4)—then the system at the heart of the nineteenth-century U.S. economy, slavery's capitalism, must in turn be considered for its connection to the national project of sentimentality. To that end, this chapter adds slavery's capitalist accounting in its fictional forms to our understanding of the national project of sentimentality by illuminating, through the nineteenth century's most famous sentimental novel, their shared logic of control.

This chapter's three main sections do not strictly follow the novel's chronology. The first section offers a fuller explanation of what I call accounting's logic of the ledger and then focuses on the long debate over enslaved versus wage labor that occurs in the middle of the novel between the southern enslaver St. Clare and his northern abolitionist cousin Ophelia Sinclair. I use this debate in chapter 19, the longest disquisition the novel offers, to establish Stowe's economic critique of slavery *as* capitalism and to establish that critique as the structuring idea that anchors the guiding problem of the novel. My reading of this debate teases out the logic of the ledger in slavery's accounting. As the cousins' discussion of the northern and southern labor systems unfolds, the rationales of both, which seek to discuss the two systems as distinct, break down. Rather than debating enslaved versus wage labor, the conversation melds the two ostensibly separate labor systems into one. Through the capitalist logics of accounting, Stowe links the two systems, and her critique of slavery becomes a critique of slavery's capitalism.

The next two sections comprise Stowe's shadow account and tarry with the ledger behind slavery's accounting. They read key scenes as a series of case studies that establish reliance on the account book by both Stowe's agents of slavery and her enslaved characters and show how Stowe attempts to create a shadow account that narrates the human story behind the ledger line. In telling the sentimental story behind the numbers, the underlying ideology operating across all of the scenes—the logic of the ledger—comes to the fore. Read as Stowe's shadow account, these scenes focus on the relationship between slavery, accounting, and sentimentalism and thus further draw out Stowe's economic critique as well as the economic operations and consequences of her novel's racial politics.

STOWE, SLAVERY, AND CAPITALISM: THE LOGIC OF THE LEDGER

When St. Clare and Ophelia begin to discuss the "abstract question of slavery" (230), the ideology of accounting controls comes to the fore as a defining essence of the institution. St. Clare opens the discussion on the definition of slavery by asking: "This cursed business, ... what is it?" (230). He answers his own question by defining slavery as a system dictated by the control of the enslaver:

> Strip it of all its ornament, run it down to the root and nucleus of the whole, and what is it? ... Whatever is too hard, too dirty, too disagreeable, for me, I may set Quashy to doing. Because I don't like work, Quashy shall work. Because the sun burns me, Quashy shall stay in the sun. Quashy shall earn the money, and I will spend it. Quashy shall lie down in every puddle, that I may walk over dry-shod. Quashy shall do my will, and not his, all the days of his mortal life, and have such chance of getting to heaven, at last, as I find convenient. This I take to be about what slavery is. (230)

St. Clare accounts for the enforced movements of enslaved people as controlled by the enslaver's "will," which is guided, of course, by the enslaver's pursuit of profit. Forced to carry out the enslaver's will "all the days of his mortal life," St. Clare tells his cousin, the enslaved worker is "under the constant eye of a master" (236), his every movement controlled by the demands of the account book.

As mentioned above, I use the word "control" here as drawn from the field of accounting—as the organizing logic of the accountant's ledger. The concept of accounting controls, fundamental to the St. Clare-Ophelia debate, helps establish Stowe's economic critique of slavery as capitalism. Before turning to the debate itself, therefore, I more fully explain the concept and examine the precise logics of accounting's control so as to underscore its resonances across slavery's and capitalism's economics as they appear in Stowe's novel. It is necessary, then, to turn to both the account book itself and the account book's history.

Since the inception of slavery, plantation owners kept accounting records, as necessitated by different aspects of the business.[9] It was not until the middle of the nineteenth century, though, just a few short years before Stowe published her novel, that these records, previously scrawled across a range of loose pages, could be more neatly organized in one place. Thomas Affleck's *Plantation Re-*

cord and Account Book was perhaps the most popular recordkeeping book of its time. It was a preprinted, bound, all-in-one accounting system for enslavers or their managers and overseers. Historians of accounting have documented the far-reaching economic potential that the techology of Affleck's books offered. For example, Jan Richard Heier has explored how the different forms allowed enslavers to keep track of all aspects of their business operations. The ruled folio contained fifteen different types of records labeled from A to O, which could be placed into four general categories: "Daily Diary," "Cotton Record Keeping," "Overseer's Record Keeping Responsibilities," and "Slave Accounting, and the Valuation of Property and Income Determination" (Heier, "Content Comparison" 134). Maintaining accurate account records, of course, made it possible for plantation owners to organize the operation of the plantation. But the account book also made it possible to leverage capital in other arenas. Thomas N. Tyson and Richard K. Fleischman have studied the role of the account book in social standing: for enslavers who lived beyond their means, for example, a labor force of enslaved workers was collateral for much-needed bank loans that maintained their social positions in southern society (384), and once enslaved persons were assigned monetary value, they could be used as collateral in home mortgages and other credit transactions (379–80). The enslaver's account book could also be transformed into records for legal transactions around inheritance, the monitoring of property, and budgeting the family's household.[10] As illustrated by Shelby's "well-furnished dining parlor" in Stowe's opening scene, slavery's accounting systems, of course, bankrolled the plantation household, itself a worksite informed by the same accounting logics (Glymph 2–3).

More recently, Caitlin Rosenthal has examined the technology of the preprinted forms as anticipating the replication, adaptation, and expansion of these accounting methods. She argues that these the records "provided the uniformity and regularity that would enable comparisons across plantations," necessary data for competitive industry ("Slavery's Scientific" 64). Such comparisons were further enabled by "pocket-books," which made enslavers' records portable. The different forms, collected and bound all in one place, could fit in a pocket, and Stowe's account books often appear on the body or in the hands of her fictional agents of slavery. Secured in a pocket, the logic of the ledger could travel not just on or between plantations, but also from the plantation to the factories of New England, which, as discussed in chapter 2, participated symbiotically with the southern plantations in the cotton market. Through the technology of the account book, in large part, Rosenthal argues, "Slavery became a laboratory for the development of accounting because the *control* drawn on paper matched the reality of the plantation more closely than that of almost any other early American business enterprise" (*Accounting* 4; my emphasis).

As a part of the accounting record, the ledger—which logged these profits and losses in human capital—was a device that wielded enormous control. The ledger helped enslavers organize their different systems of control, such as the rationing of food or medical supplies. And analyzing a ledger for the efficiency of accounting control systems helped enslavers coordinate their larger business operations. Accounting historians have long understood control as a foundational ideology for the practice of accounting. Rosenthal reminds us that "the word 'control' itself comes from an accounting document: the *contreroulle*, or counter-roll, a duplicate of a roll or other document, which was kept for purposes of cross-checking" (3–4). Today we do not immediately associate control with accounting, but accounting's origins of control can be found in the title of a corporation's top accounting officer: the controller or the comptroller (4). Nineteenth-century slavery's accounting, then, especially its deployment of accounting controls, is an important piece of why capitalist accounting practices evolved in the way they did.

This control was mapped into the pages of the account book. The ledger typically consisted of a sheet of paper drawn with narrowly spaced vertical lines spanning the length of the pages to create neat, tight spaces, which turned human characteristics into data points, simultaneously erasing laborers as people with "indeterminate" (Edwards 15) human interests, needs, and power and controlling laborers precisely because they are people with indeterminate human interests, needs, and power. The bottom line of the sheet tallied the items and rendered an account of the control system's efficiency. The tecnology of the ledger, so understood, was a means to control not only the management of finances but also the expanse of the human condition— movements, behaviors, thoughts, emotions, et cetera—by placing people in a box on a ledger line and failing to allow space, literally in the account book and metaphorically, for humanity.

The ledger's ability to control and erase the human condition is the critical target of Stowe's shadow account. Appearing in the hands of her fictional enslavers, just as they would in the hands of their real-world counterparts, the ledger is a significant metaphor for the violence it imparts and a metonym of the wider technology of enslavement that it advances. As a capitalist tool, the enslaver's ledger was designed to eliminate the human element from transactions altogether and, paradoxically, to control variables of the human element, including "psychological quirks, social desires, intellectual qualities, spiritual longings, familial attachments, community involvement—and, of course, eco-

FOR SALE wholesale and retail by B. M. NORMAN,
Bookseller, 14 Camp street, New Orleans.

THE COTTON-PLANTATION RECORD AND ACCOUNT BOOK;
No. 1, for a Plantation working 40 hands or less, $2 50.
No. 2,   do.   do.   80   do.   do. $3 00.
No. 3,   do.   do.   120 do.   do. $3 50.

— ALSO —

THE SUGAR-PLANTATION RECORD AND ACCOUNT-BOOK;
No. 1, for a Plantation working 80 hands or less, $3 00.
No. 2,   do.   do.   120 do.   do. $3 50.

By THOMAS AFFLECK.

Sent by mail, carefully enveloped and prepaid, at the above prices; and when five copies are ordered by clubs, and remitted for, an additional copy will be sent to the individual making up the club. A liberal discount, with the usual time, allowed to dealers.

These works are coming more and more into use each year.

Orders for copies to be forwarded by mail, may be sent to
THOMAS AFFLECK, Washington, Miss.

From the New Orleans Prices Current of 22d March, 1851.

We have a copy of this most useful work before us, and a glance at its systematic and business like arrangement, convinces us that no planter *who would know what he is doing and what his overseers and his hands are doing*, should be without it. The arrangement is simple, and may be understood by persons having merely a trifling knowledge of accounts.

The well-known agricultural writer, "Broomsedge," remarks of the Cotton Plantation Book in the S. C. "Farmer and Planter," for April, 1853.

"It is the completest thing of the kind we have ever seen. It comprehends everything required, and is so simple and well-arranged that you are almost obliged to go right. It will take half the price to buy a common blank book."

FIG. 1.1. Advertisement for Affleck's planation account book, which shows two of the more basic ledger pages. The ad attempts to convince the potential customer that account books are becoming increasingly popular, that they are critical to a planter's business success, and that they are accessible to all kinds of plantation owners since no prior accounting knowledge is necessary to make use of them. From Thomas Affleck, *Affleck's Southern Rural Almanac, and Plantation and Garden Calendar* (New Orleans: Office of the Picayune, 1849). Courtesy of the Rare Book Collection, Louis Round Wilson Special Collections Library, University of North Carolina at Chapel Hill.

nomic capabilities" (Huston, "Slavery" 125-26). It aimed to isolate labor, the "economic capabilities" at the end of the above list, and sought to control, because it could not eliminate, other human elements. By constructing a shadow account in novel form that defies this logic, Stowe attempts to return to the record the human stories the ledger erased by design. Additionally, in *Uncle Tom's Cabin*, this logic of control emerges as fundamental to St. Clare and Ophelia's debate over enslaved versus waged labor and thus helps to establish Stowe's economic critique of slavery as capitalism.

In the cousins' debate, St. Clare's defense of slavery is bound up in all the typical proslavery paternalist language of the time but with an interesting twist: he lays out the ways in which slavery and capitalism are in "nature, the same" (Stowe 238) and then concludes that the enslaved labor system is worse—a "more bold and palpable infringement of human rights" (237)—than the free labor system. One might expect an abolitionist author like Stowe to use her fictional enslaving character to make the straw figure's proslavery case so that she could tear it down. But St. Clare actually does not defend slavery. During his conversation with Ophelia, he explicitly negates many of the popular proslavery defenses. For example, in response to the argument that enslaved people were happier in the slave South, he says, "It's all nonsense to talk to me about slaves *enjoying* all this! To this day, I have no patience with the unutterable trash that some of your patronizing Northerners have made up, as in their zeal to apologize for our sins. We all know better" (236). And when he draws on the paternalism defense, it is in contradictory ways. For example, when he speaks of his brother, a well-off and hugely successful plantation owner, St. Clare says that his brother "takes a sort of pride in having his slaves comfortably fed and accommodated" (238). But in the same breath, St. Clare also says that his brother "would shoot a fellow down with as little remorse as he would shoot a buck, if he opposed him" (238). St. Clare's admission of the horrors of slavery—and his admission that enslaved labor is a worse system than free labor—allows Stowe to argue that the most laissez faire slaveholders, and even the ones who oppose slavery on moral grounds, are equally dangerous, if not more so, in their complicity. But the scene also allows Stowe to move beyond the moral debate and instead focus on the economics on which such morality rests.

Despite St. Clare's denouncement of the institution of slavery, he is wholly committed to it. What St. Clare defends during the conversation, then, is not the morality of institution but rather his economic participation in it, a contradiction he sums up as a "contemptible *non sequitur*" (239). He does not agree with slavery but cannot not live by it because of its economic profitability and because he is, as he says of himself, "one of the laziest of mortals" and refuses to work (239). His line of thinking defaults to the logic of an accounting system that is based on economic exploitation. The only way to sustain his livelihood is by adhering to the capitalist logics of accounting and by "*appropriating* [the lower classes], body and bone, soul and spirit, to [his] use and convenience" (237). His justification for defaulting to this way of thinking is that, he argues, it is the logic used by the American enslaver, the English aristocracy, and capitalists alike. He uses the ideology of "aristocrats" to explain the ideology of slavery, telling Ophelia that any "high civilization" is composed of two classes: a "lower class, given up to physical toil" and a higher class that rules over the lower classes in order to "acquire leisure and wealth for a more expanded intelligence and improvement" (237). The higher class "becomes the directing soul of the lower" (237) or, in the language of accounting, attempts to control the indeterminacy of human nature. According to St. Clare's justifications of slavery in this chapter, there is only one viable economic system. It simply takes on different forms in different geographical locations within a world system. The St. Clare-Ophelia scene, then, turns on questions regarding the differences between slavery and capitalism but also the similarities in the logics of accounting that they share. These questions open up space to tease out the logics of accounting, simultaneously through St. Clare's proslavery stance and Ophelia's abolitionist stance, on which both slavery and capitalism rest.

The scenes with St. Clare and Ophelia can be read as an attempt to make sense of the larger capitalist economic system that slavery is part of—as a temporary part of a world-systems approach—and the whole system of slavery as capitalism, in the classical economic sense. For example, St. Clare argues that "the American planter is only doing, in another form, what the English aristocracy and capitalists are doing by the lower classes" (237). The point St. Clare is making here to Ophelia is that U.S. slavery is not unusual in its accounting practices but is rather "a specimen of what is going on, the world over, in some shape or other" (228). St. Clare states that the U.S. South is employing the same practices as other parts of the world. Though St. Clare is not speaking to the particulars of U.S. slavery's connection to, for example, a global cotton market, Stowe's placement of U.S. slavery in a more global economic schema is significant in that it foreshadows approaches that contemporary historians use today to make similar slavery-as-capitalism arguments.

When Stowe moves the conversation back from a global to a national context, her argument becomes more explicit. As the cousins' debate goes on, these controls appear not just globally or locally, on the enslaver's ledger line, but also systemically across northern and southern labor systems. She metaphorically refers to the North and the South as brothers and "duplicates" of one another

(235). When comparing his father, an enslaver, to Ophelia's father, a northern deacon, St. Clare tells his cousin that her father is, "for all the world, in constitution and habit, a duplicate of my father" (235). He says that her father has "the same strong, overbearing, dominant spirit" as his father (235). This is generally—and correctly—regarded as a metaphor Stowe uses to drive home her sentimental argument that all men are capable of becoming evil slaveholders or agents of slavery. But this strategy is constitutive in another way: Stowe draws on the stereotype of the shrewd New Englander, adept at business, equipped with the necessary accounting skills, to show that Ophelia's father would be an ideal slaveholder were he to move South. Though St. Clare goes on to say that, in material circumstances, the two men are not the same, in that Ophelia's father did not enslave people, what is important to St. Clare is that they would have been the same because of the "dominant spirit" of their businesses' control practices. St. Clare concludes this segment of the conversation by telling Ophelia: "If both had owned plantations in Louisiana, they would have been as like as two old bullets cast in the same mould" (236). Stowe's metaphor of the North and South as "two old bullets" is apt not only for the violence it implies. Referring to the North and South as "cast in the same mould," Stowe also shows how important the development of interchangeable parts was to the economic development of both the North and South. These parts include not just bullets but also versatile, preprinted accounting forms and portable pocket-books.

To be clear, Stowe was not participating in the contemporary debate over which set of workers fared better, southern enslaved or northern free laborers. Like Frederick Douglass who commented that there was "no analogy between the two cases" ("The Irishman is poor, but he is not a slave") ("Lecture" 169), Stowe believed there was no debate on this issue. As illustrated in the following section by Stowe's shadow account—her insistence on annotating the ledger line and attempting to tell the human story behind it—the practice of accounting fully exposes the distinction between enslaved person and legal person. The enslaved worker, instead of being accounted for as a debtor, creditor, or party to a transaction like a waged worker, *is* the transaction. The fact that Stowe acknowledges both labor systems as capitalist does not lead her to position them as analogous. Ophelia's role in the scene, for instance, is to constantly reiterate this point with rhetorical questions and arguments like "How in the world can the two things be compared?" and "But it's no kind of apology for slavery, to prove that it isn't worse than some other bad thing" (Stowe 237). Ophelia also plays the role of the northerner who is forced to consider that waged labor is not the answer either. In response to St. Clare's claim that the enslaver and the capitalist both operate from the same logic of "appropriating one set of human beings to the use and improvement of another without any regard to their own" and that this makes them "nature, the same," Miss Ophelia responds: "I never thought of the matter in this light" (238). Though Stowe was not precisely a champion of workers' rights, she was beginning to touch on the conversation of capitalist critique. In this sense, the scene discussed above between the two cousins, which is written through the contemporary debate around enslaved labor and wage labor, comes to reveal a related debate around fair wage labor. That is, Stowe, at different moments in the debate, also backgrounds the comparison of waged versus enslaved labor and foregrounds the logics of accounting to show the similarity in the logics of accounting that generated both conditions.[11]

When she moves the explanatory power of capitalist accounting into the debate about enslaved labor versus waged labor, she argues that subsistence wages, like the enslaver's account books, are a capitalist fiction. This move is not to pursue the question of waged labor in and of itself but rather to point out the capitalist ethos in the logic of the ledger that subtends both labor systems. She extends the accounting controls that are embedded in the enslaver's ledger to waged labor in the industrial North, linking the southern and northern economies through their accounting practices. In this sense, Stowe inserts an abolitionist critique of capitalism into popular fiction, emphasizing the shared capitalistic logic of accounting upon which the two labor systems rest. In this sense, we can situate Stowe and her abolitionist novel not only within the slavery and capitalism debates but also within the abolition and capitalism debates, a debate that revolves around the extent to which abolition and capitalism were "concurrent and mutually reinforcing" (Beckert and Rockman 10). This debate argues, in part, that abolitionists, in their specific effort to denounce enslaved labor by praising wage labor, paved the way for the oppression of the working classes and the reign of industrial capitalism.[12] Stowe, on the other hand, begins to touch on the abolitionist conversation of capitalist critique, more broadly—indeed, she cannot escape it—in her denouncement of slavery's accounting. For all the novel's failings and its inability to live up to even its own promises, the rhetorical brilliance of Stowe's economic through line in *Uncle Tom's Cabin* is that she offers a platform for the critique of capitalism from both the proslavery and the abolitionist perspectives of the day.

When, at the end of the scene, Ophelia asks St. Clare how it will all end, St. Clare says that he foresees the end of slavery coinciding with the "mustering among the masses, the world over," that "there is a *dies iræ* coming on, sooner or later," and that the "same thing is working in Europe, in England, and in this country" (240). Stowe was likely drawing on the proslavery-anticapitalist argument that northern capitalism's subsistence wages would generate revolution, a commonplace proslavery slant of the time, found, for example, in works by George Fitzhugh or in James H. Hammond's 1858 "Cotton Is King" speech. But Stowe's quasi-Marxist rhetoric, in the context of the economic continuities she notes between slavery and capitalism, could also be read as linking the fate of the white working class with the fate of enslaved laborers and as foreshadowing Reconstruction arguments about shared economic interest.[13]

Through St. Clare, an enslaver who is antislavery and anticapitalist in logic but proslavery in behavior, Stowe emphasizes the blurred lines between slavery and capitalism, a blurriness that both abolitionists and southerners depended on.[14] It is one thing for the proslavery argument to be anticapitalist in defense of slavery—to say that slavery is "better" for the worker than capitalism. But St. Clare is not following the usual proslavery argument: he argues they are immoral in the same way—that is, in their accounting logics—and that slavery is the worse infringement on human rights. His defense of slavery rests on the argument that northern and English capitalists are operating from the same economic logic. This allows Stowe to use St. Clare's argument against slavery—he admits that it is worse—but it also allows her to critique capitalism because its logics have been laid bare in its comparison to slavery, in that they both operate from the same ideology of capitalist accounting. Stowe's argument, then, is not only about the differences between slavery and industry. The antislavery impetus of her novel makes this difference clear. Rather, the St. Clare-Ophelia scene is also about the similarities of the free market ideals and capitalist accounting practices, including practices of control, that shape both the waged labor and enslaved labor systems. By reading the St. Clare-Ophelia debate through the logic of the ledger, then, we see Stowe grapple not with whether slavery contributed to capitalism, as the question would later become, but rather with how slavery was itself capitalist. Stowe's emphasis on the shared accounting logics of southern slavery and northern industry draws out an economic analysis of slavery-as-capitalism, her understanding of slavery as part of a capitalist world-system, and her nascent capitalist critique of both proslavery and abolitionist platforms.

If the above section establishes Stowe's economic observations and critique of the continuities between slavery and capitalism, the following two sections extend that critique to her shadow account. They analyze a series of scenes or case studies in which Stowe confronts the problem of slavery by thinking through the relationship between sentimentalism and accounting. For Stowe, bookkeeping and sentimentalism together function as technologies of (accounting) control for her characters, both enslaving and enslaved. Her constant invocation of the account book in these scenes demands further attention to the inherited and enduring trope linking sentiment and accounting discussed at the opening of this chapter.

To chart Stowe's shadow account, I first read the account books of Stowe's agents of slavery, from the so-called benevolent St. Clare to the murderous Legree, including Haley, Loker, and Marks. Through these characters' bookkeeping, Stowe explores possible framings of sentimentalism and accounting, showing the profound flaws of their different approaches. As in the previous section, her explorations critique slavery, but they also critique different vexed logics of abolition. Following the close readings of Stowe's agents of slavery are close readings in which the novel attempts to escape the logics of slavery's accounting. These scenes include three of Stowe's most memorable enslaved characters, Tom, George, and Topsy, along with the newly reformed Van Trompe, a former enslaver who chooses to use his account book to moral ends. Reading for the relationship between slavery, sentimentalism, and accounting in Stowe's shadow account further draws out the economic insights, operations, and consequences of the novel's racial politics. Because, for all her creativity in crafting these economic questions and debates as a sentimental novel, Stowe fails to offer any good answers to the problem of slavery's capitalism that she so imaginatively frames. The novel's economic framework and potential for a liberatory, antislavery, and anticapitalist accounting is ultimately undercut by Stowe's own racial politics. What Stowe's racial politics instead reveal are the economic operations of her sentimentalism, demonstrated by the shadow accounts in the following sections.

ACCOUNTING FOR STOWE'S ENSLAVERS

In the antebellum period, as in Stowe's novel, the plantation staff—the overseer, the bookkeepers, and the drivers of enslaved gangs along with the agents that operated outside of and on behalf of the plantation, the traders, speculators, and catchers—were all part of what might today be called a managerial hierarchy (C. Rosenthal, *Accounting* 23–31). All of these people, like the fictional versions found in Stowe's Haley, Loker, and Marks, relied on accounting principles and records since their income depended on close attention to the attributed economic value of the men and women they kidnapped and trafficked. Plantation owners, on the other hand, like Stowe's Shelby and St. Clare, also relied on accounting systems but were more likely to focus on day-to-day productivity of the plantation business than individual workers (C. Rosenthal, "Slavery's Scientific" 80).

Like Child, Weld, and the Grimkés, Stowe had growing interest in slavery's bookkeeping and the accounting practices of slavery's managerial hierarchy. Similar to Child's *Appeal* and Weld and the Grimkés' *American Slavery as It Is*, *Uncle Tom's Cabin* also breaks down different budget areas and talks about cost-saving measures. In sentimental and narrative form, she explains how "dealers in the human article make scrupulous and systematic efforts" (Stowe 335) to control the people they enslave for the sake of the account book. Stowe's shadow account, however, is not just composed of the sentimental stories behind the ledger line. It also narrates the wider economic and historical context of how those stories are brought to the ledger line.

Stowe offers a fictional example of the type of accounting employed by traders through Haley's story line, when Haley is preparing Tom for auction. As Haley heads south with Tom and reflects on Tom's market worth, he takes account of "Tom's length, and breadth, and height" and mentally calculates "what [Tom] would sell for, if he was kept fat and in good case till he got him into market" (122). When Haley realizes that Tom's value would be higher if sold as part of a "gang," he heads to an executor's sale to "get up a prime gang" (123). In a later chapter titled "The Slave Warehouse," Stowe describes the scene inside the house where agents of slavery force upon enslaved people specific behaviors that will raise their value on auction day. Breaking away from the plot of the novel, Stowe's narrative voice explains:

> Here they are fed full daily; and, because some incline to pine, a fiddle is kept commonly going among them, and they are made to dance daily; and he who refuses to be merry—in whose soul thoughts of wife, or child, or home, are too strong for him to be gay—is marked as sullen and dangerous, and subjected to all the evils which the ill will of an utterly irresponsible and hardened man can inflict upon him. Briskness, alertness, and cheerfulness of appearance, especially before observers, are constantly enforced upon them, both by the hope of thereby getting a good master, and the fear of all that the driver may bring upon them if they prove unsalable. (335)

In explaining how the mental and physical aspects of one's appearance are manipulated in preparation for the auction block, Stowe registers these enforced outwardly physical characteristics—being fat, merry, alert, et cetera—as sources of value that contribute to a potential sum of money. When read through the lens of slavery's accounting, these scenes narrate the story behind the valuations that appear on the ledger line, showing how the number eventually recorded by the enslaver reflects a brutal and dehumanizing calculation in which the enslaved person's human needs—for instance, for food or community—are translated into a payoff on the auction block.

By narrating the ledger line, Stowe calls attention to the way the enslaver's bookkeeping hides its own logics of accounting as well as its own logics of registering human history and argues that one cannot be understood without the other. The layout of the ledger—the narrow, boxed lines drawn on paper—Stowe understood, distills and compresses information about human history and generates a certain flatness. That layout and the flatness of numbers it generates promote a present nature of history, a sense of a kind of here-and-now history that erases the past. In other words, the account book is organized by dated entries across multiple pages, which over the course of years and decades would turn into multiple books. These pages and books may, over time, be taken together to construct a larger history through their numbers and dates. But Stowe pauses on the history behind the ledger line itself.

She takes the flatness of accounting's numbers and the present nature of accounting's history and seeks to think about the human stories and histories behind it. She registers history differently from the way the account books would register it. She thinks through the history behind how a line item—one's diet, mood, facial expression, et cetera—comes to be added to the ledger. Her story lingers on why the line items in the account book exist and how the values placed in these ledger lines are brought about. Her shadow account, in this case, is of bookkeeping's own logics of accounting and history. Stowe's insistence on telling the story behind these logics reveals, in sentimental fashion, how the numbers mirror the violence of plantation practices. In this case, Stowe's shadow account of "The Slave Warehouse" attempts to make her readers see in their mind's eye scenes of slavery's accounting that they would not be able to see on the ledger line. In other scenes, her shadow account reveals to readers the even-more-hidden components of slavery's accounting, illustrated below.

Passages about Black motherhood, more recently read as Stowe's sentimental appeal to white mothers, can also be read through slavery's accounting practices. In a scene with Haley and Shelby, for example, the trader and the enslaver discuss the ethics of separating an enslaved mother from her child. Haley directs the conversation toward managerial practices that net the most profit. He tells Shelby that, though he is willing to participate in the separation of family, he is critical of the way other slave-traders "manage the business" of separation (11). He says: "I never could do things up the way some fellers manage the business. I've seen 'em as would pull a woman's child out of her arms, and set him up to sell, and she screechin' like mad all the time;—very bad policy—damages the article—makes 'em quite unfit for service sometimes" (11). Haley situates the bad "policies" that could "damage the article" in terms of the bottom line of the account book. He presents the example of a mother who "went ravin' mad, and died in a week," the result of which, Haley says, was a "clear waste, sir, of a thousand dollars, just for want of management" (12). Haley, a trader prone to taking out his pocketbook and "adding over his accounts," understands that pulling a "woman's child out of her arms" is "very bad policy" (11) and prefers that the "thing's done quietly" so as not to drawn attention to his work (11, 134). But, to underline, it is not bad policy because of the sentimental argument against family separation—it is bad policy because it is economically inefficient. Haley advocates against certain explicitly violent policies because of economic not moral ramifications. In other words, his policy ensures the mother's enforced "service" and attributed economic value are not compromised. Haley, a working-class character eager to convince Shelby that his policies reflect his business acumen, applauds his own managerial record. He says: "It don't look well, now, for a feller to be praisin' himself; but I say it jest because it's the truth. [. . .] I lose as few as any man in the business. And I lays it all to my management, sir; and humanity, sir, I may say, is the great pillar of *my* management" (12). This scene narrates how agents of slavery drew from the logics of accounting to manage mothers and family separation.

In a later example, Stowe juxtaposes Haley's "policies" of "managing the business" of familial separation with Tom Loker's. When Loker is discussing his management policy with his partner Marks, he explains: "Why, I buys a gal, and if she's got a young un to be sold, I jest walks up and puts my fist to her face, and says, 'Look here, now, if you give me one word out of your head, I'll smash yer face in. . . . I'll make ye wish ye'd never been born.' . . . I makes 'em as whist as fishes." Stowe adds, "And Loker brought down his fist with a thump that fully explained the hiatus" (71). Haley, who is listening to the conversation, criticizes Loker for policies that are "bad" for the account book. But, as Stowe highlights, though Loker employs explicit threats of violence—precisely what Haley calls "bad policy"—both rely on accounting controls.

Through the above two scenes, the first focused on Haley and the second focused on Loker, we can see Stowe explicitly comparing different types of bookkeeping. In one sense, Stowe's comparison challenges economic value as defined by slavery's capitalism. Haley's criticism of Loker, for example, exposes precisely the absurdity that a kind of hard-and-fast accounting of economic "value" can be generated by slavery's accounting and its business practices. In other words, it is not immediately clear what counts as "bad policy" or what economic value those policies generate, since not all individuals respond to the same kinds of pressures and incentives in the same way. In one case, violence might be "good for business," but in others it might incite rebellion, fugitivity, or withheld labor as forms of protest against that violence. Additionally, the above scenes show Haley advocating against explicitly violent policies because of economic, not moral, ramifications and Loker explicitly rejecting moral arguments, a slight though significant distinction in their appeals to the account book. Though Stowe comments on the moral differences and similarities between men like Haley and Loker and how their attempts to organize their account books organize their own behavior, the two passages underscore the same accounting controls used for "managing" mothers and the result of such controls recorded as profit on the ledger line.

In another sense, Stowe's comparison of bookkeeping practices can be read for its exposure of sentimentalism's economic operations, on the part of both the enslaver and the benevolent observer. For the enslaver, as Stowe shows above, the account book of one's own perception or conscience is structured by slavery's capitalism. Less evident, however, is how, in the case of Stowe's sympathetic reader, their personal (sentimental) account book is also structured by slavery's capitalism. Typical readings of Stowe's sympathetic appeal to motherhood, for example, fail to register how she is, in fact, describing emotional and physical pain, and the "management" of that pain, as folded into bookkeeping. In other words, the sentimental convention around family separation under slavery in scenes like Stowe's promotes, at first glance, a profound sentimental response of shock and horror to the violent separation of mother and child. Under the logics of sentimentalism, the benevolent observer who witnesses or reads about a child being sold away from their mother would come to understand that no monetary price compares to a mother's pain in being torn away from her child.

But what Stowe shrewdly reveals in these scenes, by telling the story behind the ledger line, is how bookkeeping, when properly mined and recast through its own shadow accounts, can tell a truer, more accurate story to the consuming observer than their own initial sentimental misperception. That is to say, regardless of any monetary price attributed to an enslaved mother, whether a trader holds the value at, say, twelve hundred dollars or drops the price to one thousand dollars because of "damage" done to the mother, the observer remains ignorant of their own understanding of the relationship between accounting and sentiment. In this sense, Haley's insistence that the "thing's done quietly" reveals that the calculation of this kind of cost (i.e., how emotional and physical pain are folded into bookkeeping) needs to be kept hidden in order to operate in an efficient economic manner. Put another way, economic analyses revealed by shadow accounts like Stowe's lead to a different way of thinking about a kind of false consciousness generated by sentimentalism and its economic logics. Stowe's attempt to show a more transparent economics through her shadow accounts emphasizes how the account book of the benevolent observer's own conscience—and even one's consciousness, is rigged under slavery's capitalism, especially in its sentimental form. Put more succinctly, a sentimental viewing of the world absent of its accounting systems is just another way to cover up the books.

In a scene that calls us back to the apparent economic versus moral distinction around the function of the account book, Haley boards a steamer and heads southbound toward the New Orleans slave market. On board, he pauses briefly to consider the increasing danger of the slave-trading business and feels a pang of distress. Upon feeling that distress, Haley "took out his pocket-book, and began adding over his accounts,—a process which many gentlemen besides Mr. Haley have found a specific for an uneasy conscience" (131). Later in the novel, in a similar scene, the account book appears with Simon Legree, where, in an effort to wind down and close out his workday, he is seen "casting up accounts" (409). The feelings of Stowe's agents of slavery are soothed by looking at their account books, and they are often seen leaning more heavily on their account books when they seek to soothe an uneasy conscience. In the scene aboard the steamer, the practice of reading through the business record, "adding over his accounts," and taking comfort in accumulated profits is enough to soothe Haley's "uneasy conscience" about the "dangerous" business. Reassured by the addition column of his account book, Haley puts the dangers of the slave trade out of his mind, and "the boat swept proudly away from the shore, and all went on merrily, as before" (131). Again, Stowe invokes the account book to undermine any sharp distinction between moral sentiment and accounting: when Haley and Legree take out their account books to sooth their conscience, they use their bookkeeping to clarify and calculate sentiment. The account book functions as a technology of the business of slavery and also as a technology of sentimental conscience conjured into physical form.

As with Haley and Legree, Stowe's other fictional agents of slavery also practice a capitalist accounting of sentiment. When slave catchers Tom Loker and Marks are negotiating a "retaining fee" with Haley for "catching" Eliza and Harry, Loker refuses to compromise as he has "business booked for five weeks to come" (74). Marks consults the account book to support Loker's claim: "Marks had got from his pocket a greasy pocket-book, and taking a long paper from thence, he sat down, and fixing his keen black eyes on it, began mumbling over its contents" (74). The greasiness of his pocketbook gives away his moral crime, and his "mumbling" reveals the kind of unkempt and unseemly accounting recorded in the book. Marks mumbles: "Barnes—Shelby County—boy Jim, three hundred dollars for him, dead or alive. Edwards—Dick and Lucy—man and wife, six hundred dollars; wench Polly and two children—six hundred for her or her head" (75). The scene is at once a negotiation tactic on the part of Marks—"I'm jest a runnin' over our business, to see if we can take up this yer handily" (75)—and an insight into the role of accounting records offered by Stowe.

Stowe's description of Mark's fictional accounting practice reproduces, for her readers, the kind of accounting kept in nineteenth-century cotton journals, turning people, and the expanse of the human condition, into numbers. In this particular anecdote, Stowe teaches her readers how to critique accounting's correlation with sentimental mathematics. The long list of names, which includes individuals and their family relations, are read down the ledger lines in a tone that appears interchangeable with the way numbers might also be read from the ledger. In this sense, for Marks, observing the situation of groups of enslaved people appears to evoke lesser emotional force than individual cases. But, ironically, in his final valuation of his accounts, he ranks the whole over the sum of its parts. In this example of Marks's capitalist accounting of sentiment (or sentimental accounting of capitalism), Stowe shows again how one's sentimental politics cannot be accurately understood without transparency around their accounting.

In "Word Become Flesh: Literacy, Anti-literacy, and Illiteracy in *Uncle Tom's Cabin*" (2017), Faye Halpern analyzes the above scene through Marks's reading practices, arguing that Stowe's novel teaches its readers not just how to "feel right" but also how to read right (253). In other words, one brings a certain ideology to the page when reading and that ideology influences one's interpretation of text. When Marks reads the long paper from his greasy pocketbook, Halpern argues, he "reads in a dehumanizing way that turns people into abstractions, slaves into dollar amounts.... These are not just any slaves that Marks is turning into dollars, but husbands and wives, mothers and children" (256). Reading is never just reading; it is tied up in "associations, from social privilege and a source of benevolence to class bounding and the power to dehumanize" (257). Reading practices, then, generate their own kind of fiction. And the combination of the fiction generated by one's reading practices and the account book, already its own kind of fiction, can have deadly consequences. If, as Sarah Robbins has contended, Stowe understood "authorship as motherly teaching, managing her readers' literacy for the national welfare" (116), then we might also argue that she is managing her readers' financial literacy as well—that she was teaching her readers how to read the fictions of slavery's accounting and the way they operated as an organizing force of sentimental thought and behavior.

A final reading in the range of Stowe's enslaving characters returns us to St. Clare, a model of the so-called benevolent slaveholder neither trained in accounting nor using accounting himself to run his plantation. Yet his familiarity with accounting practices is apparent when he negotiates the purchase of Tom with Haley and, as a kind of joke, asks himself how he himself might be read as different line items: "'I wonder, now, if I was divided up and inventoried,' said [St. Clare] as he ran over the paper, 'how much I might bring. Say so much for the shape of my head, so much for a high forehead, so much for arms, and hands, and legs, and then so much for education, learning, talent, honesty, religion!'" (Stowe 157). Joking that there would be "small charge on that last," he completes the transaction, takes Eva's hand, and introduces himself to Tom as his new master. St. Clare's seemingly lighthearted joke about "how much [money he] might bring" is, of course, Stowe's way of showing the absurdity of the ledger when it is turned on the enslaver and that even the most benign enslavers are aware of the violent logic of the ledger. Additionally, it shows how account books participated in training the good southern citizen. St. Clare lives by the logic of the ledger, not necessarily for business purposes, since his estate is not a place where the reader sees labor happening (apart from the domestic labor that Dinah does), but as a way of life.

Considered a way of life, the logic of the ledger comes to touch not just on the business practices of Stowe's enslaving characters, such as St. Clare, but also on other practices, including religion. In a novel where anything is for sale—where anything can be turned into a number on the ledger line—Christianity itself has a market value. St. Clare explains the prevailing southern opinion regarding slavery by explaining how the account book controls the interlocking systems of religion, business, and politics. He says, "Planters, who have money to make by it,—clergymen, who have planters to please,—politicians, who want to rule by it,—may warp and bend language and ethics to a degree that shall astonish the world at their ingenuity" (230). Not only is religious belief commodified in this explanation, religion itself is subsumed entirely by the logic of accounting. Like politics, religion is not just "warped" and "bent" to support the "ethics" of slavery, it is warped and bent in service to the business of slavery and "money to make." When St. Clare and Haley are negotiating Tom's price, for example, Haley makes Tom's piety a selling point to St. Clare, telling

St. Clare that Tom is the kind of pious that is "quiet, stiddy, and honest" (157). Since, in the business of slavery, even religion is for sale.

The idea that religion is part of Tom's valuation piques St. Clare's curiosity, and he tells Haley, ironically, "I don't know, either, about religion's being up in the market, just now. I have not looked in the papers lately, to see how it sells. How many hundred dollars, now, do you put on for this religion?" (157). Convinced by Eva's insistence that he purchase Tom, St. Clare, "stooping gravely over his book of bills," takes Haley up on his offer to purchase piety, telling him: "If you can assure me that I really can buy *this* kind of pious, and that it will be set down to my account in the book up above, as something belonging to me, I wouldn't care if I did go a little extra for it" (157). Indeed, Stowe takes up the role of religion in slavery's accounting—both as something that can be purchased and recorded in the account book and as something that takes account of the people who control the account book—precisely because religion was a large component of what it meant to "*feel right*" (452). In this sense, Stowe has a warning for slave traders like Haley, Loker, and Marks, and for enslavers like St. Clare and Simon Legree, for whom it is impossible to see where religion begins and slavery ends, a sentiment exemplified in Legree's threat to Tom: "*I'm* your church now! You understand,—you've got to be as *I* say ... I have called thee by name. Thou art MINE!*" (346). She also has a warning for readers who misuse numbers in their personal account books and anyone who thinks, like Stowe's agents of slavery, that they can "run up a bill with the devil all your life, and then sneak out when pay time comes!" (72). Her invocation of religious morality as somehow a part of St. Clare's transaction around Tom—that he will be rewarded "in the book up above" for purchasing piety—points upward to a different kind of account book than the ones her enslaving characters carry in their pockets. God too, as far as Stowe is concerned, has a material account book. And, earthly economic transactions, including misappropriations of the church for economic profit like Legree's, will facilitate the heavenly judgement of one's soul.

But the true irony of the scene depends on an understanding of slavery's capitalist accounting systems. Thomas Affleck, in his *Cotton Plantation Record and Account Book*, explains the line item for religion in the enslaver's account book as one that is calculated in increments of time: "You will find that an hour devoted every Sabbath morning to their moral and religious instruction would prove a great aid to you in bringing about a better state of things amongst the Negroes" (quoted in Genovese 189–90). Piety as a line item in the account book was a practice that was literally incorporated into plantation operations by enslavers and, as Stowe knew, practices of religion within one's plantation economy could not be accurately understood without transparency around practices of accounting.

ACCOUNTING OUTSIDE THE LINES OF SLAVERY'S LEDGER

Though Stowe's plot privileges the accounting systems of her enslavers, the novel also presents characters who attempt to operate outside the logics of slavery's accounting. I read these scenes as a series of case studies, which begin with John Van Trompe, the reformed enslaver, and then move to three of Stowe's most famous enslaved characters, Tom, George Harris, and finally Topsy. These scenes do not resolve the association between accounting and sentiment or provide radical solutions to the problem of slavery's accounting, but, through a different range of combinations of sentiment and accounting and a different set of characters, reading these scenes as part of Stowe's shadow account further draws out her economic voice and the novel's insights into the way sentimental accounting acts as an enabling mechanism of mainstream racism.

In the scene introducing Van Trompe, the account book takes center stage. After years of witnessing "the workings of a system equally bad for oppressor and oppressed" (Stowe 97), Van Trompe's conscience gets the best of him. An enslaver whose account book works on his conscience until he uses it to emancipate the people he enslaved, Van Trompe makes the first move in atoning for his participation in the system by taking "his pocket-book out of his desk" (97). Pocketbook in hand, Van Trompe goes from Kentucky into Ohio, buys "a quarter of a township of good, rich land, made out free papers for all his people,—men, women, and children,—packed them up in wagons, and sent them off to settle down" (97). With the same pocketbook that he used to manage his plantation practices and keep account of its financials, Van Trompe extricates himself from the plantation system. Now in Ohio, "honest John turned his face up the creek, and sat quietly down on a snug, retired farm, to enjoy his conscience and his reflections" (97). Stowe uses the Van Trompe scene to show that if one "can see to it that *they feel right*" (452), then they can also see to it that they read their account book right. Van Trompe executes a financially, logistically, and morally sound departure from the plantation business. This is an important triumvirate, since economic impracticality of immediate abolition without indemnity was often used to assuage concerns over the immorality of slavery in the South and contributed to the overwhelming apathy and willful ignorance about slavery in the North.

The extent to which Stowe explicitly centers Van Trompe's account book in the transition is significant. Van Trompe begins with his pocketbook: it is through his accounting practices that he is able to buy a quarter of a township, to account for each individual for whom he makes out free papers, and to collect and purchase the resources needed to help them re-settle their lives. Stowe's juxtaposition of Van Trompe and the other enslavers makes a moral argument in which a Protestant work ethic and good finances are tied directly to abolitionism and an ability to "enjoy" one's conscience. The juxtaposition shows the opposite is also true—bad finances and the gamble of speculation not only reflect but also constitute bad moral character.

Through the association of sentimentalism and accounting, we can also read new ways in which Tom, Stowe's titular character, might have been the author of his own account book. Similar to the real-life economic knowledge of enslaved people as documented by historians of slavery, we can read Tom as having intimate economic knowledge of his own valuation. For example, in "'We'm Fus' Rate Bargain': Value, Labor, and Price in a Georgia Slave Community" (2004), Daina Ramey Berry explores enslaved men's and women's interpretations of their own values and sales and explains that enslaved people "developed a keen understanding of their value, going to great lengths to negotiate their sale in such a way as to maintain family ties" (55). They understood the role of gender, age, and skill, among other factors, in pricing and valuation schemes and used their economic and social knowledge to persuade potential buyers to purchase their entire families (55–56). To read Tom as the author of his own account book, we can turn to two of the novel's most pivotal scenes concerning the main character: the scene where he discusses his looming sale with his wife Aunt Chloe and the scene where he is beaten by Legree to the point of death.

When Tom is on Shelby's plantation and learns of Shelby's plans to sell him, Tom is faced with the choice to escape. And when Eliza knocks on his door late at night and tells Tom and Aunt Chloe that she plans to flee, Chloe suggests that Tom join her. But Tom refuses to leave, telling his wife: "No, no—I an't going. Let Eliza go—it's her right! I wouldn't be the one to say no—'t an't in *natur* for her to stay; but you heard what she said! If I must be sold, or all the people on the place, and everything go to rack, why, let me be sold. I s'pose I can b'ar it as well as any on 'em" (Stowe 44). In her seminal 1985 book *Sensational Designs: The Cultural Work of American Fiction, 1790–1860*, Jane Tompkins reads Tom as a submissive, nonviolent, Christ-like figure and argues that the "figure of Christ is the common term which unites all of the novel's good characters, who are good precisely in proportion as they are imitations of him" (146). Tom was at the top of this list (146). This reading of Tom as an exemplar of Christian virtue has prevailed among readers and scholars. However, reading Tom as the author of his own account book creates a shadow account that gives the commodification of Tom's piety—and Tom's own accounting of it—new meaning.

Tom's much-vaunted passivity is, very significantly, enforced by his concern not to allow other enslaved men and women, and more of them, to be sold in order to discharge Shelby's debt. His refusal to flee, it must be understood, is in part informed by his knowledge of the enslaver's accounting systems. Tom understands his high valuation in the family's book, and he uses this valuation to leverage his value in order to protect his family and friends. In this way, his logic exposes the gap between economic valuations of a human life and the moral value of human life. In the account books, Tom's value is equivalent to the value of "all the people on the place." But by all accounts in a moral world, every life is valued as equal, and the preponderance of lives ruined in a mass sale would be morally worse. Here his calculations of human life act as their own shadow account. If Tom needs to be sold to save everyone else, he tells his wife, he will be: "It's better for me alone to go, than to break up the place and sell all" (Stowe 44). Tom, in committing to stay on the plantation, is in some ways passive, but it is not a supine passivity at all. If we grant his character economic agency and knowledge, we can read his passivity more accurately as a strategic one meant to subvert accounting's control.

Tom deploys a similar strategy later in the novel with Simon Legree, operating as a disruptive force in Legree's accounting system. When Tom refuses to act as a "driver" of other enslaved people (364), Legree delivers a "shower of blows" and asks Tom whether he will still defy his orders: "'Yes, Mas'r,' said Tom, putting up his hand, to wipe the blood, that trickled down his face. 'I'm willin' to work, night and day, and work while there's life and breath in me; but this yer thing I can't feel it right to do;—and, Mas'r, I *never* shall do it,—*never!*'" (365). Tom's answer, that he is "willin' to work, night and day" but not willing to be a driver of others, obstructs enslavers' strategies to incorporate enslaved workers into managerial hierarchies. His refusal to be a driver threatens Legree's profit margins. Though Tom surrenders control over his own working body, he rejects exerting managerial controls over others. This was a disruption in the system for which Legree was unprepared: "Tom had a remarkably smooth, soft voice, and a habitually respectful manner, that had given Legree an idea that he would be cowardly, and easily subdued" (365). Tom's resistance to Legree's training intended to make a driver of him, positions him not so much as a submissive, Christ-like figure but as a disrupter of slavery's accounting. His piety and Christianity, at one point highly prized, no longer hold the same kind of value. When

Tom resists Legree's efforts to control him and train him as a driver, he poses the ultimate threat. His threat to that which is most sacred to Legree, the bottom line of his account book, is met by a murderous reaction.

In general, Stowe was limited in the ways she imagined that her enslaved characters might have engaged in their own accounting practices, even though accounting practices were very much a part of daily life for all people who existed under slavery. Stowe does, however, give us more of a glimpse of such practices, however limited, in George Harris's story line. In an early scene introducing George, in anticipation of a financial transaction, George appraises his value and skill as a laborer—outside of the plantation's account book but also in capitalist terms—and tells his wife Eliza that he has decided to flee bondage. Referring to his enslaver, George tells Eliza: "I know more about business than he does; I am a better manager than he is; I can read better than he can; I can write a better hand" (21).

George, an "ingenious fellow," had invented a machine for cleaning hemp, a labor- and time-saving technology that was quite the "valuable affair" according to his boss at the manufactory (112). The patent is held by George's enslaver, and his labor is simultaneously owned and appropriated by enslaver and manufacturer, an extended metaphor for the linkage between slavery and industry. The value of George's skills shifts depending on who is authoring the account book: his enslaver, his boss at the manufactory, or George himself. Because George's knowledge of business, management, and technology threaten racist conceptions of skilled labor and expertise, his enslaver takes him away from inventive work and instead puts him to the "hardest, meanest and dirtiest work" (21). Resistance to the obstruction of Black innovation and enterprise shows up in the way that George is relocated—and relocates himself—on the ledger line. Through this scene with George, and earlier with Tom, Stowe imagines the ways, albeit limited, that her enslaved characters might have engaged in their own accounting practices. George's own accounting system—his methods of ascribing value to both himself and his labor—is a shadow account in itself, revealing accounting to be a cultural construct, not simply a mathematical one.

Ultimately, though, Stowe's attempt to reorganize the logic of the ledger through characters like Van Trompe, Tom, and George are various forms of what could be called economic escapism. In other words, the above three readings show Stowe experimenting with different ways to challenge or get outside the ledger lines of slavery's account book. But in each of the three cases she is unsuccessful. Van Trompe comes close: he finds a way to use his account book to execute the immediate abolition of slavery within his own business practices. This is an important use of the account book considering the contemporary proslavery arguments made about the economic impracticality of immediate emancipation. But even in this case, when Van Trompe relocates to Ohio, his counter-account of his own books and bookkeeping introduces a kind of local escapism to the problem of slavery's accounting rather than any real solution to it. His local economic escapism is all the more clear given Stowe's own accounting linkages between the free and unfree states, which she lays out so carefully in the St. Clare-Ophelia debate. The former enslaver trained in slavery's accounting reestablishes himself in the free states. And though Van Trompe is now reformed as an abolitionist, moving Van Trompe and his accounting skills from an unfree to a free state is an ironic reversal of Stowe's own example, in the St. Clare-Ophelia chapter, in which she draws on the stereotype of the business-savvy northerner, well-equipped with the necessary accounting skills, as an ideal slaveholder if he moves South.

Tom and George also engage accounting practices as different forms of economic escapism. Through Tom's accounting practices, he finds a way to challenge the enslaver's ledger and to protect others around him. But ultimately Tom's attempt to get outside of slavery's account book culminates in an escape to a purely religious sphere. And George's accounting systems, for all their insight and ingenuity, are not put to use by Stowe in ways that would challenge or disrupt the dominant system, despite their potential. Instead, Stowe exports them, when George looks to emigration and Liberia, and offers another version of economic escapism, where the opportunity to reinvent the logics of bookkeeping is removed to a remote place, far away from U.S. society.[15] In this sense, Stowe's sentimentalism makes an economic argument as her thematic thread of escapism aligns with the bottom line of her own account book: her turn toward colonization. Her bookkeeping models struggle to imagine practical activities for the social, political, and economic integration of African Americans. In other words, her novel-length shadow account, rather than imagining realistic solutions for African Americans' full economic rights through strategies like land ownership or suffrage like Frances E. W. Harper does (see chapter 4 of this book), instead imagines a separatist utopia or different society, somewhere far away.

While the above three cases (Van Trompe, Tom, and George) represent different kinds of economic escapism, it is perhaps Topsy, the young, enslaved girl bought as a ruse by St. Clare and brought into the workplace of his cousin Ophelia's plantation household ("You find virgin soil there, Cousin; put in your own ideas") (250), who is best able to get outside the logics of slavery's accounting. In other words, when Ophelia attempts to control her, in an accounting sense, Topsy simply refuses to be accounted for.

In a final case study of Stowe's accounting, I read Topsy as a site where the kind of literal accounting that takes place in the enslaver's recordkeeping shows up in the domestic sphere.[16] The plantation household, as historian Thavolia Glymph explains in *Out of the House of Bondage: The Transformation of the Plantation Household* (2008), is often overlooked as a site of labor relations because of sentimentalism's association with it as a private space of white women. It was, nevertheless, Glymph argues, "also a workplace, not a haven from the economic world, [and] it was not private or made so by the nature of the labor performed within it or the sex of the managers" (2–3). It was a place where "enslaved women mopped its floors, dusted its mahogany tables, made its beds, ironed, wet-nursed, and bathed and powdered their owners" and where the scene was set for "day-to-day practices of domination" and "power relations between women" (2). In *They Were Her Property: White Women as Slave Owners in the American South* (2019), Stephanie E. Jones-Rogers points out that inside the plantation household, white, enslaving women exerted their economic agency by instituting disciplinary and managerial practices to "preserve the monetary value" of the enslaved people who worked inside and outside their domestic spaces (63).

Ophelia, assuming the position of the plantation mistress, wields the power of ownership over Topsy's ascribed value as a domestic worker according to the disciplinary logic of the ledger. Ophelia and her attempt to domesticate Topsy by putting her to work "making her own bed, sweeping and dusting her own chamber" (Stowe 250) is a fictional representation of the women Glymph calls the "*controlling* force within the plantation household" (3; my emphasis), a part of the management of enslaving households like St. Clare's. It is not St. Clare, in other words, who manages and balances the accounts of the household, it is his female counterpart, the "violence and power in the great house, the female side of domination" (Glymph 2).

As plantation mistress, Ophelia brings not just domesticity but also white womanhood to the ledger line. Ophelia's success as a domestic manager and her ability to achieve a model of domestic virtue ultimately depends on her control of Topsy—her ability to box Topsy into the lines of the ledger according to the needs of her household workplace. As Glymph explains, "The plantation household was the principal site for the construction of southern white womanhood, making the place of black women [and girls] within it critically important" (65). It was through the plantation mistress's management of enslaved domestic workers—for example, her ability to control the numbers on the household's ledger lines and balance the accounts of domestic economy—

that she was able to subscribe to ideologies of middle- and upper-class white womanhood.

Throughout the story, Stowe generally gives this role to Mrs. Shelby, the novel's typical "true" woman, and highlights accounting's contributions to her true womanhood toward the end of the story. Although Mrs. Shelby participated in upholding the Shelby planation economy through her domestic practices, it is after Mr. Shelby dies that we see her most visibly engage the account book. Now the executioner of her husband's estate, Mrs. Shelby takes over his accounts. As Stowe narrates: "Mrs. Shelby, with characteristic energy, applied herself to the work of straightening the entangled web of affairs; and she and [her son] George were for some time occupied with collecting and examining accounts, selling property and settling debts; for Mrs. Shelby was determined that everything should be brought into tangible and recognizable shape, let the consequences to her prove what they might" (Stowe 423–24). Mrs. Shelby is tasked with cleaning up the messiness of her husband's accounts. At this point in the novel, the Shelbys' son has not yet announced his plans to set free those his family has enslaved. So when Mrs. Shelby takes over her husband's accounts, she uses her accounting skills not to liberatory ends but to maintain the plantation. In this case, then, it is the female enslaver who brings to bear on slavery's accounting not a moral conscience but a tidiness. Women's supposed proclivity toward the domestic or the sentimental does not counter the brutality of the business of slavery. Rather, it makes it better organized.

If a plantation mistress's ability to neatly organize the accounts of a domestic economy allowed her to subscribe to ideologies of middle-class white womanhood, her inability to manage the domestic economy had the reverse result. As Glymph notes, "Black women's noncooperation defined and marked the failure of southern domesticity and simultaneously the defeat of its accomplice, the ideology of a gentle and noble white womanhood" (6). Inverting the apparent roles of northern and south women in the novel, it is Ophelia, not Mrs. Shelby, to whom the inability of balancing the southern domestic account book applies.

When Ophelia is not able to box Topsy into a ledger line, she becomes frustrated. Stowe narrates, "Miss Ophelia had just the capability of indignation that belongs to the thorough-paced housekeeper, and this had been pretty actively roused by the artifice and wastefulness of the child" (288). Ophelia calls Topsy a wasteful child, not because she is an inefficient worker who wastes resources like time and labor or because Ophelia is not able to instill her "ideas of education" (250) in Topsy. In fact, the narrator tells us, "Topsy was smart and energetic in all manual operations, learning everything that was taught her with surprising quickness. With a few lessons, she had learned to do the proprieties of Miss Ophelia's chamber in a way with which even that particular lady could find no fault. Mortal hands could not lay spread smoother, adjust pillows more accurately, sweep and dust and arrange more perfectly, than Topsy" (257). Rather, Ophelia calls the young girl wasteful because Topsy refuses to be, in accounting terms, controlled in the first place, to be boxed into a ledger line for a regulated and functional purpose of domestic worker first confined to the kitchen and then to the "sphere of operation and instruction" of Ophelia's chamber (250). Topsy, in spite of being "raised by a speculator" (249) and later educated in the domestic upkeep of the plantation household, is wasteful because she rejects both upbringings; she attempts to live outside of the ledger.

Instead of maintaining Ophelia's chamber, Topsy turns it into a child's playground: "She would climb the posts, and hang head downward from the tops... singing and whistling, and making grimaces at herself in the looking-glass" (257). Instead of making beds, sweeping, or dusting, Topsy could be found "dancing, tumbling, climbing, singing, whistling, imitating every sound that hit her fancy" (256). It is the potential productive value of her childhood as a domestic worker and the cost of nonproductive, playful childhood that ultimately Topsy is instructed not to "waste" in order to balance Ophelia's domestic account book. Topsy's "wastefulness" was a specific kind of wastefulness—a refusal to be controlled and an insistence on being a child, not a domestic worker. Topsy, rather than escaping to a faraway place like Van Trompe, Tom, and George, simply refuses to be accounted for, even by the most determined Yankee.[17]

The smart, energetic, quick-learning young girl that Stowe describes in the above passage carries these qualities with her into adulthood. Toward the end of the novel, when Stowe is wrapping up her characters' storylines, she tells us that Ophelia brings Topsy to Vermont where, having blossomed into a graceful and pious young woman, she is eventually recommended as a missionary in Africa. Speaking of Topsy's missionary work, Stowe writes: "We have heard that the same activity and ingenuity which, when a child, made her so multiform and restless in her developments, is now employed, in a safer and wholesomer manner" (443). Topsy's "activity and ingenuity" as a child was really a refusal to be accounted for in the plantation household economy, a refusal that disrupted both the white middle-class woman's account book and white womanhood itself. Topsy posed a threat not only to the efficiency of the plantation household's account keeping and profitability but also to Ophelia's ability to perform the duties of white womanhood. Now that Topsy is a woman possessing those same qualities of "activity and ingenuity" that empowered her to get outside of the ledger line Ophelia would have boxed her in as a young girl, Stowe contains the threat Topsy would have posed as an adult by boxing her back into the ledger. With the tidiness of the plantation mistress's accounting skills, Stowe channels Topsy's potential to disrupt by employing her, as a missionary in Africa, in a manner that is "safer" for white domesticity and the kind of sentimental accounting that is complementary to racial capitalism.

The above scenes, from Stowe's agents of slavery to her enslaved characters, read *Uncle Tom's Cabin* as a sentimental shadow account and together help to offer Stowe's particular sentimental vision of nineteenth-century accounting practices. But a larger culture of accounting in plantation economics existed outside of the fictional accounting practices and capitalist ethics Stowe portrays. Beyond Stowe's novel, one might think of Harriot Jacobs, who explains her accounting practices and logics when she takes inventory of the Flints' silver candelabra, which had been purchased with money that Jacobs's grandmother loaned to Mrs. Flint. The three-hundred-dollar loan was never repaid, and the candelabra was not returned. Instead, Jacobs writes, it became part of the Flint inheritance, an heirloom that "will be handed down in the family, from generation to generation" (14). In documenting the movement of money and goods, Jacobs accounts for stolen inheritance and generational wealth. In *Behind the Scenes* (1868), Elizabeth Keckley uses accounting practices in emancipatory and liberatory ways in both parts of her autobiography. When she recalls her time in slavery, she takes account of her hired-out work and savings plan to purchase her freedom, and in the second part, when she recalls her time with Mary Todd Lincoln, she narrates it, in part, through the successful accounting practices she uses to run her businesses. And Frances E. W. Harper's 1857 poem "Free Labor" argues for individual economic action by asking consumers to take close account of their conscience and pocketbook, engage their economic agency, and boycott products produced by enslaved laborers.

Outside of an author's individual and fictional or literary accounting practices, the nineteenth-century print culture of advertisements produced postings for Black businesses and services that represented the necessary accounting skills and practices required to maintain a successful business in a broader racist economy. This print culture also produced postings such as "Wanted" ads for fugitive slaves, which represented an enslaver's ledger and his economies of loss and gain. These "Wanted" ads, posted by enslavers, contrast with "Information Wanted" ads, posted by formerly enslaved people who sought the exchange of information about family members with no monetary reward attached to it. The fact that the economic logics behind such "Information Wanted" ads and Keckley's accounting practices, for example, were a means to bring about one's literal survival brings into sharp relief how Stowe's racial sentimentality limits the emancipatory power of her own accounting. In other words, for all of her shadow accounting and for all of the abolitionist rhetoric that she uses to narrate that shadow account, her enslaved characters are not liberated or even somehow saved by her sentimental account(ing); they remain enslaved, emigrate, or die by the end of her novel.

Ultimately, Stowe reinscribes violence into accounting through her sentimentalism. For all of her focus on the economic logic of slavery's accounting—the puzzle that receives the most explicit philosophical treatment in the novel—Stowe's sentimental racist politics limit her from thinking beyond that puzzle to consider the relationship between sentimentalism and accounting in any truly liberatory way. Though *Uncle Tom's Cabin* registers continuities in the economic logics undergirding slavery and capitalism, it fails to fully register the continuities in the racist logics undergirding the capitalist accounting approaches to both slavery and capitalism, especially the version of capitalism that Stowe herself benefits from.

A focus on sentimentalism, slavery's accounting, and capitalism in *Uncle Tom's Cabin* gives us another way to make sense of Stowe's inability to follow through on her more radical statements for social reform. This is to say that, because Stowe starts with the foundation of slavery-as-capitalism, she has to critique not only slavery but also capitalism more fundamentally. As a white, middle-class woman, Stowe benefited from capitalism in ways that were more socially and politically acceptable in the abolitionist movement than slavery. This tension created by her understanding of the relationship between slavery and capitalism alongside her advocacy of abolition and inability to fully divest of or call out the privileges of white supremacy within U.S. capitalism gives us another way to make sense of the failures surrounding her problematic (and sentimental) racial politics.[18] Ultimately, then, Stowe's sentimental shadow account demonstrates the economic logics of sentimentalism as an enabling mechanism of mainstream racism: sentimentalism's critique of slavery's accounting promotes and upholds the bottom line of racial capitalism by economically disempowering Black people, while simultaneously engaging in emotional and political appeals on behalf of those racial capitalism most violently oppresses.

CONCLUSION:
THE FICTION OF CAPITALIST ACCOUNTING

Uncle Tom's Cabin is a vexed shadow account because, on the one hand, it fails (or succeeds at failing) to practice a liberating, emancipating accounting practice aimed against slavery, like the novel's project itself. The economic logics of Stowe's racist sentimentalism limit the emancipatory power of accounting in that they cannot bring to the novel's ledger a bottom line that advocates full and equal freedom for enslaved or emancipated characters. But, on the other hand, Stowe's shadow account highlights both the oppressive and liberatory potential of accounting. It marks the capitalist accounting controls used by enslavers, it demonstrates how sentimentalism can expose or complement these controls, and it also, in illustrating slavery's accounting as a fiction itself, as shadow accounts do, creates potential moments of capitalist destabilization.

Even though Stowe's novel does not deploy sentimental accounting to emancipatory ends, we can still glean economic insights from its association between accounting and sentimentalism. The above series of case studies, the accounts of both enslaver and enslaved, stress an understanding of accounting as authored and narrated. In Stowe's hands, then, the account book is exposed as its own kind of fictional genre; the story that it tells is not a definitive depiction of events but rather a series of decisions by its author. While the account book as a form tries to render everything in mathematical logic and rigid addition and subtraction, it represents a fantasy of objective, stable value that just does not exist, regardless of the commodities (or people) being transacted. Stowe's fictionalization of account books draws her readers' attention to the fictions and fantasies undergirding the economic logic practiced by nineteenth-century enslavers. By creating a world born of accounting, Stowe provides a novel-length illustration of accounting as fiction, thereby rejecting an empirically neutral framework and politicizing its practice. In this way, Stowe's shadow account challenges the logic of the ledger. The ledger, as revealed by the stories behind it that Stowe narrates, is not naturally objective and intransigent but rather an enabling fiction that, complemented by a system of sentimental accounting, authors and authorizes the system of slavery itself.

By focusing on the logic of the ledger across *Uncle Tom's Cabin*, Stowe documents slavery as a capitalist system in her novel, and the appearance of the account book throughout reflects the extent to which slavery's accounting practices permeated mainstream culture. Stowe's economic acuity around slavery's capitalism, her theorization of accounting and its economic meaning-making, facilitates a kind of literary experimentalism with sentimentality. What that experimentalism allows us to see ultimately is how Stowe's liberal sentimentalism and her critique of capitalist economics, or slavery's accounting, are bound up in one another and that sentimentalism can be read as its own economic framework that maps neatly with the economic frameworks of the marketplace and mainstream racism. Stowe, then, emerges as an author whose work, within its own limitations, foreshadows academic accounting arguments that refuse distinctions between accounting and social accounting. Ultimately, though, by showing that accounting lies at the heart of her link between the labor systems of the South and the North and by showing accounting as value-laden and authored through the logics of sentimentalism, Stowe's novel also insists that it is possible for the nation to reimagine itself through its accounting "values," even if she is not able to do so herself.

The next chapter moves us from the plantations of the South to the factories of the North, two sites that are geographically distant but linked by their shared capitalist accounting logics and practices. Chapter 2 focuses on a poem by one of Lowell's best-known "mill girls," Lucy Larcom. It goes beyond the ledger line and takes account, so to speak, of the poem's disclosure of a different kind of economic insight around slavery's capitalism: what it feels like to touch and weave cotton in the Lowell factories, with the knowledge that the cotton was previously touched by enslaved women laboring on southern plantation fields.

CHAPTER 2

Slavery's Cotton Market in Lucy Larcom's "Weaving"

> But ever as I weave, saith she,
> The world of women haunteth me.
> —LUCY LARCOM, "Weaving" (1868)

IN HER 1868[1] POEM "Weaving," Lucy Larcom draws on her time as a factory worker in antebellum Lowell, Massachusetts, and leads her readers through a mill girl's experience before the loom. As the poem's speaker observes the ways her body interacts with the machine, she begins to question the extent to which she has been conscripted in the cotton market that upholds slavery. Repeating the word "weaving" over and over throughout the poem, the speaker creates imagery of an incessant motion that turns into a compulsory act. While she performs the act of weaving to which her body is habituated, she reflects on the sensations she experiences as she weaves. After sixteen lines of weaving, at the end of the third stanza, the speaker connects her bodily movements to the larger cotton circuit of women: "But ever as I weave," saith she, / "The world of women haunteth me."

Only two types of women populate the "world" that haunts Larcom's speaker, and they perform two sets of interconnected tasks. In the North, white factory women worked with cotton as spinners, weavers, doffers, and sweepers after the raw cotton arrived from southern cotton plantations. In the South, enslaved women on cotton plantations weeded and plowed the field, dropped the seeds, and hoed, picked, dried, sorted, whipped, ginned, moted and packed the cotton that would be exported to northern factories (J. Jones, "My Mother" 240). In reality, however, the "world of women" that made up the cotton circuit was populated by more than white factory women and enslaved Black women. The cotton circuit was a vast and complex network, crossing the geographical boundaries that separated North and South, that included women outside of the factory and the field and from all stations: women enslavers, businesswomen, shopkeepers, wives and daughters of traders and merchants, widows of manufacturers, and Black and white women who did putting-out work as spinners, weavers, seamstresses, and dressmakers, all of whom were also consumers.

Larcom, however, intentionally singles out two groups of women who are not typically thought of as women in nineteenth-century conceptions of "woman"—the factory girl and the field hand—and makes them the topic of her poem. She pushes these women and their labor back into public view and centers them as not only as women but as originators of worlds.[2] I attend to her focus on these women by reading "Weaving" as Larcom's own intervention in the slavery and capitalism debates—one that documents links between the two systems by centering working women. Since, as Larcom's speaker engages in the incessant activity of weaving, it is in this "world of women" that her body participates.[3]

This chapter follows the cotton as it circles through Lucy Larcom's "Weaving" and emphasizes the bodily experience of the white, working-class woman who existed and labored under the antebellum cotton market. Thus, it rejects the fraught capitalist logic that would examine the development of raw material into a consumable commodity for sale in the market, a logic that simultaneously erases the embodied process of cotton weaving, the tactile experience of cotton itself, and the racialized and gendered significance of cotton as it makes contact with the skin. Instead, it focuses on these latter points. It follows a circuitous trail of cotton in the poem's world of weaving by exploring the speaker's "lived experience" or "lived body," in the Merleau-Pontian sense, as shaped by the dictates of the cotton market and the sensory experiences that permeated her sense of subjectivity under slavery's capitalism.[4] Through an analysis of Larcom's "Weaving," I explore how one woman from the cotton market's "world of women" perceives the world created by cotton *in* and *through* her body, thus necessitating a conception of the body as racialized and gendered. If we read, in Larcom's poem, the lived body of the weaver and if we "return" to the "thing" of cotton itself (Merleau-Ponty, *Phenomenology* lxxii), then, we return to the world as it precedes what we now understand to be so-called knowledge of slavery's capitalism and instead appreciate how slavery's capitalism was lived through by one weaver whose body was caught up in and sustained it.

Scholars of nineteenth-century white, working-class literature have explored such literature for the ways that whiteness has been constructed by a working status.[5] In my analysis of "Weaving," I extend this line of inquiry by exploring whiteness as a process of racialization that is mediated through the broader economy of slavery's capitalism. In Larcom's poem, the textual insistence on the body and the way the body feels under this economic system is remarkably pervasive. Larcom's account of moments of so-called apperception—that moment when one is aware of what Merleau-Ponty would call one's "perception" (i.e., the "immediate and first-personal givenness of experience" [S. Gallagher and Zahavi])—come into view as an awareness to her felt condition as a person. Such awareness is not described merely in terms of its tangible effect on the body, rather it is argued *through* the body. If we read in Larcom's focus on the body the apperceptive moments that reveal an awareness of one's embodied role in the cotton market, then we can read her poem with a focus on how whiteness feels, as read through those apperceptive moments that locate the body of the wage-earning, white woman both in opposition to slavery and within the cotton market of slavery's capitalism. That is, through a phenomenological analysis of the weaver's engagement with the raw cotton she weaves into thread, we can read how whiteness—as a capitalist enterprise mediated by labor, gender, and the nineteenth-century cotton market—feels. It is precisely Larcom's awareness of the link between the cotton market and her racialized and gendered labor position as a factory worker that make her writing uniquely applicable to the study of slavery's capitalism.

Before turning to "Weaving," I offer historical background on the cotton economy—contouring the expanse of the cotton market and foregrounding the overwhelming numbers of women that comprised its labor force—since it serves as a backdrop for my reading. As historians have documented, the cotton market was a wide-spanning network of geographical, material, and human connections. Historian Walter Johnson, in *River of Dark Dreams* (2013), describes those connections and the interplay between them. His description is long but, because of its intricacy, worth quoting in full:

> The "cotton market" about which they so frequently spoke, and to which they attributed an almost determinative power over their own lives and fortunes, was in actual fact a network of material connections that stretched from Mississippi and Louisiana to Manhattan and Lowell to Manchester and Liverpool. The economic space of the cotton market was defined by a set of standard measures—hands, pounds, lashes, bales, grades—that translated aspects of the process of production and sale into one another. Those tools for measuring and enforcing quantity, quality, and value produced commercial fluidity over space, across time, and between modes of production. Yet they also indexed the frictions resulting from the movement of cotton from field to factory: shifts between quantitative and qualitative valuation of the crop, between the physical processes of

producing the cotton and those of grading it, between the labor of slaves and the demands of purchasers. These measures served both as the imperatives by which the commercial standards of the wider economy might be translated into the disciplinary standards that prevailed on its bloody margin, and as markers of the nonstandard, human, resistant character of the labor that produced the value that was ultimately being measured and extracted. They marked both the extent to which the metrics of the exchange in Liverpool penetrated the labor practices of Louisiana and the extent to which the labor practices of Louisiana pushed outward to shape the practice of the global market. Rather than a pure form—"capitalism" or "slavery"—they united, formatted, and measured the actually existing capitalism and slavery of the nineteenth century. (10)

In the second quarter of the nineteenth century, the epicenter of the cotton market began to shift from Manchester factories to southern plantations. Beginning in 1846, historians Robert William Fogel and Stanley L. Engerman document, the worldwide demand for southern cotton had increased so rapidly that cotton planters were not able to keep up with it (94). This demand came in large part from New England mills, which manufactured 75 percent of the nation's textiles by 1860 (Farrow, Lang, and Frank 26). In many accounts of the cotton market, Lowell features as a central link in the symbiotic economic relationship between North and South. To meet demand, Anne Farrow explains, the eleven textile companies in Lowell strategically coordinated with each other to manufacture different products so as to minimize competition within the city: "One specialized in calico prints, for example, another in a heavy fabric called 'drillings,' yet another in fine fabrics. But the mills at Lowell also made 'negro cloth'—coarse, simple fabrics. In other words, slaves picked the cotton, which was sold to Northern textile manufacturers, who wove the cotton into 'negro cloth,' which was sold to plantation owners to clothe their slaves" (26).

The demand for cotton and the competition between manufactories had real effects on the lives of laboring women, both white and Black. The rapid increase in numbers of white women employed in the factory and Black women in enslavement reflects, in part, increased demand for production in the cotton market. In 1840 in Lowell, the textile mills employed almost 8,000 workers, most of whom were young white women. By 1860, the number of workers multiplied more than fifteenfold, rising to nearly 122,000 (Stansell 108, 260n13). The percentage of increase for enslaved women workers belies the enormity of the numbers. By the beginning of the Civil War, there were 2.25 million Black people in bondage involved, directly or indirectly, in growing cotton (Farrow,

Lang, and Frank 26), with most likely 63 to 77 percent of the women forced to work as field hands (Steckel 45).[6] This is a nearly sixfold increase from the 1790 U.S. Census, conducted three years before Whitney's invention of the cotton gin, which recorded just under 700,000 enslaved workers (Farrow, Lang, and Frank 26).

The cotton market, like other markets under slavery's capitalism, was subtended by the expanding nineteenth-century accounting culture. Numbers of factory workers and their productivity outputs were, like the numbers of enslaved laborers and their productivity outputs discussed in chapter 1, recorded in account books. Both in the factory and on the plantation, or, as Caitlin Rosenthal calls them, the "two faces of an expanding culture of accounting," operations managers relied on the account book to scale operations as demand for cotton rose and as the number of workers increased (*Accounting* 71). Because accounting practices did not develop in geographical or industry-related isolation but instead functioned as part of a trans-Atlantic print culture that included the exchange of ideas and ideologies as well as the exchange of forms, manuals, and instruction books (71–72), factories and plantations shared a similar logic of accounting. For both types of managers, Rosenthal explains, "[accounting] records made new information visible by condensing data about large numbers of workers and long periods of time into small spaces" (71), which allowed for tighter control over the time and behavior of the workers.

But the differences between accounting practices in slavery and industry matter as much as the similarities. And one crucial difference showed up *as* pages. While plantations typically used preprinted forms, factories almost always used forms that were ruled by hand (50). Rosenthal offers one reason for this: free-wage laborers could, and often did, leave these positions. Factories, unlike plantations, struggled to recruit and retain workers as the free--wage laborer, unlike enslaved laborers, could choose to terminate their employment (50). The permanence of the enslaved condition is reflected in the relative permanence of preprinted forms, especially in contrast to handwritten forms, which could be newly generated according to the changing labor force of the factory. As Rosenthal highlights, "Little less than a natural disaster could [pause plantation work]. No one quit. Even runaways were sometimes included in labor totals.... Births and purchases replaced the dead.... During a period when labor turnover in free enterprises regularly reached 100 percent or more over the course of a year, Caribbean sugar planters experienced almost none" (50). While the permanence of the enslaved condition and the related permanence of preprinted forms allowed plantation accountants to experiment with the widest range of control mechanisms on a laboring population, factory ledger lines wielded control for a different reason: they "focused on the problem of turnover and ways to manage it" (71).

The lives of the southern cotton plantation owner and the northern factory owner were dictated by the ebbs and flows of the cotton market. The same might be said of the thousands of New England farm girls who flocked to Lowell in the early 1800s to work in its growing textile industry. When Frances Cabot Lowell and his business associates established the city of mills in 1814, they combined all the machines and people needed to process raw cotton into finished cloth under one roof. The majority of this workforce was made up of young women, usually between the ages of fifteen and thirty, who were lured to the city by its promises of independence, education, and income.[7]

Labor historians and women's literature scholars continue to explore Lowell and its literary output, but in doing so they overwhelmingly background a crucial detail about the Lowell mills and those who worked in them: the mills and the mill workers existed in large part, as evinced in the above history of the cotton market, because of the economic demands produced by slavery. To talk about the mills and the women and girls who worked in them requires that we also talk about the industry's connections with the slavery industry. As Larcom's poem "Weaving" highlights, the opportunity for young white women like Larcom to participate in the public labor force was made possible by the nation's transition from a slavery-based agricultural economy to a slavery-based industrial economy. Lowell mill workers could only earn the highest wages in the female economy of the time because enslaved workers were denied them. Larcom was not the only factory worker who wrote about these connections.[8] Others, like her, understood that the wage through which factory girls felt a sense of dignity and agency was dependent on the exploitation, violence, and degradation of enslaved women's stolen labor. It is, then, against the whiteness of Lowell, the mill workers, and the wage that this chapter reads Larcom's "Weaving" for its description of the felt condition of whiteness in slavery's cotton market.

An omniscient third-person narrator opens Larcom's "Weaving" and sets the scene for the reader.[9] When we first meet the weaver, she is standing before her loom on the factory floor. From her station inside the factory, she is able to look outside a nearby window where she gazes on grassy fields, trees in bloom, and a winding river. It appears at first to be a peaceful scene, a soothing rendition of the supposed compatibility of industry and nature. But then, when the weaver begins to speak, it quickly gives way to a darker vision. The weaver's soliloquy, the dawning realization of her role in slavery's cotton market and her explanation of what it feels like to play that role is not performed by a single, identifiable factory worker. The young woman remains nameless and faceless throughout the poem, often substituting the collective personal pronoun for the singular, signaling that the role she plays is a role played by many more like her. The worker, deeply reflective and self-aware, is a feature of Larcom's poetry. As Sylvia Jenkins Cook has noted of Larcom's other work, "Larcom's poetic workers are also thinkers and writers, women whose active literary engagement enables them to form a transcendent link between the physical and spiritual realms of their existence" (Cook, *Working Women* 11). As the poem goes on, Larcom's speaker laments the inability to fully grasp the unspeakable crimes of slavery and the consequences they hold for the nation. When her soliloquy comes to an end, the third-person narrator reenters to close the scene. In the final two stanzas of the poem, the narrator observes the weaver consumed by her own thoughts as the Civil War rages on in the background. As the narrator brings the poem to a close, she leaves us with an image of the weaver, still on the factory floor. But rather than weaving before the loom as when the poem opens, she now paces before it.

Before moving to an analysis, it is worth considering the poem in full:

> All day she stands before her loom;
> > The flying shuttles come and go:
> By grassy fields, and trees in bloom,
> > She sees the winding river flow:
> And fancy's shuttle flieth wide,
> > And faster than the waters glide.
>
> Is she entangled in her dreams,
> > Like that fair-weaver of Shalott,
> Who left her mystic mirror's gleams,
> > To gaze on light Sir Lancelot?
> Her heart, a mirror sadly true,
> > Brings gloomier visions into view.
>
> "I weave, and weave, the livelong day:
> > The woof is strong, the warp is good:
> I weave, to be my mother's stay;
> > I weave, to win my daily food:
> But ever as I weave," saith she,
> > "The world of women haunteth me.

"The river glides along, one thread
    In nature's mesh, so beautiful!
The stars are woven in; the red
    Of sunrise; and the rain-cloud dull.
Each seems a separate wonder wrought;
    Each blends with some more wondrous thought.

"So, at the loom of life, we weave
    Our separate shreds, that varying fall,
Some strained, some fair: and, passing, leave
    To God the gathering up of all,
In that full pattern wherein man
    Works blindly out the eternal plan.

"In his vast work, for good or ill,
    The undone and the done he blends:
With whatsoever woof we fill,
    To our weak hands His might He lends,
And gives the threads beneath His eye
    The texture of eternity.

"Wind on, by willow and by pine,
    Thou blue, untroubled Merrimack!
Afar, by sunnier streams than thine,
    My sisters toil, with foreheads black;
And water with their blood this root,
    Whereof we gather bounteous fruit.

"There be sad women, sick and poor:
    And those who walk in garments soiled:
Their shame, their sorrow, I endure;
    By their defect my hope is foiled:
The blot they bear is on my name;
    Who sins, and I am not to blame?

"And how much of your wrong is mine,
    Dark women slaving at the South?
Of your stolen grapes I quaff the wine;
    The bread you starve for fills my mouth:
The beam unwinds, but every thread
    With blood of strangled souls is red.

"If this be so, we win and wear
    A Nessus-robe of poisoned cloth;
Or weave them shrouds they may not wear,—
    Fathers and brothers falling both
On ghastly, death-sown fields, that lie
    Beneath the tearless Southern sky.

"Alas! the weft has lost its white.
    It grows a hideous tapestry,
That pictures war's abhorrent sight:—
    Unroll not, web of destiny!
Be the dark volume left unread,—
    The tale untold,—the curse unsaid!"

So up and down before her loom
    She paces on, and to and fro,
Till sunset fills the dusty room,
    And makes the water redly glow,
As if the Merrimack's calm flood
    Were changed into a stream of blood.

Too soon fulfilled, and all too true
    The words she murmured as she wrought:
But, weary weaver, not to you
    Alone was war's stern message brought:
"Woman!" it knelled from heart to heart,
    "Thy sister's keeper know thou art!"

THE WOVEN WORLDS OF WOMEN

When the narrator opens the poem, the weaver is already at her loom. Describing the weaver's day in the factory, the narrator foregrounds her stasis against the movement of the shuttles and the river: "All day she stands before her loom; / The flying shuttles come and go: / By grassy fields, and trees in bloom, / She sees the winding river flow." Though she appears to be describing one day, the poet's description of "all day" might instead be understood as day in and day out. The "flying shuttles" might be like the days that "come and go." The "trees in bloom," one might imagine, were also watched months before when they were not in bloom. The "winding river flow[s]" like days winding and flowing one into the other. The weaver's everyday life is not dictated by a natural environment but by an industrial environment that has seemed to merge with nature itself.

In addition to a spatial awareness of the division between nature and the factory, Larcom was also attuned to the geography of a more local landscape: the factory itself and the spatial positioning of people in it.[10] Larcom knew that her location in the factory would dictate her day's sensory experience. In her autobiography *A New England Girlhood: Outlined from Memory* (1889), Larcom describes one of the machines that surrounded her: "I felt as if the half-live creature, with its great groaning joints and whizzing fans, was aware of my incapacity to manage it, and had a fiendish spite against me. I contracted an unconquerable dislike to it; indeed, I had never liked, and never could learn to like, any kind of machinery. And this machine finally conquered me" (226). Larcom, who occupied multiple jobs in the factory system in addition to weaving, also occupied different spaces associated with those jobs within the factory buildings. Her first job as a Lowell factory worker was in a spinning room, doffing and replacing the bobbins. She later tended a spinning frame, and then a dressing frame, which was near the windows and allowed her to look out toward the river. Larcom was eventually employed in a cloth room, which the women considered to be a more agreeable workstation in the factory because of its fewer hours of confinement, its cleanliness, and the absence of machinery (Willard and Livermore 448). All of this created different sensory experiences for Larcom as she worked. In *The Worlds of Lucy Larcom, 1824–1893* (1989), Shirley Marchalonis, Larcom's biographer, notes the lasting effects that the sensory experience of the machines had on Larcom: "The machines, or more particularly the noise of the machines, became intolerable, creating both a physical and psychological reaction that [Larcom] would never lose" (31). The last two years that Larcom worked in the Lowell mills were spent as a bookkeeper, keeping account of cotton in the form of cloth, recording the number of pieces and bales the mills produced (Willard and Livermore 448). In this last regard, we might imagine how Larcom's particular attention to gendered and racialized labor relations between the factory weaver and the enslaved field worker showed up on her ledger lines. Perhaps, for example, Larcom's anxiety about her role in the cotton market of slavery's capitalism might have produced its own shadow account of the inner workings of the mills.

The narrative voice in "Weaving" initially conceptualizes the weaver among two "worlds"—the natural world and the world of the factory—which places her in relation to a piece of nature she transforms through weaving. But by the end of the second stanza the narrator moves away from the general backdrop of two abstract worlds and guides us toward the backdrop projected by the weaver: "Her heart, a mirror sadly true, / Brings gloomier visions into view." Here the voice of the weaver takes over, and the poem takes a sharp turn in tone. She is no longer lost in imagery such as stars woven into the thread on her loom or a "river [that] glides along," "one thread / In nature's mesh, so beautiful!" As her body continues to weave, she realizes that her relation to the natural and industrial worlds includes a "world of women" she cannot see, a realization that transforms her way of seeing the very object—the cotton—in front of her. It is through the mirror of "her heart," through her bodily experience, that the weaver comes to understand a "gloomier vision" of the world around her.

If, as philosopher Iris Marion Young puts it, one's "lived body is a unified idea of a physical body acting and experiencing in a specific sociocultural context" (16), then Larcom's weaver can be examined as a unified idea of her physical body acting and experiencing in the specific economic context of slavery's cotton market under which her lived body labors.[11] In other words, the lens of feminist phenomenology enables a reading of the weaver's "specific body" for the way it constitutes her "facticity" (16)—that is, how she comes to understand herself as an embodied subject. In this experience of confronting a "gloomier vision" as she touches and weaves the cotton, a "truth" that is "sad" is filtered through the weaver's facticity—that is, the "material facts of her body" (16) and its relation to the specific environment she describes. Standing at the loom, absorbing through sight the separation of industry and nature, the weaver pieces together, in an integrative way, connections between the different functions of slavery and capitalism as systems that organize human labor, including her own, and gives rise to analysis of where she fits into these systems in relation to other women. Because the weaver's observations are filtered through the "material facts of her body" (16), the way cotton shows up in her lived experience positions her to uniquely make sense of her body, the staple fiber, and the reciprocity of touch between the two.

By the middle of the poem, the weaver has shifted from a dreamlike state of a laborer at one with nature to the "sad" truth of her entrapment in the emotional and physical exploitation of slavery's cotton market. It is through the action of weaving that she comes to this discovery. Standing at the loom, the weaver describes her body in motion: "I weave, and weave, the livelong day: / The woof is strong, the warp is good." Time connotations of "livelong" and adjectives like "strong" and "good" seem to vacillate between describing her body's performance at work and the product of that performance, underlining the ways in which this labor has alienated her from her own body. Trapped in a system that promotes a sense of scarcity, the weaver feels she has no choice but to weave: "I weave, to be my mother's stay; / I weave, to win my daily food."

The repetition of the word "weave" promotes a sense of a quickness, an incessant drive to weave for as long and as quickly as possible to ensure sustenance for her mother and herself. Because of the preponderance of "I" alongside an attention to the individual movements of the body, we sense her weaving as a oneness with her body, whether through the loom or through the sustenance it provides, more so than the oneness between nature and weaving that the poem appears to promote at the beginning.

The movement of the body while producing—"I weave and weave"—stands in marked contrast to the movement of the body while reflecting on her production, "up and down," pacing "to and fro." It is from within this oneness of her body and her weaving that she begins to think about functions of the system outside of herself, specifically other women laboring in the cotton market. The disappearance of the "I" over these lines, and the temporary appearance of the third-person narrator, makes room for these women: "'But ever as I weave,' saith she, / 'The world of women haunteth me.'" It is through the act of weaving—her physical experience of being in a gendered and racialized body whose skin makes contact with the cotton—that she comes to think about the enslaved women in the South who may have touched that same cotton before her.

The literal thread that the weaver touches figuratively threads together women with drastically different lived experiences and provides her an understanding of how this "world of women" was brought to be. She starts with her observations of the other weavers around her in the factory, each at a loom: "So, at the loom of life, we weave / Our separate shreds, that varying fall, / Some strained, some fair." The workers are separate from one another spatially, in the factory, and divided as "hands" within the system. They are credited or discredited in the system based on the ways in their "varying" shreds happen to "fall": some "strained," some "fair," these referring, perhaps, to those fair factory women who left the mills for marriage and those strained women who did not. And just as whiteness created the opportunity for her to participate in the wage labor system, it also offered her the opportunity—the mobility—to leave it.

In her 1875 poem "An Idyl of Work," Larcom dedicates a stanza to this fact, explaining that most every mill girl knew that part of the job description of mill work was leaving it: "Not always to be here among the looms,— / Scarcely a girl she knew expected that" (*Idyl* 34). The stanza continues, describing some of the goals held by women who choose to go into factory work:

> Means to one end, their labor was,—to put
> Gold nest-eggs in the bank, or to redeem
> A mortgaged homestead, or to pay the way

> Through classic years at some academy;
> More commonly to lay a dowry by
> For future housekeeping. (34)

Like many women mill workers who defended their rights to middle-class sensibilities, Larcom insists in her verse that the defining characteristics of mill work are that it is temporary and serves a future goal beyond the work itself. In this sense, we can see the ways in which, as historian David Roediger noted, "status and privileges conferred by race could be used to make up for alienating and exploitative class relationships, North and South" (13). While the white factory girl worked in the alienating and exploitative environment of the factory, her whiteness worked to protect her outside the factory.[12]

Regardless of one's path after leaving factory work, the poem's speaker explains, the weavers understand that while working in the factory they are part of a larger "full pattern." This pattern is made up not of fabric but of the common man or woman who "works blindly" toward some unknown, unknowable larger goal, what the speaker calls "the eternal plan" orchestrated by a kind of invisible hand, perhaps a reference to laissez-faire capitalism. This hand, likened to God, lends its "might" to the "weak hands" weaving the threads that have been imbued with "the texture of eternity." This phrase, the texture of eternity, despite its material, textural connotation might well be read as a feeling, associated with the physical sensation of touching the thread, of a ceaselessly tiresome existence with no hope of relief. The experience of the physical touch of the thread with this cosmic intuition about her bodily experience becomes the structuring metaphor of a larger metaphysical condition from which she sees no escape—"eternity."

From the factory window, the weaver's gaze falls on the winding, "untroubled Merrimack," and she follows the river "afar" to where, in the South, enslaved Black women are harvesting the cotton that she is spinning into thread. She visualizes the physical movements of these women in her imaginary world of women—"My sisters toil, with foreheads black; / And water with their blood this root, / Whereof we gather bounteous fruit"—and makes the physical connection between the touch of the enslaved women who sow the cotton seeds and the factory workers who labor with the fruit of the seed. But she also notes the saturating of that cotton, which will eventually be spun into cloth and perhaps clothing worn by the masses, with the "blood" of the woman who planted the seed. She comes to discover that the cotton she spins in stanza four is not tinted by "the red / Of sunrise" but by something far more distressing—the blood of the enslaved women working in the cotton fields.

THE PHENOMENOLOGY OF
WEAVING WHITENESS

The connections that the speaker makes are generated between elements that operate at different levels: a thread and the universe, as it were, and the touch of cotton and then of woven cloth. The lived body in Larcom's "Weaving" can be read as the speaker's opening onto the world of cotton—it is *in* and *through* the body that she perceives this world. It is the filter through which she reaches multiple dimensions of awareness of her own white subjectivity, her role in a larger network of women workers in the cotton circuit, and her location at the intersection of slavery and industrial capitalism.

Perception, for the poem's speaker, is a mode of contact with the world of cotton in which she is enmeshed. Merleau-Ponty's apt metaphor of fabric is instructive for thinking about embodied consciousness. Using textile imagery to explain how the body becomes "woven" into the world and sustains the system of significance around it, he writes: "All my thoughts and the thoughts of the others are caught up in the fabric of one sole Being" (*Visible* 110). In other words, for Merleau-Ponty, every perceptual act is a thread that connects the perceiver to the perceived, weaving them together as a "fabric of one sole Being"—that is, a whole that must always be thought of as a whole. In other words, there is no strict boundary for where one ends and where the world begins, no detached vantage point on the world. Rather, the connection between self and world is concurrent: perception weaves one into the world, but one's way of perceiving is itself woven together by the world and by the time and place and context of meanings in which one perceives.[13] The body is central to this configuration. As Merleau-Ponty emphasizes: "My body is the fabric into which all objects are woven, and it is, at least in relation to the perceived world, the general instrument of my 'comprehension'" (*Phenomenology* 273).

In Larcom's "Weaving," the weaver's body is the fabric into which all objects are woven. It is her "woven" body that becomes the general instrument of her comprehension of the perceived world around her—in this case, the world around her as shaped by slavery's cotton market. This comprehension or perception of the world is being toward a "thing," such as cotton, through the body, that is, in a bodily way rather than being as simply mentally or cognitively orientated toward a thing. At the same time, the body through which one makes contact with the world is itself shaped by the things it encounters, by the crop it picks or the fabric it weaves, which are parts of the circuitry of slavery's capitalism. Put another way, the weaver engages in a process of weaving self and world together through her contact with the "bodies" of things (cotton) and the bodies of others.

The weaver's understanding of cotton and the cotton market appears in her encounter with cotton itself, which, as she weaves, then solicits more sophisticated bodily awareness for future encounters, which then makes the cotton appear more complex in its meaning and in its affordance for more possibilities of action.[14] What such meanings and affordances of cotton are, however, depends on the particular subject position of the speaker (or author who creates the literary depiction) and her particular encounters with cotton. Larcom appears aware, for example, that her body produces knowledge that goes beyond the analytic and intellectual understandings of slavery's capitalism. In other words, as the poem evinces, Larcom is aware of the relationship between slavery and capitalism that contemporary historians are currently articulating on a more analytical level, but Larcom understands that relationship at the level of bodily awareness. Adopting a lens that privileges a woman's bodily awareness of the economic system in which she is caught up allows us to pay attention to the traces left on her body by that system. And when we pay closer attention to how she gives voice to those traces in her writing, we reach a more precise understanding of, for example, the world of slavery's cotton market that she perceives.[15]

Importantly, I am not treating these moments of the author's awareness as preexisting or guiding her writing as a consciously articulated theory or ideology that was already completely figured out. Rather, my aim is to show moments of the author's literary depictions of sensory and bodily awareness without claiming them as evidence of her understanding. This distinction between awareness and understanding allows for an analysis that originates with the here and now of a phenomenological approach rather than with analysis or intellect. Phenomenology as a theoretical framework thus enables analysis of the more intimate dimensions of slavery's capitalism, and the cotton market in particular, that invaded women's narrations of subjectivity.

One way to access the more intimate dimensions of economy is through the sensory experience of touch. Sense of touch, in part, shows that the texture of something is a function of what one prepares oneself to feel. In other words, the past—the enslaved women's touching of the cotton before it arrives in the factory where the speaker will weave it—informs the present experience, the weaver's own touching of the cotton, through an expectation that is met by the object itself, cotton. The phenomenological point here is that experience is not in a subject or a function of properties in the object but rather present as an interconnection of subject (weaver) and object (cotton). A phenomenological reading of the poem thus allows us to watch this unfold through the process of weaving and to witness the speaker's experience of the same phenomenon (cotton) altered again and again by the dawning realization of her complicity in the violent economic system that provides her livelihood.

In Lucy Larcom's case, her livelihood was perhaps connected to more than the wages she earned in the mill. While her income vis-à-vis whiteness was connected to the daily work of weaving, her family's wealth vis-à-vis whiteness was potentially connected to a family history that included her great-grandfather's business in slavery. Larcom's autobiography only briefly alludes to her ancestors' involvement in the enslavement of Black people and does not offer much detail as to its extent, but it is worth noting. In a chapter titled "Old New England," Larcom describes her hometown by recounting some of the historical influences that gave it a "character and an individuality of its own" (*Girlhood* 93). The chapter mainly discusses the town's proximity to the sea and the influence of that geographical positioning, but there is a short section in which she mentions a small Black community. Larcom writes: "Families of black people were scattered about the place, relics of a time when even New England had not freed her slaves. Some of them had belonged in my great-grandfather's family, and they hung about the old homestead at 'The Farms' long after they were at liberty to go anywhere they pleased" (96). Larcom mentions two of the women by name, pointing them out specifically because they still worked for the Larcom family. She writes, "There was a 'Rose' and a 'Phillis' among them, who came often to our house to bring luscious high blackberries from the Farms woods, or to do the household washing. They seemed pathetically out of place, although they lived among us on equal terms, respectable and respected" (96).

According to Historic Beverly, the historical society of Larcom's hometown, "Rose" was Rose Larcom, the daughter-in-law of Juno Larcom, an enslaved mixed-race Native and Black woman who was inherited upon marriage by Lucy Larcom's great-grandfather David Larcom. Though *A New England Girlhood* does not much provide further information about Rose or Juno beyond the above, an unusually detailed account of early Beverly's Black community and especially the Black people enslaved by David Larcom is found in the records of the historical society. According to the society's records, David Larcom sold three of the twelve children that Juno had with her husband, Jethro Thistle, a man enslaved by a neighboring family. In July 1774, intent on preventing the sale of her other children, Juno took David Larcom to court and charged him with "trespass and assault," stating that she and her family were "seized with Force of Arms & imprisonment kept in Slavery against her will" (Historic Beverly). The move was a risk: "If Juno's lawsuit succeeded, there was no way to be sure that they could find work to support themselves as free people. If it failed, she would have had to continue working for a man she had charged with attacking her, and enslaving both her and her family" (Historic Beverly). The courts dismissed Juno's lawsuit without a verdict when David Larcom died in April 1775. Taking matters into their own hands, Juno and her family "claim'd their freedom" and settled in a house near the Larcom farm, where they earned their living by weaving, doing laundry, and working in the fishing industry (Historic Beverly).

It is difficult to know to what Larcom meant exactly in *A New England Girlhood* when she wrote that Rose and Phillis lived among the Larcom family and their community on "equal terms, respectable and respected" because she does not elaborate on this point. Maybe the observation reflects Larcom's personal feelings toward the women, or perhaps it reflects her feelings toward the quality of the work they undertook in the community, the "luscious high blackberries" they brought to town or the household washing that they took in. Even so, the irony of this memory, and Larcom's sense that the women "were at liberty to go anywhere they pleased," is that the labor relation between the Larcom family and Rose and Phillis, even if based on an "equal" wage contract, and their location in Beverly is rooted in the history of slavery, an institution grounded specifically in inequality and immobility. Similarly, it is impossible to know what Juno Larcom thought or felt, or what she might have thought of her son and daughter-in-law's Beverly life. However, it is likely she would not have agreed with Larcom's assessment that the Black Larcom family lived on equal terms and had freedom of mobility. Other than the above brief mention in *A New England Girlhood*, Larcom does not make further mention of her family's involvement with slavery, but we might speculate that this piece of the Larcom family history contributed to her theorization of the economic relations of Black and white women's labor.

In Larcom's family history, her waged labor, and her working status we can see the ways that whiteness functions as both physical and metaphysical property. Legal scholar Cheryl I. Harris's article "Whiteness as Property" is useful here. Harris explains that the law's construction of whiteness "defined and affirmed aspects of identity (who is white); of privilege (what benefits accrue to that status); and of property (what *legal* entitlements arise from that status)" (1725). Harris adds, "Whiteness at various times signifies and is deployed as identity, status, and property, sometimes singularly, sometimes in tandem" (1725). Through Harris, we can complicate Larcom's experience: participation in the cotton circuit allowed white women like Larcom, New England cotton weavers, to access and manage their whiteness in new ways. The weaver's physical touch of cotton and her bodily movement at the loom reify her whiteness as a central property of her personhood. The process of weaving imported southern cotton initiates the female mill worker into whiteness as a system of economic value, providing a racialized and gendered way of being in the world while at the same time producing a product (cotton fabric) that reifies that symbolic economic value in a physical, tangible form. Through the act of weaving, the mill worker creates the fabric. Yet every new move she makes on the fabric as she weaves it is a function of what is already there: she is weaving her own whiteness even though it is not noticeable to her.[16]

Part of the anxiety in Larcom's narration of the weaver at the loom can be located in Larcom's recognition that her weaving had violent, potentially fatal consequences. For example, when the poem's speaker references the "loom of life," she invokes the Fates of Greek mythology—the three weaving goddesses Clotho, Lachesis, and Atropos who spin the thread of human fate and decide when to cut it, determining the course of one's life and death. We can read the speaker's factory weaving work as a rehearsal of such a posture where her work at the loom affirms the fate, as do the three Fates, of the enslaved women in the cotton circuit in which she participates. In this moment, the speaker shifts from the singular personal pronoun to the collective—"So, at the loom of life, we weave" indicting the whole class of factory girls as fatal sisters. Contrastingly, Larcom would also deploy this mythological reference to defend the dignity of women's factory work and the honor of cloth manufacturing as a "branch of feminine industry" (Addison 8). Comparing the girls' use of the "spindle and the distall" to those same "picturesque accompaniments of many an ancient legend—of Penelope, of Lucretia, of the Fatal Sisters themselves," Larcom argued for women's role in the important work of preparing "the clothing of the world" that "robes the human millions" (8). The juxtaposition of these two very different contexts for Larcom's use of the Greek myth is stark, perhaps illuminating the degree of her vexed emotions as a working-class woman who felt obligated both to acknowledge her complicity in slavery's cotton market and to defend the dignity of her labor.

When the poem's speaker shifts her focus from the female factory workers around her in the industrial North to enslaved women in the South, she does so through an association with their garments. Describing them in her mind's eye, she writes: "There be sad women, sick and poor: / And those who walk in garments soiled." The garments that the speaker references, garments made specifically for enslaved people, were produced in both northern and southern textile mills, including Lowell. Enslavers purchased from the manufacturers what they called "negro cloth," a cheap wool-cotton blend or coarse cottons. It is this cloth that comprised one of Harriet Jacobs's dresses to which, as discussed in the following chapter, she had a visceral reaction. Several formerly enslaved people have recalled their experiences wearing "lowell cloth." In an interview conducted by the Work Progress Administration in the 1930s, for example, Mariah Snyder references Lowell cloth when she recalls the clothing she was given on the plantation. Her transcribed interview reads: "We wore lowell clothes and I never seed no other kind of dress till after surrender" (52). Not only was the Lowell weaver spinning the cotton that enslaved women were harvesting, she was also part of the loop that returned the cotton back to the planation in the form of clothing for enslaved persons.

The mode of coming to realize her complicity with slavery, for Larcom's weaver, consists of trying to conjure, in a bodily way, the lived experience of the women picking the cotton she weaves. Attempting to forge a connection with those women, she notes their emotional state as one she internalizes and grapples with: "Their shame, their sorrow, I endure; / By their defect my hope is foiled." Considering that the labor conditions of picking cotton were accompanied by sexual threat, what the speaker most likely refers to as "their shame, their sorrow," the speaker's attempt at empathy reveals another linkage between the women: the relationship between white women's economic privilege and enslaved women's sexual vulnerability. These lines move the poem's reader beyond the abolitionist myth that only linked the white southern female enslaver's economic privilege and power to the enslaved women's sexual exploitation and vulnerability and shows how the economic power of white northern working-class women, like Larcom's weaver, was linked to enslaved women's sexual vulnerability as well. She ends the stanza asking who bears this responsibility: "The blot they bear is on my name; / Who sins, and I am not to blame?" The weaver's use of "blot" conjures the imagery of a kind of stain, be it on one's reputation ("my name") or metaphorically on a garment produced in the New England factory in which the weaver worked. When she asks herself whether or not she is to blame for such sins, she pauses in a seemingly rhetorical stance to allow her readers to ask themselves the same question.

The rhetorical stance that implicates her readers lasts only briefly before the speaker returns to reflecting on her own complicity. Turning from the linkage between her economic privilege and the sexual vulnerability of Black women, she attends to the linkage between her economic privilege and the physiological vulnerability of Black women. The speaker acknowledges her awareness that in "quaff[ing] the wine" and "fill[ing] [her] mouth" with bread, she is taking—

stealing—food and drink that would ensure the destruction and demise of one human being in order to provide sustenance for the continued bodily existence of another. And while she marks these instances of individual responsibility and participation, she also recognizes that she was cast in and exploited by a larger capitalist system that encompassed both the northern and southern labor systems, a larger system upheld by many more people beyond herself.

Larcom's speaker first asks the question—"and I am not to blame?"—of herself, using the personal pronoun "I," and then extends her accusation of collusion to those who weave alongside her, eventually using the personal pronoun "we" in her answer to the question. Perhaps earnest in her question, she refuses to sit alone with the burden of collusion. Invoking the other mill workers in her "world of women," she writes: "If this be so, we win and wear / A Nessus-robe of poisoned cloth; / Or weave them shrouds they may not wear." The poem's speaker and her fellow factory workers were purchasing and wearing the "poisoned" cloth that they themselves were spinning. Though she includes herself here by using the plural personal pronoun—"we win and wear"—by extending the accusation beyond herself, she also shifts some of the responsibility onto a larger class of people and thus creates for her readers an opportunity for self-awareness.

We can get at least an anecdotal sense of the numbers that comprise this class from Jennie Collins, a mill worker writing to the woman's rights newspaper *The Revolution* a few years after Larcom published her poem. In her 1870 letter, she enumerates the numbers of this class and quantifies their purchasing power via threat of boycott, writing: "There are forty-eight thousand factory girls in Massachusetts. They consume on the average six calico dresses a year, ten yards in the dress. From this you can see that the factory girls are the largest patrons of their employers.... We working women will wear fig-leaf dresses before we will patronize the Cocheco Company" (20). Collins's threat speaks to the amount of business made from the purchase of women's dresses by "factory girls," dresses they themselves helped produce.

But Larcom's line does not only allude to the amount of "poisoned cloth" worn by northerners and mill workers. It also alludes to the "shrouds" that the mill workers "weave" that travel back to plantations—the "mass-produced clothing for slaves" that both northern and southern textile mills competed to supply. Larcom describes the "shroud," a literal piece of cloth as well as a metaphor for garments of living death that the mill workers weave, garments that deceased enslaved people "may not wear" since their enslavers often did not give them a proper burial. But the reach of the "poisoned cloth" extends beyond the speaker, the class of factory workers, and the enslaved laborers who wore the Lowell-spun clothing. Larcom's reference to the "Nessus-robe" indicates another interpretation of the cotton that the mill workers wove, beyond the bodies that donned it.

Nessus was a centaur who was fatally shot by Heracles with an arrow that Heracles had previously dipped into the poisonous blood of the Hydra. Before Nessus died, he convinced Heracles's wife that his blood would ensure Heracles's fidelity. Not knowing Nessus's blood was infected with poison, the wife gave Heracles a robe with Nessus's poisonous Hydra-infected blood on it and it kills him. The poison that Heracles used to kill Nessus circulates and is transmitted back to him in a final, fatal act. As with the story of Heracles and Nessus, the poison of slavery, the multiheaded Hydra, which saturates the nation's cloth, circulates through and on the national body and kills its own people. In the second half of the stanza, the speaker turns to the war: "Fathers and brothers falling both / On ghastly, death-sown fields, that lie / Beneath the tearless Southern sky." The speaker's reference to a Nessus-robe, through which Nessus took revenge on Heracles through his blood, argues for a parallel story of revenge: one in which the nation fabricates its revenge upon itself—"Fathers and brothers falling both." The poison of the cloth created by northern factory workers out of the suffering of enslaved women is then transmitted to the "fathers and brothers" who die on the battlefield in a war waged to end slavery. Cloaked in clothing produced by the female mill workers, either shrouds or proper clothing, the women, fathers, and brothers of the poem die in the theater built by the cotton market: above the "death-sown fields," scattered with the poisonous seed of slavery's cotton and "beneath the tearless Southern sky"—tearless in its disregard for the suffering and loss of human life.

In the weaver's last mention of war in the poem, before the narrator intervenes and offers the final conclusion, she proclaims that the "the weft has lost its white." The weft is woven over and under the warp (the threads that stretch across the loom). Together, these produce cloth. So when the weft loses its white, so too does the entire piece of cloth into which it is woven. The weaver narrates the expansion of a "blot" across the cloth produced by the interwoven weft and warp: "It grows a hideous tapestry / That pictures war's abhorrent sight:— / Unroll not, web of destiny!" What Larcom calls "the blot," the national stain of slavery that metaphorically bleeds into the cotton she weaves, grows larger, covers the whole "hideous tapestry" and eventually bleeds into the fabric of the national consciousness. Allusions to whiteness and white anxiety can be found in the poem even if Larcom's language itself does not explicitly record whiteness. Her use of the word "blot" might betray a white anxiety about the mixing of races, for example, or the ways the manual labor of the mill might compromise white womanhood by being a little too close to the enslaved labor of Black women.

Nonetheless, Larcom understood that the different threads, in this case women, interwoven by slavery's capitalism were underestimated—erased, even—by those narrating the history of the period. Her weaver, for example, laments: "Be the dark volume left unread,— / The tale untold,—the curse unsaid!" Such erasure of women's contributions, as Larcom knew, was easily achievable considering that patriarchal culture dismisses women's work in the public sphere and capitalist culture renders the labor of production invisible. This erasure that Larcom notes is ironic since northern abolitionists argued that one of the biggest obstacles to converting people to abolitionism was precisely the invisibility of what plantation labor looked like to people in the North. When this is coupled with the need to remove women's labor from sight because of white bourgeois ideals of womanhood, entire worlds under slavery's capitalism get erased. Rather than allowing this erasure—an indication of the undervaluing of women's labor as well as an attempt to hide the necessary exploitation of women's labor that is essential to capitalism in general and to the cotton market under slavery's capitalism in particular—Larcom highlights the worlds of the weaver and the field hand and pushes them and their labor back into the center of that history. Within the context of the poem, Larcom understood the significance of the weaver's relation to enslaved women as a thread, connected by the material nature of cotton and cloth, in the economy of the cotton market. It is on this note that she closes out her poem.

The final four lines of "Weaving" reinforce an understanding of the phenomenological connection, through cotton, between the two groups of women. Larcom writes: "But, weary weaver, not to you / Alone was war's stern message brought: / 'Woman!' it knelled from heart to heart, / 'Thy sister's keeper know thou art!'" The weary weaver knows herself to be connected to other women as functions in slavery's capitalism, the major issue leading to the Civil War. It is to her and other women that "war's stern message [is] brought," a message that underscores the raced and gendered labor relations that make up the cotton market. Through material connection via the experience of touch, Larcom, a free white woman, attempts to bring her white readers inside the system of slavery. And while her good intentions are not the same as being fully immersed in the material conditions of enslavement, following the cotton allows her to share a rare insight that arises from her work and her economic relation to other women workers—how whiteness feels when complicit with slavery's capitalism, no matter how involuntary.

THROUGH THE FACTORY WINDOW

Toward the end of the poem, the third-person narrator reenters, pulls back from the narrow perspective of the weaver at her loom, and pans out to a view of the larger factory. The weaver, ruminating on a literal and metaphorical thread, paces about the factory floor through the day until sunset: "So up and down before her loom / She paces on, and to and fro, / Till sunset fills the dusty room." Appearing to return to natural imagery, the narrator recasts that natural imagery as blotted by slavery. The sunbeams that backlight the dust of the factory and fill "the dusty room" also change her view outside the factory window. The same sunset "makes the water redly glow, / As if the Merrimack's calm flood / Were changed into a stream of blood." The blood-red color fills the Merrimack River, which, like a thread itself, connotes movement and connection.

The incessant weaving that the poem narrates suggests the sensation of normalcy, the idea that the weaver is doing what she is supposed to be doing. But this act of weaving to which her body is habituated is a kind of distraction that, rather than allowing for focused exploitative capitalist productivity, becomes a meditation on exploitation. The pace of her work would typically woo her into a trance of production and promote a sense of normalcy, as defined by a capitalist culture. Instead it warps time and place. For, while it brings her inside slavery via the cotton circuit, it also grounds her outside of slavery, concretely anchored in the physical space of the factory even as she imagines herself within the world of enslaved women.

The tension I want to focus on now, however, is not Larcom's critique of her relative privilege or her recognition of white female mill workers' economic and material connection to enslaved women field workers but rather her inability to escape her whiteness. This inability is illustrated in the poem through Larcom's literal weaving of cotton. As much as the weaver wants to make sense of her relation to enslaved women in the South, she is unable to do so. Her attempt to identify with enslaved women is undermined by the ongoing process of the white female body's interpellation into dominant modes of white womanhood. Philosopher George Yancy explains: "Being a white antiracist is never completely in one's control because such an identity is deferred by the sheer complexity of the fact ... that the white body is constituted by racist habits that create a form of racist inertia even as the white body attempts to undermine its somatic normativity, and that the white self undergoes processes of interpellation even as the white self engages in agential acts of racist disruption"

(*Black Bodies* 231). As Larcom's weaver paces up and down the factory floor, she experiences a dissonance between the givenness of supposed white, female innocence and the sin she has trespassed as she comes to "perceive that the racial parameters that structure whiteness" (Alcoff 187) within slavery's cotton market of women—and from which she benefits—cannot be made coherent with her preferred sense of self. Larcom wants to identify with the women whom she calls "my sisters" and wants to endure their "shame" and "sorrow." She wants to take responsibility for her "sin" and "blame." But while she critiques slavery, it is the very thing that gives her a livelihood and all the opportunities she lauds (income, education, independence, the benefits so ubiquitously promoted to recruit women to the mills). Her critique expresses disillusionment with the very organization of a labor system that allows her to live, to eat and drink and breathe, and more—to "pay a mortgage," "put gold nest-eggs in the bank," to "redeem a mortgaged homestead," to "pay the way at some academy" or to "lay a dowry"—at the expense of the Black woman worker who suffers and starves (*Idyl* 34; "Weaving").

This disillusionment is partly due to the confusion caused by the fact that even though the weaver seems aware of her whiteness, she does not know what to make of it. Just like the white of the weft that disappears as she weaves, whiteness hides itself as whiteness and becomes normalized to the point where it becomes invisible. So while the weaver is aware of the exploitation of enslaved women, she is perhaps unaware (or does not fully understand) how her own investments in whiteness are also complicit in that exploitation, represented, in part, by the third-person narrator whose external frame removes us from fully accessing the weaver's interiority of self. The weaver's awareness of her complicity ends with her labor. What is passed off as her "identification" with the enslaved woman's experience is really a form of her failed imagination and inability to fully divest herself of her whiteness. In other words, her identification with enslaved women does not interfere with factory production or the operations of the cotton market or change her material world. Nor does the weaver give voice to the enslaved woman, the subjectivity of whom is a glaring absent presence in the poem even as she is the subject of circumlocution. Rather, the weaver's identification is characteristic of what Charles W. Mills calls an "epistemology of ignorance," which involves a "particular pattern of localized and global cognitive disfunctions (which are psychologically and socially functional), producing the ironic outcome that whites will in general be unable to understand the world they themselves have made" (18). The weaver's unanswered questions—"Who sins, and I am not to blame?" and "how much of your wrong is mine[?]"—that aim to "understand the world" anchor the poem. Unable to make sense of her whiteness, the weaver is unable to answer her own questions about the extent to which she is conscripted in the cotton market. What begins as an observation about a tethered economic relation transitions into a moral observation. Though she points to the cruelty endured by enslaved women and the exploitation of the "world of women," she ultimately asks her reader to feel sympathy for the weaver who feels irreconciled guilt about such cruelty.

By the end of the poem, the weaver can no longer sit with her whiteness and the disruption of sense of self it calls forward. The poem chronicles this restlessness: "So up and down before her loom / She paces on, and to and fro." The weaver paces, engaging the body in a physical movement that also renders her fixed in place on the factory floor. Rather than sitting still with the problematics of whiteness, the body is jerked into motion. She becomes trapped by its limitations. Though Larcom's weaver attempts to give an account of herself and critique her relative privilege, she stops just short of reimagining herself when she encounters the "limitations and failures" of white allyship (Yancy, *Look* 175). She cannot abide the tension she feels in what Linda Martín Alcoff would call the "disjuncture" or tension between her white body and a sensibility that attempts to exist outside of the logics of slavery's capitalism from which it arose.[17] She releases herself from this disjuncture by moving her "sin" outside of the individual sphere and into the national sphere, where it erupts in "war's stern message." Ironically, the final message on the "world of women" comes from "war," not from the weary weaver who has narrated its haunting.

The point here is not to condemn Larcom's intentions as a white abolitionist. I do not dispute the authenticity of her antislavery sentiment.[18] And I agree with literary scholars who note the poem's political significance. Karen Kilcup has argued for Larcom's "cultural power and authority" and the "political thrust of her work" ("Something" 17) and suggestively places "Weaving" within "the tradition of women's political poetry that includes Lydia Sigourney's 'Indian Names' and reaches forward to contemporary work by Gwendolyn Brooks, Lucille Clifton, and Carolyn Forché" (*Nineteenth-Century* 174). Joe Lockard convincingly argues that the radicalism of "Weaving" can be found in its "newly-forming multiracial class consciousness" (153), one that had yet to significantly take root in nineteenth-century U.S. society. That is, Larcom's final stanza, in which the plight of the enslaved woman worker is moved out of the weaver's individual sphere of consciousness and into the public sphere of war, asks its national readership to consider its own class consciousness. As Lockard argues, what is now seen cannot be unseen: "Through the agency of [the poem's] images, the mill—powered by the invisibilities of exploited and slave labour—is visible now in its entire systemic extension" (152). To be sure, Larcom has a long and undisputed record of abolitionist sentiment, verse, and action and, as a daughter of the mill from the age of eleven, the added dimension of working-class consciousness.

The point, rather, is to mark one instance in which the lived experience of white female abolitionism, against the backdrop of slavery's capitalism, manifests in literary form. More generally, Larcom's reflection on and theorization of the cotton market's "world of women" serves as one instantiation of how the lived experience of time gets racialized in that world. Yancy stresses, "Even as whites take the time to theorize the complexity of whiteness, revealing its various modes of resistance to radical transformation, Black bodies continue to endure tremendous pain and suffering.... The sheer weight of this reality mocks the patience of theory" (*Black Bodies* 229).

Indeed, as Larcom, who was "not always to be here among the looms" (i.e., she was aware that she could choose to leave the mills), was theorizing the complicity of her whiteness within the cotton market, Black women were being terrorized by this market. Larcom's poem is one form of evidence for the limitations of white activism. And when juxtaposed with Harriet Jacobs's *Incidents in the Life of a Slave Girl* in the next chapter, it opens a larger conversation about the nineteenth-century, white, antislavery movement and the dual forces of white supremacy and capitalism that made the lived experience of slavery inaccessible to someone like Larcom. Despite Larcom's attempt to bring herself and her white reader inside the condition of slavery, an attempt spurred by the phenomenological experience of touching cotton (and an ironic reversal of the typical migration from slavery to freedom), her poem reveals a gap between her proclaimed intimacy with enslaved women and her proclaimed access to the vast world of slavery which she did not know much about. Because, in the phenomenological sense, a world always exists beyond one's ability to touch, see, experience, and express it in any given moment; when one speaks about one's world, one refers to a whole that is only ever partially expressible. No experience is, in other words, complete, nor is any description or expression of the world.[19]

And such is the case for Larcom—apart from the poem's narrator and weaver—as the author of the poem; her perspective on the world of women of slavery's cotton market is only partial. So while Larcom can bring into view some aspects of the world of an enslaved woman's experience, she cannot bring that experience as a whole into view. Part of it is always invisible to her. This has to do, in part, with the fact that the world always exceeds particular expressions; the world or a world can never be brought wholly into view. But it also has to do with the fact that Larcom's way of seeing or experiencing the world is informed by the context in which her perception unfolds: her world will always be the world of white women rather than the world.

CONCLUSION:
INVISIBLE ECONOMIC WORLDS OF WOMEN

Larcom's literary depiction of a weaver's embodied experience theorizes how the developing nineteenth-century U.S. economic system literally and metaphorically passed through the female body. When women's bodies are foregrounded as "woven" into the world of cotton and "caught up in the fabric of one sole Being" (Merleau-Ponty, *Visible* 110), they become more visible, as both a part of the world and coextensive with it, constituting but also constituted.[20] However, this "Being" overflows our ability to express it and is therefore only ever partially expressible. It is at once "thick" and present but also "silent" and "invisible" (Merleau-Ponty, *Phenomenology* 453). The bodies that made up Larcom's "world of women," bodies that become more visible when read as the "flesh of the world" of cotton, become the background against which we can better attempt to see the invisible—including entire worlds of laboring women that would be otherwise erased by slavery's capitalism.

Cotton itself, as this chapter has shown, is connected to an invisible world, originated by women, that is ignored by any kind of empirical thinking—including the framework of traditional economics. That which appears to be a fungible commodity (cotton) is in fact a material in both coarse and refined form that is different when part of the weaver's world from when it is part of an enslaved woman's. When we follow the cotton through Larcom's poem, we see how cotton circulated within an invisible world of slavery's capitalism and functioned as whiteness, even when there were no white people around.

But, if the cotton market represents a shared corner of slavery's capitalism for Larcom and the enslaved women of her imagination, it also necessitates the need to recognize more than simply the historical and material differences between an enslaved woman and a factory woman in that market. It necessitates recognizing the ways such difference is constructed in relation to one another. The people in Larcom's "world of women" were not part of a web of womanhood. Enslaved women were denied access to the racialized experience of womanhood to which white women were granted access. Women like Larcom, because they were white and because they were working-class, were granted a relative degree of access to hegemonic constructions of womanhood. This relational difference appears in the inability of "Weaving" to fathom Black women as girls or mothers, only invoking the image of the stereotypical enslaved person laboring as a field hand on a plantation and unable to fully conceive of the brutality of the system that permeates every aspect of Black female subjectivity, including motherhood, a dimension of Black womanhood that does not occur to Larcom's weaver.[21]

The next chapter turns to *Incidents in the Life of a Slave Girl* by Harriet Jacobs and continues to explore economic insights of the cotton market as attained through the author's bodily awareness and engagement with the materiality of the staple fiber. In stark contrast to the image of an enslaved woman field hand invoked by Larcom's poem, Jacobs engages with cotton as a seamstress, mother, businesswoman, and author. Chapter 3 examines what it means not just for Jacobs to work with cotton in these capacities but also what it means for Jacobs to possess or own cotton in these capacities.

CHAPTER 3

Property Knowledge in Harriet Jacobs's *Incidents in the Life of a Slave Girl*

According to Southern laws, a slave, *being* property, can *hold* no property.

It was the most valuable thing I owned, and I
thought none more worthy to wear it.

—HARRIET JACOBS, *Incidents in the Life of a Slave Girl* (1861)

THE OPENING PARAGRAPH OF *Incidents in the Life of a Slave Girl* (1861) spends considerable time laying out what Harriet Jacobs's family and father possessed. A highly skilled yet enslaved carpenter, her father "managed his own affairs" and kept a "comfortable home" with her mother (9). By discussing her father's possessions and earnings at the outset of her narrative, Jacobs points to a central tension that she explores throughout, a tension highlighted by the two opening epigraphs: though enslaved people had no property rights, they often owned "property." Of course, the objects they held in their possession were, as my scare quotes signal, distinguished from property as defined under antebellum law. However, close attention to this tension reveals a discussion in the text revolving around the main protagonist Linda and her ownership of property, much of which was in cotton fabric.[1] It was the bed quilts and table cloths that she and her grandmother sewed, the clothing that she wore, the children's playthings that she crafted, and the sailor suit that aided her escape. Under slavery's capitalism, cotton, in its ubiquity and especially in its fabric form, was an object that fundamentally structured Linda's life and the material culture around her. It was an object, central to slavery's economics and the nineteenth-century institution of property, that acted upon her in violent, menacing ways and one that she acted back upon in liberatory ways.

Linda's experience with cotton, specifically her ownership of property in cotton fabrics, adds to the historical record alternative ways that nineteenth-century Black women understood—and made use of—their relation to the

85

staple fiber. It also serves as an intervention in mid-nineteenth-century property debates. When Jacobs was writing *Incidents*, U.S. debates about the definition of property were reaching their height. Saidiya V. Hartman writes that, between 1830 and 1860, "in an effort to combat the abolitionist polemic about the degradations of chattel status and the slave's lack of rights," the "law attempted to resolve the contradiction between the slave as property and the slave as person/laborer or, at the very least, to minimize this tension by attending to the slave as both a form of property and a person" (93). During this same period, in the late 1830s and 1840s, the Married Women's Property Acts began to appear, and, by the middle of the nineteenth century, numerous U.S. jurisdictions passed acts for the protection of married women's property (Chused 1359).[2] This period also saw the "free suffrage" movement, the demand that property requirements for voting be done away with (Ashworth 91). Historian James L. Huston notes that "southern secession grew out of the irreconcilability of two regimes of property rights: one in the South that recognized property in humans and one in the North that did not" ("Property Rights" 251). Huston argues that the battle between the North and the South leading up to the Civil War was, more than anything else, about a crisis of definition—a "battle for control over the power to define property" (252n12).

The moment in which Jacobs was writing was one in which property was a highly contested category, not only legally and economically but also ontologically. These debates raised questions around the meaning of property: What is property? Who gets to own it? What does it mean to own something? And perhaps most important to Jacobs, what can property do? As the North and South battled for control over which side would ultimately define these terms, Jacobs crafted her own definition of property by literally taking it into her own hands.

By emphasizing Linda's relational experience of property, this chapter extends the broader scholarly discussion of property in both *Incidents* and in the slavery-capitalism debates beyond traditional contexts. For example, many discussions tend to focus on the institution of chattel slavery—that is, of enslaved people as property. Others document enslaved people's relationship to property such as animals, money, crops on allotted land plots, and personal belongings like clothing, the holding of which was subject to the consent of the enslaver, who maintained legal rights over everything the enslaved possessed. A third context for the discussion of enslaved people's property is often found in a social framing: that is, property as defined by relationships and communities, through kinship and social ties that were inextricable from economic and material culture.[3]

The legal and economic dimensions of property in the slavery economy certainly cannot be divorced from a discussion of property, and they exist in the background of my readings. However, focusing on legal or market-based conceptions of property means working inside the narrow limitations of what nineteenth-century law and economic policy, shaped by slavery's capitalism itself, defined as property and whom it defined as property owners. These limitations are too narrow to express what property is or means to Jacobs though she was fully aware of these conceptions. And while the social dimensions of property are always present for Jacobs, in that her characters often disclose their awareness of the social relations between objects and communities, my readings privilege her main character's individualized experience of property: what it means for Linda to wear cotton fabrics or use a needle to make them.

This chapter establishes a unique approach to what makes objects count as property—a form of economic meaning-making outside of definitions contoured by slavery's capitalism—by analyzing how Linda's experience with property, including the objects and commodities that she comes into contact with, change her relation to the material world around her. Linda's acquisition, possession, and deployment of her knowledge of property, what I term her "property knowledge," moreover, allows her to access property's more liberatory functions.

My exploration foregrounds the meaning-making of property in how Linda experiences objects themselves, where experience is itself a relation between person and object. I rely on an object's double relationality to read Linda's narrated account of this experience: an object's being property is inherently relational—an object cannot be property without being the property of someone. Similarly, something being a property of an object is relational—it has to be the property of something.[4] In the close readings that follow, I explore how Linda experiences an object as defined through its properties (such as texture, shape, color) and defined as property, where it is meaningful to Linda both because of *its* properties and because it is *her* property. Significantly, these terms—*properties* of objects and objects as *property*—both share the root "proper" in the sense of something being "proper to" something else, in the sense of belonging to it. The *Oxford English Dictionary* lists one definition of "proper" as "belonging or relating to a specified person or thing distinctively or exclusively; characteristic; particular (to)." My exploration bridges these meanings in exploring how property's properties make that item meaningful to Linda.

My readings also explore how Linda experiences her relation to her property and its properties, an approach that necessitates a focus on her conscious, sensory experience of an object. To this end, I explore Linda's experience with objects and property as a relationship mediated against the broader economy of slavery's capitalism. Linda's understanding of property arises not from legal or social definitions under slavery's capitalism but rather from her experiences as a seamstress possessing an active interrelationship between her thoughts, her body, and the materials with which she works. For example, *Incidents* persistently records moments in which Linda reaches for, touches, or creates fabric objects and property under this economic system. Through a phenomenological analysis of these moments, Linda's understanding of property and its properties, as an oppositional project to slavery's capitalism, comes into being. Moreover, by reading in Linda's focus on her bodily relationship to things the apperceptive moments that reveal an awareness of her embodied relationship to fabric objects and property, this chapter reads her narrative with a focus on what property ownership can do. As similarly discussed in chapter 2 with regard to Larcom's weaver, Linda's account of moments of apperception—that moment when one is aware of one's own "perception," that is, of the "immediate and first-personal givenness of experience" (S. Gallagher and Zahavi)—comes into view as a felt awareness of her condition as a person who reaches for, touches, and owns certain things in certain ways. It is precisely Linda's awareness of the links between her property, her property's properties, and her racialized and gendered enslaved position that makes her narrative—and her meaning-making around property—uniquely applicable to the study of slavery's capitalism and how it shows up in women's lives and literature.

To think through the significance of this active interrelationship between mind, body, and property, Sarah Ahmed's examination of how bodies move through the world by orienting themselves in time and space and toward or away from objects is instructive. Ahmed theorizes that space, race, and sexuality makes "certain things, and not others, available [to certain people]" (*Queer* 14). She explains that, for example, "we inherit the reachability of some objects, those that are 'given' to us, or at least made available to us, within the 'what' that is around" ("Phenomenology" 154). Ahmed clarifies, "By objects, we would include not just physical objects, but also styles, capacities, aspirations, techniques, habits. Race becomes, in this model, a question of what is within reach, what is available to perceive and to do 'things' with" (154). The type of meaning-making that Linda generates with and around her property—that is, her gendered and racialized relation to those objects through action and perception—thus creates lines of direction, what Ahmed calls "lines of thought as well as lines of motion" (*Queer* 16). By reading for how Linda turns her body toward the objects around her, and which objects she turns toward, this chapter follows the lines of direction she creates for herself, both metaphorically as she orients herself in the direction of certain objects and literally as she orients herself north in the direction of freedom.

※

This chapter pays special attention to the way Linda narrates incidents involving objects and property as she narrates her relentless pursuit of freedom, a pursuit marked by constant efforts to evade sexual harassment by her enslaver Dr. Flint in the South, a seven-year period spent hiding in her grandmother's attic, and an escape to the North, where she lives when the Fugitive Slave Act of 1850 is passed. This chapter tracks her relation to objects both chronologically over the different periods of her life and conceptually as they represent slavery/fugitivity in the South and fugitivity/emancipation in the North. The majority of the chapter locates Linda in the South. It tracks her relation to objects and property, which mainly comprise cotton fabric—quilts, clothing, and children's playthings—and documents the corrosive effect of Linda's property knowledge on her enslavement. Each engagement with an object that is not in the enslaver's interest moves Linda further from an identity that enslavement would impose on her and toward one she creates for herself. Over time, her interactions with objects, facilitated on her own terms and through her own meaning-making, become integral components of the very process of fleeing and are thus constitutive components of Linda's own freedom from slavery. Moving beyond the South, the final section of the chapter locates Linda in the North and again tracks her relation to objects and property, which are now mainly composed of emblems of freedom—money, levies, books, her bill of sale, a home, and, finally, writing—and document the revelatory effect of Linda's property knowledge on her understanding of "freedom" as a relative term in the antebellum North. Each engagement with such an emblematic object both reveals her distance from freedom and encourages her continued pursuit of freedom, even in the so-called free North.

OBJECT(S) OF FREEDOM IN THE SOUTH

This section tracks Linda's relation to objects and property in the South, both as enslaved and as fugitive and locates her engagement with property as being meaningfully on property, either Flint's or Aunt Martha's. It begins on Aunt Martha's property with the scene in which the slave patrols invade her home, focusing on the relationship between property (refined fabrics in the form of bed quilts, sheets, and table cloths), domesticity, and freedom. It then moves to Flint's property, focusing on issues of dressing not the home but the body, and, moving from women's clothing to men's clothing, showcases the contrasting disciplinary and liberatory properties of Linda's clothing as property.

When Nat Turner's revolt broke out in Southampton County, Virginia, in 1831, it stoked white fears of slave insurrections over sixty miles away in North Carolina. In response, Linda's hometown of Edenton, North Carolina, commissioned patrol bands to search the homes of its Black residents. Linda, expecting the patrols to arrive at her grandmother's house any moment, adopts what at first seems a curious preparation. She narrates: "I put white quilts on the beds, and decorated some of the rooms with flowers. When all was arranged, I sat down at the window to watch" (62). Tidying and decorating the home seems, at first, an incongruous course of action when faced with the violence to be expected from the bloodthirsty "bullies and the poor whites" who would invade her home. But, after narrating the scene outside of her grandmother's window—"the wild scouts [who] rushed in every direction," the martial music from drums and fifes, and the captains shouting orders to their companies (62)—Linda tells her reader with confidence: "We were ready to receive the soldiers whenever they came" (63).

Something in laying out these objects, the white quilts and flowers, made Linda feel she was "ready" for the soldiers who would invade her grandmother's house. It was perhaps her knowledge that, as she says, "nothing annoyed them so much as to see colored people living in comfort and respectability" (62). With this in mind, she arranges the house as neatly as possible and, in doing so, performs precisely the right sort of ritual of domesticity that one ought to perform when receiving guests. She positions her property to signal a proper performance of femininity vis-à-vis homemaking that, according to the racist and classist tenets of the cult of domesticity, is not accessible to Black women, especially enslaved women. Placing this property strategically around her grandmother's house, she weaponizes her possession of the accoutrements of domesticity and the rituals of domesticity itself. This move on Linda's part is received by the solders as a subversive act.

As Linda expects, the amount and quality of the linens she and her grandmother possess trigger the patrollers. When the patrol bands search the house, they seize not on the household goods that Linda ostentatiously displayed in preparation for the raid but, ironically, on the presence of stowed linens, sets of household fabric goods that were not even on display. Linda narrates: "My grandmother had a large trunk of bedding and table cloths. When that was opened, there was a great shout of surprise; and one exclaimed, 'Where'd the damned n****** git all dis sheet an' table clarf?'" (64; my asterisks). Reacting to the accusation that she had in her possession refined cloth that she should not have had access to, Linda's grandmother responds that she rightfully owns the linens. Upon hearing her response, a "grim-looking fellow without any coat," riled by her display of ownership, tells her: "You seem to feel mighty gran' 'cause you got all them 'ere fixens. White folks oughter have 'em all" (64). The "fellow without any coat," characterized expressly through his lack of possession in cloth, acknowledges that Aunt Martha owns the linens, but in doing so he uses a framing of criminal trespass to describe her ownership—making a kind of legal claim that only white people should own such refined household goods. In other words, Aunt Martha's ownership of the linens offends the soldier so much because, in part, it is really only legible to him as a trespass against a "natural" order of property ownership. Despite the fact that Aunt Martha is free and that they are discussing her linens in her home, the patroller's insinuation is that as Black seamstresses reduced in his eyes to instruments of cotton production, Linda and even her free grandmother cannot be owners of high-quality, refined cotton. Because it is the signs of Black domestic respectability and success in Aunt Martha's home—the confluence of her claim of ownership and the high quality of the objects she owns within the house that she owns—that set the patrollers off, the scene highlights Linda's vulnerability as a property owner as she orients her relation to objects in ways that allow her to feel free within her grandmother's home. Additionally, the scene with the linens highlights the violence that free Black people, like Aunt Martha, were in danger of because of the work they did, the items they could make, and their ability to own those items.

However, the scene is not about what Black people, enslaved or free, are allowed to touch, since the seamstress necessarily touches the linens as she makes them. Rather, it is about *how* Black people are allowed to touch—under what conditions, in what way, and when. According to the patroller, Linda and Aunt Martha were not meant to possess the linens, only to make them, and those who make them ought not to be the ones who possess them. Touching cotton under the claim of ownership—rather than under the claim of production or for the care of white enslavers—makes the women's sociopolitical legitimacy precarious under the gaze of the patrollers. What sets them off, in other words, is not that Linda and her grandmother had the ability to make things or even to make things of high quality. The men who enter Martha's home, representing the interests of the propertied enslaving class while simultaneously marked by their own lack of property, accept the women's sewing abilities and skills inasmuch as they want to use and exploit them. What angers them is that the "fixens" in Aunt Martha's house, her property in cotton fabric within the property of her home, are the same domestic items that could be found in the upper-class homes of white people like the Flints but not their own, an indignity that is critical to their ire.

The scene with the linens highlights the way gender, race, and property are mutually constitutive in a literal sense, in that Linda and her grandmother ostensibly crafted the linens and domestic items themselves.[5] The quilts and linens in this scene constitute property in that their fabrication is associated with the cooperative labor and custody of the women who sewed the items. The scene also highlights the way gender, race, and property are mutually constitutive in a metaphorical sense, in that the women lay claim to those items within the property that is Aunt Martha's private domestic space. The linens are objects that are meant to disappear into one's private sphere. However, understanding that Martha's private property is going to be made public by the patrol's invasive violation of the private sphere, Linda makes more property visible. In a kind of performative prolepsis, then, the linens, meant to be private, become associated as property publicly when the patrols arrive and Linda claims ownership of them in front of the white patrollers and within the Black space of Aunt Martha's home.

Patrolling because of Nat Turner and therefore already anxious about the fragility of slavery's racial order, this "unnatural" allocation of property and these performances of property ownership through domesticity are all the more unsettling to the patrollers. As Koritha Mitchell emphasizes in *From Slave Cabins to the White House: Homemade Citizenship in African American Culture* (2020), "Dominant culture attacks African American achievement of every kind, but nothing seems to inspire more hostility than black domestic success.... Because the nation insists on linking citizenship to traditional domesticity, homemaking has long defined who is and is not a citizen, so the traditional domestic success of those who are not straight, white, and male is routinely attacked" (16, 17–18). Linda, who lays claim to the linens in the private space of her grandmother's house and then makes that claim publicly, accesses this link between domestic success, property ownership, and subjecthood, a proximity to freedom that the patrolmen view as a threat.

Moving from Martha's property to Flint's property, Linda's relation to objects made from cotton fabric when she is inside her grandmother's home offers a striking contrast to when she is on Flint's plantation. On Flint's plantation, Linda is not only legally considered property but also confined to the space of another person's property. Even so, she continues to forge her relation to objects as her own property within Flint's property-space. The objects she makes or possesses while living on and as Flint's property are meaningfully different from the objects she makes when she lives as Flint's property but in her grandmother's house. But, in both cases, her ability to make or claim objects of a certain kind eventually facilitates her escape from Flint's property and thus facilitates her escape from being his property.

A juxtaposition of Linda's relationship with the fine material of the linens in her grandmother's house against her relationship with the coarse material of the dress Mrs. Flint issues her further emphasizes the contrast of Linda's relation to property on Flint's property. Speaking to her experience of fabric within enslavement, Linda discusses her relationship with the dress she is forced to wear, writing: "I have a vivid recollection of the linsey-woolsey dress given me every winter by Mrs. Flint. How I hated it! It was one of the badges of slavery" (14). Before turning to Linda's engagement with the linsey-woolsey dress on Flint's plantation, the below section takes a brief excursion to contextualize the linsey-woolsey material and outline some of the market conditions of slavery's capitalism that shaped the production of such dresses.

Mass-produced clothing for enslaved workers, like the "shrouds" that Larcom's speaker weaves in the preceding chapter, made up a significant share of the output of northern textile mills. Historian Seth Rockman explains that the plantation and the factory were connected not just by cotton but also by the coarser fibers that made up what was called "negro cloth": "an ill-defined category of textiles varying by composition, texture, color, and pattern, but united by its explicit purpose of outfitting enslaved people" (170). Mass-produced clothing for enslaved workers made up a significant share of the output of northern textile mills, and southern mills wanted a piece of that market. For example, in the May 19, 1849 issue of *Friend's Review*, an article titled "A Southern Cotton Mill" by Mr. Bryant gave an account of an Augusta, Georgia, cotton mill that provided ready competition for the cotton mills of the North. Bryant reported, "Only coarse cloths are made in these mills—strong thick fabrics, suitable for negro shirting—and the demand for this kind of goods, I am told, is greater than the supply. Every yard made in this manufactory at Augusta, is taken off as soon as it leaves the loom. I fell in with a Northern man in the course of the day, who told me that these mills had driven the Northern manufacturer of coarse cottons out of the Southern market" (558). This market was lucrative and competitive. And though the New England mills are better known, southern mills were also a part of this larger cotton market.

Just as significant as the amount of competition for market share among manufactories is the amount of research and development that went into creating the industry. According to Seth Rockman in "Negro Cloth: Mastering the Market for Slave Clothing in Antebellum America" (2018), "firms aggressively solicited information on the qualities of successful slave textiles, sent experimental fabrics to plantation markets to be tested, and cultivated reliable merchants and enslavers who would recommend American-made goods to their clients and neighbors" (173). They used capitalist accounting practices to seek out the most efficient and most profitable methods in the product design, manufacturing, marketing, and distribution of the cloth. Rockman's exploration of the "research and development" process for negro cloth documents connections between the plantation and factory that are rarely considered in the history of American capitalism (171–73).

A physical manifestation of the economics of slavery's clothing market, dress worn by enslaved people, like Linda's linsey-woolsey dress, was also, according to historian Stephanie M. H. Camp, used by planters for disciplinary purposes. In "The Pleasures of Resistance: Enslaved Women and Body Politics in the Plantation South, 1830–1861" (2006), Camp writes, "Planters imprinted slave status on black bodies by vesting bondpeople in clothing of the poorest quality, made of fabric reserved for those of their station" (105). Sylvia Jenkins Cook's explanation of the meaning-making involved in clothing the human body highlights Camp's argument on planters' use of "clothing of the poorest quality" for the people they enslaved. In *Clothed in Meaning: Literature, Labor, and Cotton in Nineteenth-Century America* (2020), Cook writes, "The uniquely human action of clothing our physical bodies is the first and most literal manifestation of the material culture of our lives" (1).

The dress, given to Linda by Mrs. Flint, a piece of property whose economic meaning-making is foisted upon her body along with the status of enslavement it signifies, stirs an emotional reaction in Linda. For Linda, both the market relations of slavery's capitalism and the enslaver's disciplinary intent are embedded in, become properties of, her dress. In Linda's dress, then, definitions of property under slavery's capitalism take fabric form.

If the possession of fine linens signals Linda's potential access to a kind of freedom, the properties of the coarse fabric—the origins of the material, its role in slavery's clothing market, the physical feel of the utilitarian fabric, and the status it signifies—perhaps remind her of her distance from it.[6] Cook's explanation of the relationship between the clothed body and one's sense of self offers further insight into Linda's reaction to the linsey-woolsey dress. Cook writes: "The clothed body paradoxically stimulates our awareness of the mental aspect of our self that is least easily defined in material terms. Clothing registers palpably on the body and cognitively in the mind in a symbiotic connection" (1). The feeling of the textile material, woven from a mixture of flax and inferior wool, against one's skin is a particular one—one very different from refined cotton. Though Linda does not document her sensations or thoughts, we might speculate that she sensed the feel of the rough, coarse linsey-woolsey against her skin and experienced it as punishment and a signifier of her enslaved status, a public marker that ensured her vulnerability.

The dresses that Linda owned, given to her by Mrs. Flint, her grandmother, or made by her own hand were sites from which Linda engaged in a battle for freedom over her personhood. Linda emphasizes this point early in her story when she links the comfort of her being to the clothing Aunt Martha provides her: "I was indebted to *her* for all my comforts, spiritual or temporal. It was *her* labor that supplied my scanty wardrobe" (14). Her italicization insists on her possession of her wardrobe as a battlefield for the possession of her personhood. There is a physical intimacy to clothing and the way it drapes our bodies and an emotional intimacy to clothing and the way it "attires our bodies yet cloaks a more abstract inner self" (Cook 1). That intimacy between clothing and oneself appears as comfort and security when Linda wears the clothes supplied by her grandmother. To wear dresses and outfits sewed for her by her grandmother or herself was to challenge her enslaved status and Flint's control over her body and her movement.

Historians and literary scholars have previously commented on the relationships between clothing, enslavement, and freedom. Thavolia Glymph offers the example of Virginia Newman, a formerly enslaved woman. Glymph writes that for Newman, the idea of freedom was "a blue guinea with yaler spots" (10). Glymph explains that the blue dress with yellow spots was "Newman's first 'bought dress,' and it represented, for her, control over her 'whole life' and, concomitantly, the diminished control white people had over it" (10). Cook extends Glymph's analysis of Newman's dress, noting that Newman "released a more open-ended series of metonymic meanings for the garb of her liberated selfhood. Literally, she could wear vividly colored clothes rather than the drab attire of servitude. Figuratively, the blue-and-yellow dress might reveal righteous resentment of bondage, or her yearning for beauty, or even her preoccupation with trivial matters of fashion at a momentous time in history" (*Clothed* 9). Camp also contextualizes enslaved women's dress as a site of contested terrain. She explains that, "under cover of night, women headed for secret frolics wearing their best fancy dress, marking on their bodies the difference between the time that belonged to the master and the time that was their own" ("Pleasures" 105). Camp describes the homemade dresses that enslaved women designed and created as a mark of skill, craft, and ownership, writing that most women held "fancy dress" in their possession by "eking out time at night to make it, from beginning to end: they grew and processed the cotton, cultivated and gathered the roots and berries for the dye, wove the cloth, and sewed textiles into garments" (106). In these cases, women owned the entire process of production—from growing to processing to sewing, entirely in service of themselves, fully removed from their enslavers. This sense of removal from the enslavers enabled a sense of ownership not just of the process of clothing production but also of oneself.

Conversely, however, for these same reasons, enslaved women's dress could also place them in peril. Clothing that challenged Linda's enslaved status and liberated her from it placed her in a precarious position. Referencing a dress most likely given to her by her grandmother, she narrates, "I rarely ventured out by daylight, for I always went with fear, expecting at every turn to encounter Dr. Flint, who was sure to turn me back, or order me to his office to inquire where I got my bonnet, or some other article of dress" (67). For enslavers, new clothing generated suspicion and was perceived as a threat, so Linda's adoption of bold sartorial choices was doubly dangerous given Dr. Flint's jealousy and constant surveilling of her. As Camp explains, "Fancy dress offered a challenge to status-enforcing clothing because dressing up was heterodox behavior" ("Pleasures" 106). For Dr. Flint, who desired control over every aspect of Linda's being, including what clothed her body, the production of cloth for any purpose outside of plantation operations was itself a threat, and a dress not issued by him signaled a lack of control over Linda.

Jacobs's real-life enslaver, James Norcom, who is portrayed as Dr. Flint in the narrative, disclosed the threat that Jacobs's dress posed to him and his fear of losing control of her by way of her dress in an ad he composed in his attempt to recapture Jacobs (see fig. 3). "Being a good seamstress," the ads states, "she has been accustomed to dress well, has a variety of fine clothes, made in the prevailing fashion, and will probably appear, if abroad, tricked out in gay and fashionable finery." Associating her ability to access refined cloth with her ability to move North, Norcom understood Jacobs's dress itself as her proximity to freedom. In Jacobs's narrative, Linda's proximity to fabrics puts her in precarious situations in the above readings, since, as Norcom sensed in real life, it could also be—would also be—the thing providing her opportunity to escape.

In Linda's case, this opportunity took the form of a sailor suit. Linda does not mention the type of fabric that the suit was made of, except for the tarpaulin hat, made from canvas, which is a fabric usually made of cotton. But we might imagine that the different parts of the suit were made of coarser fibers and weaves such as denim, canvas, "negro cloth," or kersey wool. The "suit of sailor's clothes" (Jacobs 106) that she wears when she moves via boat from the

$100 REWARD

WILL be given for the apprehension and delivery of my Servant Girl HARRIET. She is a light mulatto, 21 years of age, about 5 feet 4 inches high, of a thick and corpulent habit, having on her head a thick covering of black hair that curls naturally, but which can be easily combed straight. She speaks easily and fluently, and has an agreeable carriage and address. Being a good seamstress, she has been accustomed to dress well, has a variety of very fine clothes, made in the prevailing fashion, and will probably appear, if abroad, tricked out in gay and fashionable finery. As this girl absconded from the plantation of my son without any known cause or provocation, it is probable she designs to transport herself to the North.

The above reward, with all reasonable charges, will be given for apprehending her, or securing her in any prison or jail within the U. States.

All persons are hereby forewarned against harboring or entertaining her, or being in any way instrumental in her escape, under the most rigorous penalties of the law.

JAMES NORCOM.
Edenton, N. C. June 30

FIG. 3.1. James Norcom's ad seeking the capture of Harriet Jacobs, *American Beacon* (Norfolk, Va.), June 30, 1835. The ad is noteworthy for its remarkable focus on Jacob's "very fine" clothing as well as her ability to craft high-quality clothing. Courtesy of the State Archives of North Carolina, Raleigh.

house of her white benefactress to the crawl space of her grandmother's house, a mixture of various fabric forms, literally moves her closer to freedom.

While Linda is hiding in the crawl space of her benefactress's house, an enslaved cook named Betty aids Linda in her escape by bringing her the sailor suit. Linda says, "I tried to tell her how grateful I felt for all her kindness. But she interrupted me" (106). More interested in how Linda wears the clothing than receiving appreciation for it, Betty instructs Linda how to move her body underneath the clothing: "Put your hands in your pockets, and walk ricketty, like de sailors" (106). Betty's instructions to Linda, a kind of property knowledge itself, take advantage of the town's maritime industry and its geographical location as a port city on the Albemarle Sound. Linda's hometown of Edenton "exported herring and other fish, tar, naval stores, and other timber products to cities like New York and Charleston," and, at the time when Linda disguised herself as a sailor, much of the town's commerce was handled by enslaved seamen (Schermerhorn 127). So, when Linda "blackened [her] face with charcoal" to give herself a darker complexion, she was more likely to go unnoticed among the sailors and more likely to throw off those who would have been searching for a person with a lighter complexion (130–31).[7]

Equal in significance to the jacket, trousers, and tarpaulin hat that clothe Linda's body, Betty knows, is the way her body moves under those clothes. Betty's instructions to Linda on how to wear the sailor suit are really instructions on how to wear clothing in ways that make her appear free, where such freedom is racialized and gendered. Linda, a domestic worker conditioned to constant surveillance, must learn to wear clothes like a maritime worker used to a relative degree of mobility. By putting her hands in her pockets, perhaps in a relaxed way, Linda performs familiarity with the feel of a more-refined cotton on her skin, as if the alternative would give her away. And Betty's instruction to "walk ricketty" meant for Linda to walk in a masculine way, a way of wearing clothes associated with the relative ease with which sailors moved in clothes and through space to perform their duties. When Linda wears the sailor suit that allows her to blend in with Edenton's enslaved seamen, she accesses a particular kind of freedom, one attached to a laboring class of Black men granted limited mobility, to which she did not previously have access.

In *Black on Both Sides: A Racial History of Trans Identity* (2017), C. Riley Snorton reads the scene of Linda's escape in the sailor suit as a scene not just about gender but about a "cross-gender fugitive practice" (57). The scene, he argues, is an example of "how the ungendering of blackness became a site of fugitive maneuvers wherein the dichotomized and collapsed designations of male-man-masculine and female-woman-feminine remained open—that is fungible—and the black's figurative capacity to change form as a commoditized being engendered flow" (59). So, when Linda darkens her complexion and moves her body under the clothing in particular ways, she is not just wearing a disguise. Nor is she just performing the limited amount of gendered freedom or mobility given to and associated with the local enslaved seamen. She uses the sailor suit to get to a "site of fugitive maneuvers" and then uses it again to move herself literally in the direction of freedom.

Having performed a sailor's strut to Betty's satisfaction, Linda makes her way to the wharf where she will be smuggled onto a ship and hidden. As she walks outdoors for the first time in a long time, Linda notes her sensory reactions as she continues her performance: "The fresh air revived me. It was also pleasant to hear a human voice speaking to me above a whisper. I passed several people whom I knew, but they did not recognize me in my disguise" (106). For Linda, the feeling of the fabric is connected to how the body moves under it. It is through cotton, woven into the form of a sailor's uniform, that Linda is able feel the pleasures of freedom, to breathe "fresh air," to hear a "human voice" that is not whispering, and to see people in ways that are particular to her relation with cotton fabric in this instance. No longer wearing the rough linsey-woolsey dress that grates her skin, she is, in a sense, freed for other kinds of sensory experience—ones connected to freedom of movement and social freedom as she goes "boldly through the streets," passing acquaintances who do not recognize her (108). Linda used clothing to access this specifically racialized and gendered (or ungendered) freedom of movement not just to move under her clothes and between hiding spaces in ways that make her feel free but also to move herself toward eventual freedom, geographically toward the North.

Because Linda likely did not make the sailor suit she wore, the scene with Betty that is at first glance about Linda's flight is also a scene about the seamstress work of other enslaved women and about the production of textiles in the slavery economy more broadly. In other words, it is a scene about fabric, the stitching that makes that fabric useful, and the person who does that stitching. As historian Alexandra Finley writes, sewing and dressmaking required "considerable craft knowledge" (58), an inheritance often passed down, as in Jacobs's case, from mothers and grandmothers but sometimes acquired from training schools to which enslavers would send young girls.[8] It was skilled and time-consuming work, laborious and physical, requiring women to sit in uncomfortable positions for hours hunched over fabric (58).

Enslaved women's ability to sew brought value to the plantation economy in terms of the domestic resources they provided, and it also brought value to their sale on the auction block. Finley writes, "Slave traders regularly advertised enslaved women as seamstresses, and potential purchasers regularly requested enslaved women with sewing abilities" (64). The activity of sewing forced the seamstress to participate in a scheme by which not only her own body but also the bodies of other enslaved persons were themselves valued as property. Enslaved seamstresses were forced to sew everything from "the sale outfits that the enslaved people on the auction block wore" (4) to "slaves' every-day clothes"—the dreaded linsey-woolsey fabric that Linda calls the "badge" of slavery—"to the masters' and mistresses' intricate evening wear" (V. Reynolds 6). Indeed "enslaved women often became competent dressmakers with a sense of what modern readers might recognize as fashion design" (6). Sewing skills like Jacobs's thus had enormous value in the reproduction of slavery.

But the skill of sewing holds paradoxical value in another way. Just as this skill brought value to the enslaved seamstress as property, it also enabled her to participate in the production of freedom by sewing garments for escape or providing comfort, as with the clothing Aunt Martha sewed for Linda. The scene with the sailor suit thus highlights the ambivalent status of the possession or inheritance of this particular craft knowledge. In Linda's case, however, sewing facilitates her escape and operates in direct opposition to the way it functions in the slavery economy. In this context, Jacobs's escape through her use of the sailor suit is not just an individual line of direction toward freedom but also one made possible by the labor and craft knowledge of generations of enslaved women.

OBJECT(S) OF FREEDOM IN FUGITIVITY

While the previous section looked at scenes of dressing the home and dressing the body as examples in which Linda held property in cloth fabric on spaces of property, this section looks closely at one specific property-space. It returns to Aunt Martha's property, not to her parlor but to her attic, where Linda spends nearly seven years in hiding. This section reads the attic and its properties as a site of production for Linda's seamstress work—and mothering through seamstress work—that continues to move her and her children, Benny and Ellen, in the direction of freedom. If, as Sara Ahmed suggests, how we perceive the world is in part a function of the degree to which objects come into our space of action (*Queer* 51–63), then paying attention to which objects come into Linda's space in the attic, which objects she reaches for within that space, and the properties of that space brings us closer to an understanding of Linda's world and how she moves herself and her family through it toward freedom.

In the attic, Linda sews, reads, and mothers as she hides in the crawl space that demands the contortion and disfigurement of her body. The physical nature of sewing that required women to sit in uncomfortable positions for hours, hunched over fabric, takes on a new meaning in the cramped dark space of the attic. Linda hides in "that little dismal hole, almost deprived of light and air, and with no space to move [her] limbs" (Jacobs 138), performing the physicality of seamstress work and crafting objects that she hopes will help move her children toward freedom. This is hard physical labor but also, for Linda, part of the production of freedom. Because the way the attic contorts her body is in part what constitutes her world, I attend to the attic and its properties before moving to Linda's sewing, the relation between the space of the attic and the objects she sews, and the "lines of thought as well as lines of motion" (Ahmed, *Queer* 16) toward freedom that she draws for her family from the garret.

In the cramped space of the attic ("nine feet long and seven wide" and "the highest part ... three feet high"), Linda has no "room to stand erect" and is unable "to feel the earth under [her] feet" as she did when she moved in the sailor suit (Jacobs 108, 113). Instead, her condition of fugitivity with bitter irony anchors her to the wood panels of the attic, where she is unable to "stretch [her] cramped limbs" and where time appears "countless" and immeasurable (113, 138).[9] The action-space of the attic dictates not just the sensation she feels under her feet and what she feels her feet to be anchored to but also how much "fresh air" she is allowed to take into her lungs and the length of sleeping periods due to being "restless for want of air" (114). She logs this bodily experience, moving from season to season and describing each season's effect on her body in the attic. During the second winter, Linda narrates, she suffered much more than during the first: "My limbs were benumbed by inaction, and the cold filled them with cramp. I had a very painful sensation of coldness in my head; even my face and tongue stiffened, and I lost the power of speech" (115). Larcom's poem in the preceding chapter creates imagery of the "blood of strangled souls" watering the root of cotton, a description based on bodily attributes but metaphorical, not corporeal. Linda's narrative, on the other hand, documents how the circulation of blood in her veins slows. Striking too is Linda's interaction with the passing of the seasons in contrast with Larcom's weaver, who sees the trees in bloom while weaving inside the factory, through a window. The passing of time and the changing of seasons for Linda literally change the space of the attic itself, thus changing the way her body experiences that space. For Linda, the weather fills her body: it might send a small draft of fresh air to her lungs, a degree of light to assist her eyes, or a cold cramping to her limbs. The attic, as a space of production on Martha's property, and the attic's properties, the degrees of light, the temperature of the air, and the volume of the sound that it holds, all contribute to which objects Linda is able to reach for and the kind of work she is able to do with those objects.

She performs this work under the limited daylight entering through a square-inch aperture she bores into the wall (109), its minuteness a violence of its own kind. Linda describes the limitation placed on her vision and her ability to read: "the little loophole" constrains her line of vision to just a "glimpse" (138) of the distance from the attic to a single star and the width of that distant star. Reminiscent of the stars in the fabric woven in Larcom's poem, which disappear as the weaver begins to recognize her complicity with slavery, the stars here in slave territory are almost totally excluded from Linda's view by her having to hide from the slave patrols. In the attic, crowded not by people but by sounds, Linda describes hearing the language of the "patrols and slave-hunters" (138), a language of words and intonations, filtered through the body's auditory system, that is specifically constructed to ensure the lifelong captivity of the very body through which that language is filtered. Like Larcom's weaver, whose work with cotton at the loom occasions the opportunity to meditate on labor relations, so too does Linda's work with cotton and the needle lead to related meditations. The image of Linda cramped in the attic space contrasts starkly with Larcom's image of the mill girl in the open space of the factory, her muscle memory, and the habituation of her body to the routine labor of her weaving. Larcom's weaver is always able to see objects in the factory and through the window; the brutal working conditions of enslaved women, embodied in the properties of the cramped attic in which Linda labors, lie beyond the weaver's view.

Linda, sitting or lying at the aperture, with a needle in hand and thread or fabric in arm's reach, creates relations to these objects through action and perception aimed to move her and her children toward freedom. When Aunt Martha brings cloth and thread to her in the enclosed space, Linda puts it to use immediately. She describes the scene with a sense of urgency: "Grandmother brought me materials, and I busied myself making some new garments and little playthings for my children.... How I longed to tell him [Benny] that his mother made those garments, and that many a tear fell on them while she worked!" (111–12). Not simply producing new garments and playthings by way of her needle, Linda senses a relation between the material she processes and her acts of motherhood. Fabric and motherhood blur into one another, for within the garments she crafts are a mother's longing for her child, literally, as the material she works with absorbs her tears and is invested with a substance from her own body. Through cotton fabric as motherhood, given her physical absence, Linda illustrates the relationship between objects and knowledge passed down to her: Linda can make cloth toys for her children because she possesses the knowledge handed down by her mother and grandmother. In this way, the object she makes embodies or incarnates a kind of intergenerational property knowledge; her grandmother did not just bring her materials, she also imparted what to do with them.

When Linda crafts children's clothing and playthings in the space of the attic and passes them on to Benny and Ellen, she engages in an intentional relation to fabric that allows her to claim a kind of freedom for her children by claiming them as children.[10] The text's attention to the vexed nature of enslaved women's potential "ownership" of their own children highlights the significance of this act. Phillip refuses to let his mother use her savings to purchase his freedom, Linda and her brother John hold "daily controversies" on the subject of purchasing family members (14), and Aunt Martha considers a plan to buy Linda and her children as an alternative to Linda's plan to flee. In this context, when Linda crafts clothing that will drape Benny's and Ellen's bodies in ways that protect and present them to the outside world, she claims her children *as* children rather than as property, and she also claims a childhood for her children. Linda crafts the toys and clothing that will structure their time and script their scenes of play amid the ever-present threat that their childhoods could be stolen from them.[11] In *Stolen Childhood: Slave Youth in Nineteenth-century America* (1995), Wilma King argues, "Enslaved children had virtually no childhood because they entered the work place early and were more readily subjected to arbitrary plantation authority, punishments, and separations. These experiences made them grow old before their time. Furthermore, parents tried to protect their offspring, who learned that mothers and fathers were also vulnerable to cruelties" (xx). The toys that Linda's children play with, the "new suits" that they wear, and the items that fill their Christmas stockings to their "surprise and joy" (Jacobs 112), all crafted by their mother, structure the material culture of their childhood and afford them a degree of freedom under her care. Embedded in Linda's engagement with the cotton materials as she crafts objects of possession for her children is her intentional reach, in the direction of her children's protection and freedom, toward those objects.

In addition to the influence of the intergenerational property knowledge passed down to her, the intention behind Linda's reach is also located in her property knowledge around the violent origins of the cotton she works with. The materials Aunt Martha brings Linda did not exist as garments and playthings before Linda gives them to her children. This fact re-scales (and shortens) the metaphysical distance between the violent origins of the cotton and the final form of that cotton once Linda crafts it into children's toys and clothes. Those origins still exist in the clothes and playthings, of course, though in an importantly different way. To emphasize that part of Linda's craft was her knowledge of the violence that surrounded the production of cotton is also to emphasize the intentional way she reaches for and makes use of the material in the cramped attic space, an attempt to also craft for her children a kind of freedom.

Though Linda was not directly involved in working with cotton in its raw form in Flint's cotton fields, she was aware of the kind of labor performed by field workers. Having spent several months on Flint's plantation, she observed the plantation operations involved in producing cotton and the day-to-day suffering of the "men and women [laboring on the plantation] who were unpaid, miserably clothed, and half famished" (90). In the narrative, Linda writes that the moment she learned her children "were to be brought to the plantation to be 'broke in'" was the same moment that "nerved [her] to immediate action" (90). Flint's threat to send Linda and her children to the plantation and presumably to be forced to work in the fields is one of the catalysts for her escape to the attic. By escaping to the attic, Linda intentionally chooses the kind of interaction she has with cotton, working not in the field with her children but with the material in the cramped garret, sewing objects for her family. Linda does not give a full description of the kind of field labor these men and women endured, but we can get a sense of the scenes that Linda might have witnessed—and the conditions she fled, choosing, instead, the conditions and properties of the attic space—through Solomon Northup's *Twelve Years a Slave* (1853).

In his narrative, Northup describes scenes of forced labor in the cotton fields. He explains that the cotton is planted in March and April and that the picking season begins about five months later in late August. In the early months of spring, Northup writes, "A plough drawn by one mule is then run along the top of the ridge or center of the bed, making the drill, into which a girl usually drops the seed, which she carries in a bag hung round her neck. Behind her comes a mule and harrow, covering up the seed, so that two mules, three slaves, a plough and harrow, are employed in planting a row of cotton" (123). After describing the planting season, Northup describes the daily schedule of a field hand's work of cotton picking, through the example of an enslaved woman named Patsey. He begins by explaining that each field hand is given a sack to hold the picked cotton. His description centers on the relationship between the sack and the body: he notes how the sack becomes a kind of appendage of the body, describing how each part of the sack attaches to a specific part of the body and uses anatomical terms to describe the object of the sack. He writes: "A strap is fastened to [the worker], which goes over the neck, holding the mouth of the sack breast high, while the bottom reaches nearly to the ground. Each one is also presented with a large basket that will hold about two barrels. This is to put the cotton in when the sack is filled. The baskets are carried to the field and placed at the beginning of the rows" (124). The sack is made of a type of "Negro cloth" and, with all of its components (the strap, the mouth, and the bottom), physically covers the body from head to toe. In this, it is reminiscent of the linsey-woolsey dress Linda is given to wear and metaphorically cloaks the body in the economic ideology of slavery's capitalism.

Patsey, as Northup introduces her, was "the most remarkable cotton picker" on the plantation (125). Operating out of fear and knowing that her safety was attached to her productivity but not guaranteed by it, Patsey "picked with both hands and with such surprising rapidity, that five hundred pounds a day was not unusual for her" (125). Alongside the other field hands, Patsey worked in the cotton field "as soon as it [was] light in the morning," was given ten or fifteen minutes "at noon to swallow [her] allowance of cold bacon," and was not "not permitted to be a moment idle until it [was] too dark to see" (126). When it was no longer possible to see, field hands were forced to attend to other chores, "feed[ing] the mules ... and swine," cutting wood, and preparing their food for the next day in the field (127).

Accompanying the physical labor of women's work on and off the cotton field was fear for the safety of their children, who often labored alongside relatives in the field (King 31). As Wilma King writes, "If mothers did not strap the smallest children who could not keep up on their backs, they left them on pallets at the end of rows, near fences, or under trees away from the hot sun. They also made swings in trees or hammocks between trees to keep the babies up off the ground" (13). Along with fear for their children's safety was fear for their own and the constant threat of physical and sexual assault. "The enslaved victim of lust and hate," Northup wrote, referencing Patsey's licentious master and jealous mistress, "Patsey had no comfort of her life" (143).

Jacobs was not a field worker and does not describe field work in her text. While it would be a mistake to take one person's account of women's field work as representative of women's experience in general, Northup's discussion of Patsey gives us at least a sense of the working lives of women that Linda may have witnessed on Flint's plantation and the conditions with which Flint threatened her and her children. Northup's passages on Patsey's experience help us better understand Linda's property knowledge around the gendered and racialized production of cotton that influences her relational experience between objects, property, and motherhood, and the way she intentionally reaches for cotton materials in the attic as she pursues freedom for her family.

Though Linda does not trace step-by-step the transportation of cotton from the field to the attic in her text, the material that Linda crafts into garments and playthings would surely have originated in southern cotton fields where enslaved women like Patsey harvested the cotton that would be exported to northern factories. The day-to-day toil experienced by women and children in the cotton fields and the brutality and violence that existed in the background of the production of the material with which Linda sews in the attic recasts the meaning embodied in the clothing and toys she makes for her children. In other words, part of Linda's escape plan was to ensure that her children were not subjected to the kind of enforced field labor that people like Patsey had to endure. Inhabiting the position of a kind of financial speculator under slavery's capitalism different from the agents of slavery we are more used to hearing about, Linda leverages her economic knowledge of Flint's valuation of her and her children as his property, speculates on the rate of Flint's pursuit of her against Flint's cost for the support of her children, and wagers that, based on her economic awareness of his plantation's operations, the attic gives her the best chance to pursue her plan.[12] By escaping to the attic, Linda chooses the kind of interaction she and her children have with cotton: to craft and play with cotton as new toys and clothes rather than work with cotton as forced laborers on Flint's plantation. She reaches for and repurposes cotton for practices of mothering and transforms the cotton, implicated in and surrounded by regimes of violence, into objects of comfort and protection. Because "action depends on how we reside in space with objects" (Ahmed, *Queer* 52), by sewing for Benny and Ellen in the space of the attic, orienting her reach and thoughts in the particular ways described above, she continues to create lines of direction toward freedom for herself and her children.

However, not all objects in *Incidents* are inherently liberatory to Linda, though they have liberatory potential that Linda puts to intentional use.[13] The importance of Linda's reach toward objects or property in the attic becomes clear when she finds herself in the absence of objects. As cognizant as Linda is about what it means to hold or own objects, she is also aware of the meaning of the absence of objects. She comments: "O, those long, gloomy days, with no object for my eye to rest upon, and no thoughts to occupy my mind, except the dreary past and the uncertain future!" (Jacobs 110–11). The absence of objects on which to rest her eye makes more present the absence of opportunity. Linda's lament connects objects to thoughts and time and shows an understanding of her ability, when the opportunity is present, to project intentions onto objects in ways that organize moments in time, whether present or future.

The extent to which Linda mothers with cotton fabric from the attic space is highlighted by scenes in which her children engage in play, beyond her ability to observe them from the peephole, that do not involve the objects she crafts for them. In "The Play of Slave Children in the Plantation Communities of the Old South, 1820–1860" (1980), based largely on WPA narratives, David K. Wiggins maintains that "play taught [enslaved children] the values and morals of the adult world" (King 44). In *Incidents*, the relationship between play and the values and morals of the adult world is visible in a scene with Benny, who knows his mother is living above him in hiding. After Benny tells his mother that he has known she was there because he heard her cough, she asks him if he told his sister Ellen. She narrates his reply: "He said he never did; but after he heard the cough, if he saw her playing with other children on that side of the house, he always tried to coax her round to the other side, for fear they would hear me cough, too" (Jacobs 145). Benny's answer reflects the intertwining of his childhood play—outdoors, and not with objects crafted by his mother—with fear for his mother's and sister's safety as well as hope that her hiding will facilitate her escape and lead to their freedom.

In another scene, Linda's children are offered other types of objects as playthings that hold the potential to constitute a different kind of play for them. Dr. Flint, in an effort to bribe Benny and Ellen to tell him where their mother is, "took them into a shop, and offered them some bright little silver pieces and gay handkerchiefs" (111). The potential eruption of violence surrounds them as Flint attempts to manipulate their knowledge, with gifts of various objects, in ways that puts their and their mother's lives at risk. Through the potential engagement with these objects, Linda's children are presented with the choice between their mother, whose love and care for them is represented in the form of crafted objects that have no history as property and no market value, and Dr. Flint, whose authority and power are represented by his capacity to buy property for them (or buy them objects on the market), which is, of course, the same power he has to buy them.

These contrasting scenes of child's play throw into relief the relative comfort, protection, and freedom that Linda's relation with cotton fabric and materials generates for her children, within the space of her grandmother's house, when and how she chooses to work with cotton material in the garret. This relation, however, is never far from the economic dynamics that created it. And though we are talking about a physical fabric, Linda's experience turning the material into garments and playthings also allows us to see the larger fabric of related economic and labor systems she and her family are caught up in. Through fabric—Linda's grandmother's passing of material to her, Linda's craft work with material, and Linda's passing of objects to her children—and contoured by the space of production in which that fabric is crafted, Linda creates an experience of play around her children's possession of objects. In this experience of play, she also creates for her children a relative degree of freedom— outside of meanings of property (relative both to her children and to objects as possessions) as defined by slavery's capitalism.[14]

Linda's experience with objects in the South highlights how she leverages her knowledge of the relationship between property, race, and gender to reshape property toward liberatory ends.[15] In other words, her gendered and racialized experience of spaces and objects leads to her understanding of the liberatory properties of those spaces and objects and property's potential to be liberatory. Thus she participates in the meaning-making of property outside of its meanings at the intersection of slavery and capitalism. In "Finding Sojourner's Truth: Race, Gender, and the Institution of Property," legal scholar Cheryl I. Harris writes, "Because of the institution of slavery, the relationship of Black people to the idea of property proceeds from a radically different history and perspective than the dominant class, racially defined. From this perspective, property is not simply liberating but is also the conceptual and material instrumentality of subordination" (388). This dual dimension makes Linda's property knowledge—her acquisition, possession, and deployment of property—all the more remarkable. Her relationship with objects as an enslaved woman and then as fugitive in the South undermines the principles of property under slavery and capitalism and moves her, literally and figuratively, closer to freedom. She brings this property knowledge with her as she moves north, the setting of the following section.

OBJECT(S) OF FREEDOM IN THE NORTH

Though the material conditions of her relationship with property change as she moves from the South to the North, Linda engages objects and property in ways that continue to move her toward freedom. The incidents involving objects and property she narrates in the North, though, have less to do with cotton fabric and more to do with objects that would be considered emblematic of freedom, such as money or the bill of sale. If the previous two sections documented the corrosive effect of Linda's property knowledge on her enslavement, in that each engagement with an object oriented her metaphorically and geographically in the direction of freedom, this final section tracks her relations with objects and property both as fugitive and emancipated, and her orientation toward those objects in the "free" antebellum North. It documents the revelatory effect of Linda's property knowledge on her understanding of freedom as a relative concept, in that each engagement with such an emblematic object reveals her distance from freedom and returns her to her pursuit of it. Linda reflects on freedom as a relative concept in the penultimate paragraph of her narrative, when she writes: "We are as free from the power of slaveholders as are the white people of the north; and though that, according to my ideas, is not saying a great deal, it is a vast improvement in *my* condition" (186). The final section of this chapter draws out those ideas through her experiences with objects and property. It begins with Linda's relation to money and to money as an object itself and then moves to spaces of property, first the abolitionist reading room of which she is a business owner with her brother John and then the home space which she still does not own. The section closes with the bill of sale and a concluding discussion of Linda's property knowledge, her understanding of property and property's properties.

When Linda lands in Philadelphia after a long boat ride, her first errand is to furnish herself with clothing that will offer her yet another disguise, illustrating again the extent to which her movement toward freedom, even in the North, was structured by fabric. She goes in search of gloves and double veils (149) and pays for the items with coins and paper currency that her grandmother gave her before she left North Carolina. Aunt Martha, who supported Linda in enslavement and in fugitivity, gave her granddaughter enough money to pay her expenses "to the end of [her] journey" to freedom (151).

One might imagine how money felt in Linda's hands as she participated in the shop transaction. If it was a coin, she might have felt the weight and texture of the metal and understood its color, whether copper, silver, or gold, to signify value as attached to the property of the metal it was made of. If it was paper money, she might have likewise experienced its weight, perhaps noting its property of physical lightness in contrast to the metaphorical weightiness it carried as a tool to aid her escape, its value backed not by metal but by the financial and political institution of banking. Dylan C. Penningroth emphasizes that one "way slaves secured their ownership of money was to pay attention to how the bills and coins looked and felt" (*Claims of Kinfolk* 97). And, like many Americans in the middle of the nineteenth century, formerly enslaved people drew distinctions between the different kinds of money that circulated in the United States, distinguishing "'bank money' from 'confederate' money, coin from paper, and 'good Yankee Money—old kind of money' from the quickly worthless new bills that the rebel government issued during the war" (97–98). When Linda exchanges the money that her grandmother had given her in the South for the gloves and veils, she might have been handed back a different kind of money from the northern shopkeeper. In addition to the tactile experience of the money's weight and texture, Linda might have experienced a different feeling about the money that passed through her hands depending on what kind of money it was.

When Linda pays for her items, the shopkeeper adds "so many levies" to the total price (149). Never having heard the word "levy" before, Linda is unsure of the meaning of the price and its relationship to the "levies"—that is to say, their exact properties—and gives the shopkeeper a gold piece to cover the cost. When the shopkeeper returns the change, she counts it to figure out how much the levy is.

In the South, the purchase or possession of new or nice clothing was itself suspicious. While Linda's purchase of clothing in the North is not suspicious in the same way, it is an event that is likewise highly racialized because of how it draws in Linda as an economic agent in a larger, racialized tax system. Money (the levy) here does the work of registering suspicion as Linda's distance from authentic freedom or even, rather, from democratic economic participation. In other words, Linda's first experience in the North, involving money and objects, and money (coins or paper currency or "levies") as objects themselves with different properties, highlights the irreconcilable difference between the democratic promise of freedom in the "Free States" (Jacobs 153) and its deeply undemocratic, often opaque economic operations.

Though Linda is unfamiliar with the systems of levies in the North, she soon adds an understanding of this system to an already clear understanding of the capitalist meanings of money. Even so, her interaction with money and exchange in the Philadelphia shop represents a lesson about capitalism that was unavailable to her in the garret, where she held not gold coins but cotton fabric and thread. While enslaved, she documented the changing valuations attributed to people and things and understood the speculative nature of markets. But in the exchange in the shop, she learns just how disconnected the freedom of economic participation is from the freedom of legal emancipation. As the coin is passed from hand to hand it imparts a lesson that is not passed through the circulation of cotton fabric in the South: economic participation is not emancipatory. Aunt Martha's money may have carried Linda to "the end of her journey" in the North, but it could not take her far enough to carry her to the end of that journey, to "freedom" (151). Instead, Linda moves from a world where her participation was apparently limitedly engaged with pure economic transactions to one where economics becomes openly applied, clearly involving taxes and state intervention. For Linda, the ability to transact exchange, the tactile experience of holding money and passing it from hand to hand, and her consequent fast-growing understanding of how money's properties engage in complex interactions between the state and individual parties, are moments in which she acts on money's liberatory properties and money's oppressive properties act on her. The transaction is a step toward freedom in that it purchases a disguise for her flight, but it also illuminates properties of the nation's early racialized taxation system.

Clearly, for Linda, a single, disenfranchised fugitive woman, to be taxed meant that she was paying taxes without representation. And while property and income tax are different from sales tax, in that all people are subjected to sales tax whether they are a citizen or not, the scene is an example of how Black people, like Linda, and money earned by Black people, like Aunt Martha's, which Linda uses to purchase her gloves, were subject to a larger racialized taxation system.

In *American Taxation, American Slavery* (2006), Robin Einhorn explores how American taxation systems and policies, from their earliest inception in the colonial period, were shaped by slavery and enslavers' interests. For example, the three-fifths compromise, which is best known for apportioning representatives and presidential electors to the states, was also a compromise in the apportionment of direct taxes (Einhorn 158). The 1787 document ratified at the United States Constitutional Convention read, "Representatives *and direct taxes* shall be apportioned among the several states which may be included within this Union, according to their respective numbers, which shall be determined by adding the whole number of free persons, including those bound to service for a term of years, and excluding Indians not taxed, three-fifths of all other persons" (my emphasis). The compromise is intimately bound up with debates concerning the meaning of property, since enslavers did not want to pay property taxes on enslaved persons, but to not consider slaves property meant jeopardizing a core proslavery moral argument. Viewed through the taxation clause of the compromise, the South's concession to the North was that slaveowners would be taxed on their property in enslaved persons between the ages of twelve and fifty, and the North's concession to the South was that enslaved people, which the law considered three-fifths of a person, would count toward the representation apportioned by population. The direct tax was only applied four times: "[In 1798, 1813, and 1815 the direct taxes] were national taxes on land, houses, and slaves; the 1861 tax was a national tax on real estate" (158). But it is not difficult to see how, in regard to taxation, the compromise ultimately served the interests of the proslavery South: it gave the South more representatives in the House and therefore more control over how taxes would be spent. On the local level, enslavers in North Carolina were subjected to a slave tax, which was a revenue source for city, county, and state governments.

In the moment in which Linda pays the full levy on her gloves and veils, she lives out or exists as this double compromise: her very being is a revenue source for the North Carolina state government (since, according to the law, she is considered property on which a levy is placed), and her partial being (according to the three-fifths compromise) contributes to the state's apportionment of representatives who decide how levied funds will be used. Not only is her being—her body considered as property—taxed in North Carolina, but also the means she must purchase to support her own being (in this case fabric again—the double veils and gloves that offer her a disguise as she flees to freedom) are taxed in Pennsylvania. The southern states generate revenue from her being, and the northern states generate revenue from her need to survive. In addition, the money she uses to make that purchase holds a depreciated value as an economic unit since the earnings of a free, Black businesswoman like Aunt Martha would have been subjected to what Christopher J. Bryant calls a "freedom tax" (99). According to Bryant, the freedom tax was a tax system on free Blacks meant not for public revenue generating purposes but "to discourage the growth of their free Black populations" (99). Thus, the scene in which

Linda pays the levy on her purchased items and becomes owner of a newly acquired piece of clothing does not represent a liberatory moment marked by Linda's participation in free-market capitalism as an economic agent. Rather, it is representative of a degree of freedom, since the very property of this transaction marks it as the moment in which Linda is first conscripted to participate financially in a larger taxation system designed not just against her political, social, and economic interests but also against her very being.

When Linda becomes a business owner—the antislavery reading room she establishes with her brother John has a business side from which they sell books and stationery—she turns the knowledge generated by her intellectual and physical engagement with objects, such as money and cotton fabric, into a physical site of knowledge. Scaling up her experience, and increasing control of her politics of property, the space of the reading room becomes a physical manifestation of Linda's engagement with property as a site for the production for freedom. We might imagine, for example, that some of the books she read in the attic—"holding my book... in a certain position near the aperture" (110)—were added to the collection of materials housed on either side of her business. Perhaps those books and her experiences reading them, once shaped by the properties of the attic, reappear to Linda in new forms as altered by the properties of the reading room. The distance between the cotton field and Linda's newspapers, books, and stationery is shorter than one might think when we consider that the paper of many books was often made from cotton rags.[16] But the books of Linda's antislavery reading room, to the extent that their paper is made from cloth rags, offer her a material metaphor to leverage her property knowledge: the abolitionist books in Linda's reading room hold antislavery arguments in their pages and antislavery arguments *as* their pages. The knowledge produced by her experience with property as mediated through cotton (linens, clothing, and playthings) becomes knowledge made available to the public also as mediated through cotton (in the form of paper in books) in a physical property-space that she owns and can make her own.

Space as property that can move Linda toward a closer engagement with freedom, not as a public business space but as a private home space, appears in the final paragraphs of *Incidents*. Yearning for a domestic space of her own, she asserts: "I do not sit with my children in a home of my own, I still long for a hearthstone of my own, however humble. I wish it for my children's sake far more than for my own" (186). Previous critics have read this passage as Linda's desire to participate in and stake her claim in a northern, industrial, capitalist landscape as a property owner.[17] But she positions the home not as a source of wealth but as a basic right needed to care for and protect her family—it is not property for property's sake but property for her children's sake, so that she will have something more than cloth toys to pass on to them. Linda gave her children objects made of cloth as property, for example, but she longed to be able to have a space to share with them—to have property of her own in which to be free with them. The home, for Linda, is a site of production from which the meanings of objects are made. One can make and remake fabrics into homemade things, but the homemade, without a free home, is limited in what it can do. Linda's understanding of a domestic space as a site of production for meaning-making that moves her in the direction of freedom, rather than position her as a property owner in a way that marks a static state of freedom, is the culmination of a life in which her experience with objects and property across captivity, fugitivity, and emancipation help her acquire an increasing understanding of the properties of freedom and its degrees.

Linda's access to objects and property is largely determined by her struggles during slavery, but her experience with those objects and pieces of property is also shaped by her struggle toward freedom. Her physical and mental activity around things—how she touches, uses, and thinks about things—is part of an effort to use things in ways that bring her closer to freedom. But if her relation to objects and property that I considered in the first half of this chapter represents the unfreedom of slavery but is also a means to freedom (literally and figuratively), what is her relation to that object most emblematic of those things, the bill of sale at the close of her narrative when she is legally free?

Conditioned by an understanding of property that arises from the role of things in her relentless pursuit of freedom, Linda returns to that understanding of property in the North when she realizes that she is emancipated but not free. In this context, Linda describes the bill of sale—an object (and idea) created without her knowledge or permission—as having the "inestimable boon *of* freedom" (186; my emphasis), the properties of freedom but not freedom itself. The bill of sale has a profound effect on Linda, then, not because it moves her closer to freedom as a legal or economic status but because it discloses to her the distance between emancipation and a genuine freedom of being. In *Ontological Terror: Blackness, Nihilism, and Emancipation* (2018), Calvin L. Warren offers an apt metaphor for understanding Linda's relationship to the bill of sale when he argues that "Black ~~being~~ only has access to emancipation, never freedom. Emancipation is an *aperture* on the domain of terror and not self-adequation" (63; my emphasis). Warren explains that conceptions of freedom associated with emancipation and rights, which freedom papers represent, "neglect the ontological horrors of antiblackness" by the very assumption that "freedom can be attained through political, social, or legal action" (15). In other words, the legal mechanism of Linda's emancipation effectively confirms her status as unfree. For Linda, then, the bill of sale is yet another aperture, reminiscent of the aperture of the attic, through which she understands that the meaning of freedom would require an alternative self-definition.

CONCLUSION:
PROPERTY KNOWLEDGE AS SHARED PROPERTY

This chapter has shown how Linda's theorization and meaning-making of property arises from and grows out of her developing personal and intimate experience with property, much of which, especially in the South, is in cotton fabric and cloth. It has explored how Linda experiences an object as defined through its properties (such as texture, shape, color) and defined as property, where it is meaningful to Linda both because of *its* properties and because it is *her* property. To this extent, Linda's understanding of property arises from her individual experiences as an enslaved seamstress with an active interrelationship between her thoughts, her body, and the materials with which she works. Moreover, these experiences of property—and the property knowledge that she acquires from these experiences—are part of the process of accessing freedom and exist outside of the legal or economic conceptions of property in which property is traditionally understood. Property has monetary value and can be subject to taxation, for example, but it is ontologically more than this: it has its own properties that can transcend economic value and summon up ethics.

It is worth underlining here, then, how this conception of property is a reframing of that term, one that adds Jacobs's meaning-making of property to the historical record on nineteenth-century property debates. The logic of property undergirding both the proslavery and antislavery sides of these debates arose in large part from Locke's central premise that "every Man hath a *Property* in his own *Person*" (Locke 287). In "The Prehistory of Possessive Individualism" (2012), Jennifer Rae Greeson argues that "the concept of self-possession rests on a prior assumption that selves are possessable objects—an assumption that was generated, before and alongside liberal political theory, in the practice of Atlantic slave capitalism" (918). She emphasizes that Locke's central premise is not a claim that simply explains how everyone rightfully owns their own labor potential: "Surely," Greeson argues, "the entity of the 'Person' cannot be fully reduced to 'the *Labour* of his Body, and the *Work* of his Hands.' Instead, Locke's premise seems to rely on the unspoken assumption that persons are possessable objects, commoditized and entered into the market alongside the objects that their labor allows them to appropriate" (919). So, on the one hand, Lockean doctrine justified southern claims to own people whom enslavers turned into legal property. On the other hand, the Lockean doctrine of "possessive individualism" justified northern claims to an exploitative free wage system since one was free to alienate one's labor and therefore free to sell it.

Linda's pursuit of freedom attempts to exist outside of the logics of Lockean definitions of property and self-possession on which the South and North relied. Instead, it originates in the experience of self-knowledge that refuses to conceptualize property and freedom in either southern or northern terms. For Linda, the logical progression toward freedom is not toward economic or legal conceptions of self-possession or property or in the direction of market relations at all. Rather, property, for Linda, is a practice of being, a practice of orienting herself toward objects and their properties and choosing lines of thought and motion around those objects that move her toward a future she creates. In her reach toward objects, property, and freedom, Linda imagines property as an oppositional project to slavery's capitalism and thus reveals the way power dynamics are not inherently embedded in property but rather granted to property as properties by people with power. Her continual challenge to property as an ideological category structured by slavery's capitalism troubles definitions of property and its associations with slavery and/or freedom by reminding us that property is an idea or ideology before it is a thing or an institution. Linda may not be able to change the larger power relations of property within slavery's capitalism, but Linda's reach, at the very least, is, to borrow from Saidiya V. Hartman, guided by her "yearning to refashion and transform the given" (112), to remake the meaning of property outside of the logics of slavery's and capitalism's economics.

Harriet Jacobs's *Incidents* thus participates in the theoretical work of defining property as it is in flux—both as part of a national debate and as part of Linda's experience as enslaved, as fugitive, and as emancipated. Each of these subject positions, particular to Linda at different moments and places in her life, changes her relation to and understanding of what property is under slavery's capitalism. Focusing on Linda's experiential relation to objects and property across these different phases of the narrative allows us to move outside of a binary discussion of property in terms of slavery and/or freedom, since her experience, being enslaved in the free North, for example, troubles that binary at every step. The intervention of *Incidents* into the property debates, then, is one that immediately moves beyond this binary and instead reveals meanings of property—and freedom—as themselves in flux. In this context, it is Linda's property knowledge, arising from her experiences with things, and not an economic, legal, or even social framework of property, that is foundational to her meaning-making of property.

Besides the needle, Linda's relationship with the pen perhaps best illustrates her property knowledge. Throughout *Incidents*, Linda tells us that her sewing often occasioned her time to think. As this chapter has argued, Linda's experience of property, in phenomenological terms, is not located in the subject or in a function of properties in the object but rather in the interconnection of the subject (seamstress) and the object (cotton).[18] As she sews her cloth, she sews together her thoughts. It is precisely because she at once "reads and sews" (Jacobs 110) and sews and thinks throughout her narrative that she comes to think the thoughts that move her toward freedom, thoughts that she later puts down in writing on paper.

If we consider the material object of *Incidents in the Life of a Slave Girl* as the textual presentation of Linda's experience of property, then we can think of Jacobs's distribution of this property (the physical text), not in capitalist economic terms that cast Jacobs's ability to claim authorship as ownership over a thing that could be bought and sold in the marketplace, but as something meant to be shared. It is a sentiment she speaks to in her preface to the book when she states that her purpose in writing is to share her experience and "arouse" in her readers "a realizing sense" (3). Jacobs's ultimate piece of property is her claim to knowledge, which, made manifest in *Incidents*, she makes into, not her property, but rather into the shared knowledge of her readers—all of it our property.

In the next chapter I continue an exploration of the meaning of property under the long shadow of slavery's capitalism by showing how, in Frances Ellen Watkins Harper's Reconstruction-era writing, and as directed to her Black readership, property appears again in significantly different forms. Chapter 4 explores how Harper's novel *Minnie's Sacrifice* depicts inheritance—in cultural, historical, and financial senses—and considers Harper's vision for reclaiming that inheritance for the Black community, a necessary and strategic tenet of economic citizenship during Reconstruction.

CHAPTER 4

Reconstruction's Inheritance in Frances Ellen Watkins Harper's *Minnie's Sacrifice*

> We have money among us, but how much of it is spent to bring deliverance to our captive brethren? Are our wealthiest men the most liberal sustainers of the Anti-slavery enterprise?
>
> —FRANCES E. W. HARPER, "Our Greatest Want" 1859

> We have wealth among us, but how much of it is ever spent in building up the future of the race? in encouraging talent, and developing genius?
>
> —FRANCES E. W. HARPER, *Minnie's Sacrifice* 1869

FRANCES ELLEN WATKINS HARPER knew the value of money. But, more than that, she understood the meaning of money. She was particularly attuned to the way meaning became attached to money as it circulated through society, and she used her writing to theorize the moral, political, and economic implications of money as a financial instrument and to strategize its role in racial uplift discourse. As evinced by the opening epigraphs in which she poses similar questions ten years apart, Harper's concern with money and wealth and its meaning for the Black community traversed time. This concern appears in striking force in her 1869 novel *Minnie's Sacrifice*,[1] written and published in the immediate years after the Civil War, as the nation transitioned from a socioeconomic infrastructure subtended by slavery's capitalism to one subtended by racial capitalism.

By the time Harper published *Minnie's Sacrifice*, as Frances Smith Foster notes, she was "the leading African-American writer and a social activist of international stature" (*Brighter* 122). A poet, novelist, essayist, lecturer, and activist, Harper contributed to every major social reform movement of the nineteenth century, including those during Reconstruction. The relationship between the abolition of slavery and the emergence of a postbellum-era capitalism created the backdrop against which reform efforts, including education and reparations, labor and land ownership, and suffrage and citizenship, were debated—all debates in which Harper participated.² Reconstruction presented her the opportunity to think through the "shadows of the past" (Harper, "Affairs" 124) and to imagine, along with her Black readership, where the nation might go after the war.³ One of the ways she did this was through *Minnie's Sacrifice*.

It was a novel that her readers waited for in anticipation, according to a notice in the *Christian Recorder*, the newspaper of the African Methodist Episcopal Church, in which the novel was serialized. On March 13, 1869, a week before *Minnie's Sacrifice* debuted on the front page of the paper, the editors of the *Recorder* announced: "MINNIE'S SACRIFICE is the title of a serial story to be contributed by Mrs. F. E. W. Harper. We congratulate our readers on making this announcement. As a writer, whether of prose or poetry, Mrs. Harper stands foremost of all the colored women of our day.... 'Minnie's Sacrifice' will commence in our next issue. Let our friends be on the look out." As Eric Gardner writes in *Unexpected Places: Relocating Nineteenth-Century African American Literature* (2009), in the mid-1860s and under the editorship of Elisha Weaver, the AME Church's flagship paper was becoming the most important Black periodical in the nation. At that time, Weaver, who desired to place the *Recorder* "among the first-class reading papers" in the nation, attributed the paper's success to the fact that he had made the *Recorder* "a paper adapted to the wants of the times" (quoted in Gardner 133). Weaver broadened the paper's secular content, attended to politics, and facilitated a great number of Black voices on the Civil War (133). Though Weaver was not the editor when *Minnie's Sacrifice* was published, he helped set the stage for its reception. Harper's story, then, was placed in the hands of *Recorder* readers poised to receive the most relevant stories of the time. And because the *Christian Recorder* "was conceived by African Americans, edited by African Americans, written primary by African Americans, and largely distributed by African Americans to an almost completely African American audience" (Gardner, *Black Print* 4), it was a literary forum that allowed Harper to "speak about and to African Americans themselves" (Foster, "Introduction" to *Minnie's Sacrifice* xxviii), about a range of issues—many of which were economic.

This chapter traces the economic dimensions of *Minnie's Sacrifice* to draw out Harper's exploration of economic meaning-making around two pivotal issues—inheritance and citizenship—that were shaped during Reconstruction, at the intersection of slavery's aftermath and an emerging postbellum capitalism. By crafting a story that historicizes slavery's inheritance economically, but also in relation to people and values, Harper challenges the effort of racial capitalism to generate new categories of economic citizenship for Black people during Reconstruction, categories of citizenship that would be "stripped bare" (Kelley xvii) of a Black historical consciousness. In this way, Harper's story is a story about racial capitalism different from the ones we are used to reading. *Minnie's Sacrifice* is not a story that narrates how the economic system expropriates value from the labor, talent, or skills of racialized people; rather, it is a story about Black economic incursion.[4]

In *Minnie's Sacrifice*, Harper suggests how free-born Black and formally enslaved subjects can rehearse alternatives to proffered models of postbellum citizenship defined by the logics of slavery's capitalism. She imagines new methods of economic meaning-making by using conventional nineteenth-century literary tropes in unconventional ways. Her versions of the tropes of the inheritance plot and the "tragic mulatta" lead to models of economic citizenship that then act on economy.[5] More precisely, Harper contests sentimental attachments to money and instead shows how Black subjects can participate in, create, and invest in Black development to solidify a communal economic position in the midst of white supremacist violence.

Carla L. Peterson has previously noted Harper's concern with economics. She writes, "Undergirding Watkins Harper's sweeping moral vision of universal freedom lay her awareness of the raw economic issues surrounding slavery, giving rise, for example, to a speech in defense of the free labor movement" (*"Doers"* 134). Peterson summarizes Harper's call for vigilance in the boycotting of rice, cotton, and sugar produced by enslaved laborers and argues that Harper's economic awareness "provided the framework for [her] racial uplift program," one that hinged on the "establishment of a network of social institutions dedicated to racial uplift—schools, newspapers, churches" (134). Following Peterson, this chapter emphasizes Harper's awareness of the "raw economic issues" that frame *Minnie's Sacrifice* to locate the author as an integral figure in the story of African American economic history and activity during the Reconstruction era.

Harper's attention to the economic, however, is not only found in *Minnie's Sacrifice*. Harper attended to a wide range of economic issues in her writing and speeches before the publication of *Minnie's Sacrifice* and would continue to do so after its publication. In perhaps her best-known examples of economic analysis, the poem "Free Labor" (1857) and the short story "The Two Offers" (1859), Harper critiques the political and social meanings of the commodities and marriage markets, respectively. In her antebellum essay "Our Greatest Want" (1859), the sentiment of which reappears as part of the conclusion in *Minnie's Sacrifice*, Harper lingers on the biblical story of Moses and Moses's resistance to the seduction of the Pharaoh's riches, making resistance his most admirable characteristic of all. In "Moses: A Story of the Nile" (1869), a long poem published the same year as *Minnie's Sacrifice* and one that she draws on throughout the novel, she more fully develops Moses's resistance story. In her 1866 speech "We Are All Bound up Together," Harper, who was then widowed, critiques debt as an abstract notion of wealth that, like credit, is imbued with social meaning, exclaiming: "Had I died instead of my husband, how different would have been the result!" She understood that the debt placed on her shoulders as a widowed Black woman accrued interest that compounded on the basis of gender and race. And in other nonfiction pieces published after *Minnie's Sacrifice*, like "Our People" (1870) and "Land and Labor" (1870), Harper speaks to industrial and business pursuits, landownership, and strategies for mutual aid and Black development. She would continue to pursue economic themes and critiques in her fictional works as well, talking to her Black readers about economics concerns in *Sowing and Reaping* (1876–77) and *Trial and Triumph* (1888–89), which were also published serially in the *Christian Recorder*, and through the last decade of the century in her best-known novel, *Iola Leroy* (1892).[6] Economic concerns, then, are found throughout Harper's oeuvre, but it is in *Minnie's Sacrifice* that all of these issues come together strikingly in one story.

This chapter extends previous scholars' observations on Harper's economic acuity by situating *Minnie's Sacrifice* at the intersection of slavery and capitalism. It foregrounds Harper's concerns with the raw economics of slavery as well as the raw economics of its aftermath, and it shows how these concerns undergird the economic meaning-making strategy for inheritance and citizenship that she presents in novel form to her readers.

The plot of *Minnie's Sacrifice* revolves around the lives and marriage of Louis Le Croix and Minnie Le Grange, both of whom who live most of their early lives believing they are white, not knowing they are Black and legally enslaved. Unbeknownst to them and unknown to one another, their early lives take parallel paths: both are born to enslaved mothers and enslaving fathers in 1840s Louisiana, both are raised as white, and both are educated in the North. There, Minnie is raised by adoptive, antislavery Quaker parents, while Louis is "adopted" by his biological father who wants to "care for [Louis] as a son, without acknowledging the relationship" (11).[7] Unlike Minnie, who fully embraces her adoptive parents' peace-seeking, antislavery spirit, Louis, despite being raised and educated in the North, more staunchly digs in his heels as a proslavery, "real hot-headed Southerner" (42). In young adulthood, Louis's and Minnie's parallel plot lines eventually merge in the North, when they are introduced, still believing they are white, by a mutual friend intent on matchmaking. Because of archival absences, some crucial romantic exchanges between the protagonists may be missing for the contemporary reader, but the novel appears to move through a double proposal plot.[8] Most likely, Minnie refuses Louis's romantic advances when they both believe themselves to be white and later accepts his proposal after the two, Moses-like, denounce their "white blood" (80) and choose to live as Black people. It is only after both learn of their ancestry and claim racial solidarity with the Black race that they marry. Once married, Minnie and Louis dedicate their lives and their inheritance, furnished by Louis's wealthy enslaving father, to Black development in the postbellum South.

Though *Minnie's Sacrifice* opens in antebellum Louisiana, the external—and economic—framing of *Minnie's Sacrifice* is located in a more distant time and place. Further historicizing Louis's and Minnie's ancestry, Harper moves from 1840s Louisiana to 1790s Saint-Domingue. It is here, a few short months before the Haitian Revolution, that Louis's paternal grandparents of Spanish and French descent, the Le Croixes, marry and then flee to New Orleans to escape the looming revolution. As with Louis, Minnie's white grandparents, the Le Granges, are also of Spanish and French descent and flee the Haitian Revolution. While the remainder of Minnie and Louis's story takes place in postbellum Louisiana, Harper's historiographical narrative of their biological fathers' family histories provides the backdrop to her story, wending through the French colonization of Saint-Domingue, the Haitian Revolution, U.S. slavery, and the Civil War. This backdrop is important because the racial uplift work Minnie and Louis perform after they marry, their education, suffrage, labor, and land reform work, is only made possible by the Le Croix family fortune that Louis inherits from his enslaver father, wealth accumulated across the slavery economies of Saint-Domingue and New Orleans. The first section of the chapter, then, takes up the issue of inheritance.

INHERITANCE AS WEALTH, PEOPLE, AND VALUES

Inheritance as a capitalist economic instrument is critical as a category of analysis because issues of inheritance during Reconstruction were in many ways also issues of reparations. Before the war, enslaved children born into the system of slavery (like Louis and Minnie) were born into an economic and legal system that denied them inheritance rights because it denied them property rights in the first place. As the preceding chapter shows, enslaved individuals, families, and communities made decisions on their own terms about the meaning and value of property and who had access or rights to it. But under antebellum law it was one's status from a matrilineal inheritance that most governed ideas around property, family, and inheritance for enslaved children: the legal doctrine of *partus sequitur ventrem* dictated that children inherited the legal status of their mothers. Children born into slavery were not only denied inheritance rights in a legal sense but also denied it in a familial sense, in that they could not inherit property from their wealthy white enslaver fathers.[9] In *Minnie's Sacrifice*, Harper challenges the operations of inheritance as a capitalist economic instrument by rewriting the meaning of inheritance around wealth, people, and values.

The story line around inheritance as wealth was, for Harper, a fictional rendition of the economic system working the way it should, while in real life the advances of Reconstruction were being actively complicated and undermined. Her inheritance plot, no mere literary device, purposefully governs everything economic that happens in the novel, much of which is put into motion by Louis's Black grandmother, Miriam. But before discussing how Miriam's economic agency acts on Louis's monetary inheritance, I examine how Harper historicizes the inheritance as wealth.

Part of Harper's project, to offer a fictional rendition of the economic system working the way it should, starts with her invocation of the history of the Le Croixes' and Le Granges' fortunes, beginning in the eighteenth-century French colony of Saint-Domingue, where the families of Louis's and Minnie's enslaver fathers built their massive fortunes. Harper outlines in detail for her readers how these fortunes came into being for each family. Writing about Bernard Le Croix's upbringing and the inheritance he would pass on to his son Louis, Harper narrates: "[Bernard's mother] was about ten years old and Bernard was twelve, and in their childhood was commenced a friendship which ripened into love and marriage. Bernard's father and mother lived long enough to see their first and only grandchild, and then died, leaving their son a large baronial estate, 500 slaves, and a vast amount of money" (9). Minnie's family has a similar history. Due perhaps to archival absences, we do not know if Minnie receives any financial inheritance from her enslaving father, but the transnational path of his accumulated wealth is worth noting. Minnie's biological father, Louis Le Grange, also inherits a fortune built by enslaved laborers in Saint-Domingue, and he gains additional wealth upon marriage to his first cousin, which his mother arranges. In preparation for the cousins' first meeting, Mrs. Le Grange tells her son: "I want you to be all attention to your cousin, for she is very rich. She has a fortune in her right, which was left her by her grandmother, and besides she will have another one at her father's death" (25).

In addition to his new wife's inheritance, Louis Le Grange, Minnie's father, also receives a fortune his family had accumulated in Saint-Domingue as a wedding gift: "His father made him a present of a large plantation, which he stocked from his own purse, with three hundred slaves" (26).

On the eve of the Haitian Revolution, both families flee and resettle their estates outside of New Orleans. Le Croix, Louis's grandfather, "foreseeing the storm which was overshadowing the land, contrived to escape, bringing with him a large amount of personal property. Preferring a climate similar to his own, he bought a plantation on Red River, and largely stocked it with slaves" (9). Like Le Croix, Minnie's grandfather Le Grange "had also been a Haytian refugee" (22), and like Le Croix, Le Grange resettles his plantation on Red River.

Harper was, as John Ernest has pointed out, an author whose work was meant to "influence readers' understanding of history and progress" (*Resistance* 6). Her historicizing of the inheritance's origins is significant in two ways. First, she situates the inheritance as part of the transnational and domestic circulation of wealth created by the labor of enslaved people. In the last few decades of the eighteenth century, when Le Croix and Le Grange would have been plotting their escapes, Saint-Domingue was "one of the greatest wealth-producing colonies of the world" (Fick 22), producing massive amounts of indigo, sugar, coffee, and cotton through enslaved labor (21–25). Thus, haunting both Le Grange's and Le Croix's personal property, and the inheritances that they pass on, are French legacies of human trafficking, robbery, and exploitation of land and resources. And by choosing Louisiana as the location to which Le Grange and Le Croix flee and relocate their fortunes, Harper memorializes in her novel what historian Dale Tomich terms "Second Slavery," a paradigm for considering transnational and imperial frameworks and the history of capitalism, particularly in the wake of the Haitian Revolution. The idea of Second Slavery suggests that instead of slavery being weakened in the decades after the Revolution and the abolition of transatlantic slave trade in 1808, it found a second life in the U.S. South, Cuba, and Brazil, a repercussion of Haitian emancipation and decolonization. Louisiana, the U.S. epicenter of Second Slavery and the setting of *Minnie's Sacrifice*, was a central site through which capital accumulated and flowed.[10] Continuing to trace the national circulation of Le Croix's fortune, Harper writes that "Le Croix, before his death, had sold the greater part of his slaves, and invested the money in Northern bonds and good Northern securities" (33). In this way, Harper also emphasizes the economic relationship between the slave South and the industrial North by connecting the economies through the circulation of money from Haiti to New Orleans and also to the northern United States.

By following the history of the family fortunes in such detail, Harper gives attention to another aspect of the economics of slavery—that is, money and wealth marked by slavery cannot be erased or removed from the economy, not even in fiction. By locating the accumulation of that wealth across time, place, and generations with such specificity, Harper memorializes the capitalist links created by slavery that connected Haiti, New Orleans, and the North and offers her readers a story about Black economic meaning-making around inheritance: what that wealth means to the Black community when attached to a Black historical consciousness.

The second significance of the inheritance's origins is its connection to the Haitian Revolution.[11] Because so much of the inheritance plot originates at the time of the revolution and is shifted to the United States because of it, and because Harper is writing in the immediate years after the Civil War, Harper links these two historical moments of the revolution and the war for her readers. Aligning these two events would have highlighted not only the Haitian achievement of Black political autonomy but also Black economic agency and would have foregrounded the possibility of Black political and economic revolution during Reconstruction in the United States.[12]

The invocation of the Haitian revolution in Harper's work was part of the wider literary culture of her day. In the 1860s, when Harper was writing *Minnie's Sacrifice*, African American literary culture was revisiting Haitian history. Brandon Byrd summarizes the role of writers, activists, and historical figures in this endeavor. He explains that texts like William Wells Brown's *The Black Man: His Antecedents, His Genius, and His Achievements* (1863), for example, which contains biographies of men like Toussaint Louverture and Jean-Jacques Dessalines, show that African Americans found lessons for their future in the Haitian past (549–50). In addition to connecting the Haitian past to the future, African American writers were also connecting it to the present. For example, in the March 1863 edition of the *Douglass Monthly*, Frederick Douglass reported on the reception of Haitian diplomat Colonel Ernest Roumain in Washington. Douglass noted that Roumain's visit was not only a welcome acknowledgment of a sovereign black nationality but also an "unmistakable sign of the doom of caste and dawn of higher civilization" (quoted in Byrd 547–48). And Carla L. Peterson, writing specifically on *Minnie's Sacrifice* and the *Christian Recorder*, has noted, "In Harper's literary imagination, Southern slaveholding culture has its origins in the foreign Creole culture of pre-revolutionary Haiti and is characterized by ostentatious displays of wealth and moral self-indulgence. As such, it stands in negative contrast both to the many accounts of the independent black Republic of Haiti published in the *Recorder* and to

Harper's vision of the North as a site of industrious free labor" ("Reconstructing" 314). *Minnie's Sacrifice* draws lessons from Haiti's past by invoking the history of Louis's inheritance, connects it to the present by calling for Black revolutionary movement during Reconstruction, and uses it to look toward the future by signaling Black economic possibility.

Significantly, in the novel it is only because the inheritance is historicized by its origins in Saint-Domingue and its circulation in the slavery economy that it becomes as a tool for Black development. In other words, it is when Louis and Minnie learn of the history surrounding their racial and financial inheritance that they decide to disseminate it back into the Black community. In lieu of a missing chapter that perhaps holds more telling dialogue, Colleen O'Brien offers the most plausible explanation of this moment in the novel. O'Brien surmises that "Minnie and Louis identify a debt that they, and perhaps all Americans who benefited from slave labor owe the South's former slaves" ("White Women" 615). O'Brien concludes that Minnie's assertion "I will help you pay it" (Harper, *Minnie's Sacrifice* 65), which is part of the recovered text, is likely Minnie's response to Louis telling her "that he must repay his debt to the black men and women whose work built his father's fortune" ("White Women" 615).

Harper's story line about debt and inheritance participated in contemporary economic debates since debt played a central role in discourses and counter-discourses of freedom after emancipation. As Saidiya V. Hartman theorizes in *Scenes of Subjection: Terror, Slavery, and Self-Making in Nineteenth-Century America* (1997), "The very bestowal of freedom established the indebtedness of the free through a calculus of blame and responsibility that mandated that the formerly enslaved both repay this investment of faith and prove their worthiness" (131). In other words, debt was lifted from the ledger lines of slavery's account books, discussed in chapter 1, and transferred onto the ledger lines in the account book of freedom. But as the formerly enslaved asserted, they had not incurred debt but rather were owed one, and in "counterdiscourses of freedom, remedy was sought for the injuries of slavery, not through the reconstruction of the Negro—in other words, the refashioning of the emancipated as rational and docile individuals—but through reparations" (131–32). Through Louis and Minnie, Harper introduces another class of people into the postbellum debates around debt. Because she viewed the economic fate of Blacks across all classes as linked, Harper called on the "growing black professional and business class" (Peterson, "*Doers*" 198) to help transform the conversation about debt into one about inheritance and reparations.

But, crucially, before that inheritance passes on to Louis and Minnie from Louis's enslaving father, it passes through the hands of Miriam, Louis's grandmother. Not coincidentally, it is Miriam who initially figures out how to take the old economic structure of slavery's capitalism, now in the emblematic form of Louis's inheritance, and place it in the hands of Louis and Minnie so that they can restructure it. In this sense, Miriam's maneuverings, from the very beginning of *Minnie's Sacrifice*, make her one of the most economically strategic and revolutionary characters of the novel. She paves the way for other Black women, like Minnie, to later build on economically what she begins. Miriam's contributions to the inheritance plot begin at the novel's outset, which I revisit here.

When chapter 1 of *Minnie's Sacrifice opens*, Miriam is mourning the death of her daughter Agnes, who has recently died giving birth to Louis. Louis's biological father, Le Croix, is also the man who enslaves all three. While Miriam is mourning, Camilla, Le Croix's white daughter and Louis's half-sister, enters. Camilla is immediately vexed to learn that the baby—who looks white and has "golden hair, bright blue eyes and [a] fair complexion"—is Agnes's (4). Miriam purposefully prods Camilla's confusion, pulling on her heartstrings and reasserting that, despite his complexion, Louis is, after all, "only a slave" (4). Miriam's words grate "harshly on [Camilla's] ear" and accomplish their purpose (4). Horrified at the thought that a white baby could be a slave, Camilla vows to save Louis from a life in bondage. She makes up her mind to take Louis "to the house, and have a nurse for him, and bring him up like a white child, and never let him know that he is colored" (5). Miriam supports Camilla's decision, as Foster notes, and she "encourages, even manipulates" Camilla to carry out the plan ("Introduction" to *Minnie's Sacrifice* xxx). When Camilla doubts she will be able to carry off the scheme with her father, Miriam goads her again. "And why can't you have your way?" she presses. "I'm sure master humors you in everything" (Harper, *Minnie's Sacrifice* 5). This move on Miriam's part works: Miriam gets Louis into the house of Pharaoh, so to speak, and, employed by Camilla as his nurse, Miriam oversees Louis's upbringing to the extent she can once they are both inside the house.

This scene echoes a verse in Harper's poem "Moses," published in the same year as Harper's novel. Reading the poem as a paratext for the novel allows us to hear Miriam's voice in ways we do not in *Minnie's Sacrifice*. In the verse, Moses's mother explains to Moses how she hid him when she heard that the Pharaoh called for the death of all Israeli sons. In part, the verse reads:

> I hid thee when the bloody hands of Pharaoh
> Were searching 'mid our quivering heart strings,
> Dooming our sons to death; by faith I wove

> The rushes of thine ark and laid thee 'mid
> The flags and lilies of the Nile, and saw
> The answer to that faith when Pharaoh's daughter
> Placed thee in my arms, and bade me nurse the child
> For her (147)

For Moses's mother, the "answer" to this call for the death of her son is to place Moses in the house of Pharaoh, by way of the Pharaoh's daughter, and to watch over and protect him while in the employ of the Pharaoh as Moses's nurse. For Louis, as with Moses, it is inside the house of Le Croix, as his "adopted" son, where he gains access to all the resources available to the southern white sons of wealthy enslavers such as money, education, economic agency, and political power—all resources with which Harper's novel is concerned. Miriam figures out how to deal with the old economic foundation of the antebellum period by placing Louis in the house of Pharaoh and positioning him (and later, Minnie) to inhabit economic structures of power differently from what his birth would have dictated. In exchange for separation from her grandchild, Miriam gives Louis access to all the resources that will later allow him and Minnie to emerge as leaders in the Black community. Despite the novel's title, then, Minnie is not the only female character who makes a sacrifice. Miriam's sacrifice creates the economic framework for the novel and enables the later economic portion of the novel to be set into motion.

Later in the story, Miriam plays a crucial role again around Louis's potential for economic agency. Harper writes:

> Le Croix is dead; but before his death he took the precaution to have Louis emancipated, and then made him a joint heir with his daughter. The will he entrusted to the care of Camilla; but the deed of emancipation he placed in the hands of Miriam, saying, "Here are your free papers, and here are Louis'. There is nothing in this world sure but death; and it is well to be on the safe side. Some one might be curious enough to search out his history; and if there should be no legal claim to his freedom, he might be robbed of both his liberty and his inheritance; so keep these papers, and if ever the hour comes when you or he should need them, you must show me." (32–33)

In the above passage, Miriam holds Louis's "liberty and his inheritance" in her hands literally and metaphorically. From her own extremely tenuous economic position, Miriam continually protects and ensures Louis's access to a range of economic resources and opportunities. From the time of Louis's birth and over the course of his life, while enslaved by his father and half-sister, Miriam manages to get out of Le Croix the very least of what Le Croix owes Louis because of the crimes he committed against Louis and his mother. Louis is still in the North and close to completing his education when the papers change hands. And, once he does, Harper narrates, he will "have no difficulty as to choosing the means of living; for he was well supplied, as far as that was concerned" since "he had a large amount of money in the North, which his father left him when he came of age" (61). It is Louis's inherited fortune, initially secured by Miriam and then protected by her, that makes possible Louis and Minnie's racial uplift work in the second part of the novel. To the extent she could, Miriam negotiates what would seem to be impossible circumstances and makes possible anything Louis might do economically for the rest of the novel.

But for Harper there is a second kind of inheritance outside of a financial one—an inheritance that has to do with people rather than wealth or capital. *Minnie's Sacrifice* recasts the meaning of inheritance under slavery's capitalism to reclaim not just what but also who belongs to the Black community. In other words, Harper was just as interested in returning people to the Black community after the Civil War as she was interested in returning the wealth and resources they generated. She was concerned with both the reunion of families and relatives lost to one another in slavery (Gardner, "African American" 446) and the racial reclaiming of people.

Harper's variation of the "tragic mulatta" trope insists on the racial reclaiming of those Black women whom the trope centers. She speaks directly to her readers on this point when she inserts her authorial voice into her novel and says of Minnie: "While some of the authors of the present day have been weaving their stories about white men marrying beautiful quadroon girls, who, in so doing were lost to us socially, I conceived of one of that same class to whom I gave a higher, holier destiny" (91). Minnie is central to the novel's Black uplift work; indeed, it could not take place without her. Because Minnie's decision to not pass is crucially linked to the marriage and inheritance plot and to her racial uplift work, Harper's previously white-passing characters represent what becomes possible when they do not reproduce whiteness but rather disinvest of it. Harper's concern with racial reclamation can be attended to by the theme of inheritance as people in at least two ways—the inheritance of people back into the social community and the inheritance of people as resources who bring talent and capital to bear in the community. As Cassandra Jackson has previously noted: "Frances E. W. Harper calls attention to the necessity of personal sacrifices, including financial ones, in the communal effort to build free black communities after the war" (*Barriers* 7).[13]

In relation to the theme of inheritance as people, the economic possibility for Harper's near-white characters lies in their individual racial trajectories. For Louis, this trajectory is set in motion when his grandmother Miriam presents his free papers to him. Louis reads the papers "like one who might read a sentence of death to see if there was one word or sentence on which he might hang a hope of reprieve" (Harper, *Minnie's Sacrifice* 60). He accepts the authenticity of the papers but feels unanchored, like a "mariner at midnight on a moonless sea, who suddenly, when the storm is brewing, finds that he has lost his compass and his chart" (60). The scene marks an inherent contradiction to personhood under the logics of slavery's capitalism: the very existence of Louis's free papers reinscribe his status as property even as they act to undo that status. Harper does not address this contradiction to personhood and self-ownership in Louis's inheritance transference in great depth, but we see that contradiction play out in Louis's actions after receiving the papers. The sense that Louis "owns" himself but does not makes him flee the immediate scene. It conjures an overpowering mixture of complex emotions, "horror and anguish" (59), disbelief, confusion, and anger for Louis as he wrestles with the contradictions implicit in an identity that emerges from ideas of capital under slavery.

On the one hand, this scene allows Harper to give her character a site from which to reappropriate the kind of family structures that slavery was set up to mystify and to partially redress the social and economic injustices that occurred at that intersection of slavery, capitalism, and inheritance. Put another way, in an ironic reversal of the capitalist and white supremacist logics of inheritance within the system of slavery, Louis, who lived as the adopted white son of Le Croix, inherits his father's fortune as his Black son. On the other hand, Louis is only able to reclaim his identity when he shifts away from meanings of identity defined under slavery's capitalism and its intertwining principles of white supremacy, inheritance, and property ownership. Ultimately Louis comes to reject ownership of what Cheryl I. Harris would call "white identity as property," which serves to affirm "the self-identity and liberty of whites, and conversely, den[y] the self-identity and liberty of Blacks" ("Whiteness" 1743). Louis purposefully abdicates his racial inheritance of whiteness while claiming its monetary inheritance and, after selectively choosing what he inherits, turns toward meanings of identity that were formed by Miriam's own economic vision from the time he was a baby. When Louis allies himself to his mother's race, he has the opportunity to formally reunite with his family, including his grandmother Miriam, and to establish new family and community networks. Louis's racial trajectory, with its combination of emancipation, inheritance, and allyship, creates new economic conditions and opportunities, especially when he and Minnie marry.

Minnie also rejects ownership of her "white identity as property," though we do not see her granted self-ownership as we do with Louis. (If there is a similar scene for Minnie, we do not have access to it in what has been recovered from the archive.) Like Louis, she becomes aware of her Black ancestry through a maternal figure. When her mother Ellen heads North in search of Minnie, she serendipitously runs into her daughter on the street during one of Minnie's afternoon walks. Minnie is in shock when Ellen first reveals her true identity. Though she at first grapples with her racial identity, she soon embraces it fully. Minnie, who always felt there was something missing from her life, some "mystery which enshrouded her young life" (50–51), cherishes her reunion with Ellen, and a "ripening love [arises] between those two long-suffering ones" (53). When asked how she feels about now living as a Black woman, Minnie responds: "When I found out that I was colored, I made up my mind... that I would live out my own individuality and do for my race, as a colored woman, what I never could accomplish as a white woman" (72). As Koritha Mitchell notes of a similar story line in *Iola Leroy*, "Harper's characters count the cost and decide that what they would lose if they were estranged from African Americans would not be sufficiently compensated, despite how handsomely the country rewards whiteness" ("Introduction" 39). Part of what living as a white-passing woman in white society would cost Minnie is her relationship with her family (including her mother), her identity, self-respect, and individuality, and the opportunity to contribute to Black uplift from within the Black community.[14]

Though Minnie and Louis believe they are white for most of the novel, they come to fully abandon whiteness as an identity and political ontology. Harper draws Louis's and Minnie's characters as exemplars of resistance to the incentives of whiteness and wealth that would destroy the Black activist and economic networks that had coalesced through the antebellum period and decimate the numbers of people who could contribute to postbellum networks of economic incursion. In this way, Harper directs her fictional inheritance to carry reparative elements, not based on Mr. Le Croix's decisions or beliefs, but on Louis's and Minnie's: *what* Louis and Minnie inherit (wealth and identity) is just as important as what they *do* with that inheritance. When he is named heir, Louis knows he does not inherit Le Croix's massive fortune for himself; he inherits it on behalf of his family and his community. Rather than using the inheritance to reproduce capital, Louis and Minnie reinvest it back into the communities whose exploited labor, skill, and talent created the conditions of those profits.

Minnie and Louis, now aligned with the Black race, marry as the residue of their former white lives begins to fade. When they marry as a Black couple, they inherit a generational wealth that positions them as mobile, educated, and monied. Whereas marital love in nineteenth-century women's novels often represents a point of arrival, in *Minnie's Sacrifice* it represents a point of departure. Though aspects of the romance and marriage plots are missing, perhaps due to archival absences, we can surmise that Harper intended their union to be central to the novel's economic argument since their marriage signals a major turning point in the plot.[15] Black love is also central, as Koritha Mitchell notes, in Harper's later novel *Iola Leroy*, which follows a similar though longer and more fully developed story line than *Minnie's Sacrifice*. Referencing *Iola Leroy*, Mitchell writes, "Given that African Americans will bring love into the future, even if slavery has robbed them of everything else, Harper's novel suggests that the strength of the race's future will correspond to its homemaking success. However, because black love had strengthened slavery's chains, the challenge in freedom is to find ways to make homebuilding not simply a response to familial and romantic connections but also a locus of strategies for building dignified black futures" (*From Slave Cabins* 65). Similarly, for Minnie and Louis, Black love is accompanied by Black purpose in *Minnie's Sacrifice*. It is precisely when the two marry that they begin to change the world around them. Once married, Minnie and Louis decide together to invest their inheritance in Black development. As a married couple, they activate Louis's inheritance as a site of Black economic disruption and futurity by building on Miriam's effort to reconstruct the antebellum foundation and using it to create a communal economic base for the Black community from which social and political power will flow.

Harper purposefully roots her characters' transformative politico-economic actions in the fact of their mixed-race identities. In her story, unassuming characters—children of an enslaved mother and enslaving father—become economic actors who interrupt the traditional flow of money meant to maintain a hegemonic economic order. Harper activates the ebbs and flows of her characters' racial fluidity against a background of shifting economic circumstances, an example of what P. Gabrielle Foreman terms "histotextuality." For Foreman, histotextuality is "a method for interpreting sophisticated historicized tropes in narratives whose meaning has previously been thought to be produced by relying on the texts' thin and putatively singular or seemingly impoverished mimetic referents" (14). In other words, the histotextuality of Louis and Minnie includes a distinct relation to the economics of slavery's capitalism, and their literary figures accrue meaning in specific, historicized economic contexts across the antebellum, war, and postbellum periods. At the beginning of the story, both children, born into the chattel slavery system, would have been considered legal property. Before and during the first few years of the war, their northern educations and livelihoods, which make possible their marital match, are funded by the accumulated wealth and social networks of their enslaver fathers. And after the war, Louis and Minnie distribute to the Black community a substantial inheritance from Louis's enslaver father. Each phase of their lives can be read within particular economic contexts rooted in slavery's capitalism.

If the mixed-race characters in *Minnie's Sacrifice* exist at the intersection of racial instability and economic shifts in national infrastructure across the periods before, during, and after the Civil War, then the culmination of these figures' meaning lies in the economic context of Reconstruction. If we read the inheritance plot as also about inheritance as people, then the inheritance plot is not only about a story line that is economically reparative. As noted above, it is also about the people who receive the inheritance and what they do with it. Harper's characters with white ancestry, when they declare and affirm their Black identity and bring their talent and resources, including financial resources, to bear in the community, become logical bridges between the economics of slavery's capitalism and the economic future of Black development. Thus, Harper's redirection of inheritance by way of her mixed-race characters can be read as a metaphorical overthrowing of the father-master's economic logics.[16]

Part of Harper's economic meaning-making around inheritance, finally, involves inheritance as values. Minnie and Louis's homemaking, as mentioned above, is a site of economic disruption. Through this site, Harper creates a value scheme that explicitly recognizes the economics of the domestic sphere and the economics of the marketplace as linked, rather than a value scheme, like in *Uncle Tom's Cabin* as discussed in chapter 1, that appears to mystify those links. In Stowe's novel, as in other popular women's fiction of the time, as Nina Baym has argued, white authors centered domesticity as "a value scheme for ordering all of life, in competition with the ethos of money and exploitation that is perceived to prevail in American society" (Baym 27). For Black women like Aunt Martha in chapter 3 and the enslaved women of *Minnie's Sacrifice*, it was impossible to separate, or even mystify, the domestic sphere from the ways it was vulnerable to and structured by the logics of slavery's capitalism. Rather than showing Minnie and Louis's domestic sphere as structured by market forces or "competing" with the ethos of money, Harper reorganizes the ethos of money entirely. Once again centering economic meaning-making by Black women, as she does in the early part of the novel with Miriam, Harper creates this ethos through Louis's and Minnie's inheritance of values, especially the values they inherit from their mothers and grandmothers.

The third and final meaning of inheritance in this section is the inheritance of values passed on to Louis and Minnie, particularly from Black women, an inheritance that guides the way the couple reinvests that money in Black development. As Brigitte Fielder has argued, "Harper's anti-passing politics positions racialized matriliny as foundational for the deliberate, radical racial reproduction of Blackness" (*Relative Races* 140). In *Minnie's Sacrifice*, an inheritance of values, crucially, comes from Black maternal figures. Miriam's and Ellen's care work around people and relationships, the families, communities, and social networks that they create, is also economic work. It is work, informed by their personal and laboring histories under slavery's capitalism, that structures the value systems they pass on to Louis and Minnie. This inheritance of values ultimately structures decisions the couple make around their inheritance of wealth. By relying on a set of values that arise from the economic knowledge and experience of Black women, Harper disrupts the operations of patriarchal capitalism and rewrites the economic values that direct the community's economic operations.

Making up for lost time and making use of what little time she has with her grandson, Miriam acts as a maternal figure to Louis, giving him attention, sharing life lessons, and literally and metaphorically putting him on a path that sends him back to the Black community. For example, when Louis renounces his whiteness and deserts the Confederate army to join the Union, he becomes a wanted man. As Miriam helps him prepare to flee, she instructs him on how to evade the white people who would capture him and send him south. She teaches him how to secretly locate and communicate with the Black people who will protect him and assist him north. As Louis races to get beyond the borders of the Confederacy, he meets people along the way who perform heroic, superhuman acts of stratagem, bravery, and selflessness, including, for example, a man who throws the bloodhounds off Louis's path by cutting his own feet so that his blood would deepen the scent on another track (64). Louis learns from lessons in Black courage along his escape northbound, as well as from the political knowledge of the Black community, which Harper describes as having "deeper intuitions" and a better understanding of the nation and the war than the politicians who "did not or could not read the signs of the times aright" (65). Despite the obstacle of distance due to Louis's upbringing in the North, Miriam, who literally sets Louis on the path to reconnect with the Black community, ceaselessly works to pass on her values and knowledge to her grandson.

Though there are not many scenes in the novel where Louis acknowledges Miriam's influence, we can hear that acknowledgement in Harper's poem "Moses" if we read it, once again, as a paratext for *Minnie's Sacrifice* and if we read

Louis as a Moses-like character. Speaking of his mother, Moses says, "from her lips I / Learned the grand traditions of our race" (143).

> The blessed hopes and glorious promises
> That weave their golden threads among the somber
> Tissues of our lives, and shimmer still amid
> The gloom and shadows of our lot" (148).

At this point in the poem, Moses has turned his back on the Pharaoh's riches and "cast [his] lot among the people of [his] race" (149). Like Moses, Louis finds his way back through the lessons and values of a mother figure.[17] But, more specifically, he finds his way through Miriam's lessons on the "grand traditions" and "blessed hopes and glorious promises" of the people who came before him and brought him into being. Miriam once again saves Louis's life, literally by directing him north to freedom and spiritually by directing him back to the Black community.

Minnie's inheritance of values is also complex. Critiquing, perhaps, the abstruseness and ambiguity of the concept of inheritance during Reconstruction, Minnie selectively cobbles together a value system passed on to her from her northern education, her adoptive Quaker parents Josiah and Anna, and her mother Ellen. From a classical education and "hard study," she receives the "knowledge of books" (74). From Anna's domestic economy, she learns to plant "the roots of progress under the hearthstone" (74). As a child in the home of Quakers, a station of the Underground Railroad, she meets road-weary antislavery lecturers, learns "a reverence for humanity" (31), and is "educated in peace principles" (66). As part of the Quaker community, she experiences the Quakers' ability to form communities, and even economies, that largely function outside or on the margins of society.

Minnie also inherits values from her mother. Ellen and Minnie's mother-daughter relationship is a bridge that connects one who has lived most of her life enslaved with the other who was born enslaved but has never experienced life under slavery. From her mother, Minnie learns about herself and her family's history and legacy. Ellen also teaches Minnie a carefully crafted lesson about understanding and channeling one's emotions to productive ends. It is perhaps this lesson that makes Minnie such an effective leader later in the novel. In the scene with the most dialogue between Ellen and Minnie, the two discuss the relationship between forgiveness, religion, and the protection of Black life. The conversation is spurred when Ellen notices her daughter's "sinking spirits" (82) as Minnie questions what the future holds for people living under a government that does not protect the lives of its Black citizens. In response, Ellen hides her own "disquietude" to try to "keep Minnie's spirits from sinking" (82) and explains to her daughter how she deals with her own kind of sinking spirits. Ellen says that that she used to feel bitterness toward the people who treated her so cruelly until God taught her forgiveness: "I used to suffer until my heart was almost ready to burst, but I learned to cast my burden on the Lord, and then my misery all passed away. My burden fell off at the foot of the cross, and I felt that my feet were planted on a rock" (82). Ellen's lesson is not one of forgiveness in the sense of absolution but of forgiveness as strategic self-interest and self-preservation, that puts one on more stable ground—or, as Ellen says, with one's feet "planted on a rock"—and is connected to the larger interest and preservation of family and community. It was, perhaps, this strategy that encouraged and sustained Ellen's relentless pursuit to reunite with her daughter. Harper uses the religious trope of forgiveness to almost militaristic ends: it is a mechanism that strategizes the protection of Black life and family and one that Minnie later uses in her uplift work.

The importance of the knowledge and work generated by characters like Miriam and Ellen is more visible in Harper's Aunt Chloe poems, which were published a few years after the novel in a collection of poetry entitled *Sketches of Southern Life* (1872). The poems center the voice of Aunt Chloe, an older, grandmotherly figure and formerly enslaved woman who recounts the history of slavery through Reconstruction. Her history touches on many of the issues that appear in *Minnie's Sacrifice*—money and commodities, education, suffrage, governmental politics, and family—but through her eyes and through her personal history. The character of Aunt Chloe is, as Frances Smith Foster notes, a significant contribution to nineteenth-century African American literature:

> She is probably the first black female protagonist, outside the tragic mulatto tradition, to be presented as a model for life. Mrs. Chloe Fleet is not the young, talented, cultivated middle-class heroine of the sentimental novel, nor is she the weeping, shivering slave girl. She is "rising sixty," a mature ex-slave, one of the many who survived the auction block, separation from her children, and the toil and tribulations experienced by "ordinary" slave women. After slavery, Aunt Chloe went to work and learned to read "the hymns and Testament." Barely literate and unsophisticated, Aunt Chloe is a folk character, a no-nonsense woman of moral strength and great common sense." (*Brighter* 137)

What makes Aunt Chloe a "model for life" is also what makes Miriam and Ellen models for Louis and Minnie: the ability to offer astute, carefully crafted, "no-nonsense" analyses of social, political, and economic issues that can only come from her individual lived experience and perspective. Aunt Chloe, like Miriam and Ellen, has an awareness of such issues that we do not often get from other fictional characters in the nineteenth century. Louis and Minnie carry the values they inherit from their mothers and grandmothers, characters similar to Aunt Chloe, into their uplift work.

One of the themes that arises from Aunt Chloe's analysis, according to Foster, is that "freedom requires unified, continuous struggle" (*Brighter* 236)—a theme that also reverberates through Miriam and Ellen's lessons in Harper's novel. Their inheritance of values is later complemented by lessons of "faith and trust" that they learn in the South. Harper narrates: "Some of the most beautiful lessons of faith and trust they had ever learned, they were taught in the lowly cabins of these newly freed people" (75). Louis and Minnie step into activist leadership positions because they inherited financial, educational, and social privileges, but they ground their activism in cross-class conversation.

Harper prizes the couple's partnership, grounded in mutual admiration and purpose, and the values Minnie and Louis each bring to their marriage and to their activism. But her novel, as the title attests, really centers the thought and action of Black women. It is Minnie, and the Black women around her, who hold the ideas to enact radical change in the postbellum moment of national rebuilding. Harper's move to generate economic value and change through the care work of women like Miriam, Ellen, and later Minnie anticipates feminist economist Nina Banks's research, which argues that, as with critical, scholarly arguments about women's unpaid housework, Black women's community work has rarely figured as economic work. But if we place Black women's experiences at the center of economic analysis, we can "reconceptualize Black women's *community activism* as unpaid, nonmarket 'work,'" with "work" defined as those "activities that produce and reproduce material life" (344). Reconceptualizing community work like Miriam's, Ellen's, and Minnie's as a site of production makes visible the economic contributions of that work, which creates social and economic value. It also makes visible their economic knowledge. The knowledge Black women gain from their economic work and the social and economic value that work produces contributes to their value systems passed on as inheritance.

Harper's move to center Black women as economic agents in her fiction aligns with the historical role of women in Black economic activism. Across the nineteenth and twentieth centuries, as political economist Jessica Gordon Nembhard reminds us, "African American women played significant roles, held leadership positions, and often formed their own organizations throughout these periods and across almost every kind of organization. As founders and main participants in many mutual-aid societies, women were instrumental in organizational development, fund-raising, day-to-day coordination, and networking for cooperatives as well as other organizations" (29). Drawing on women's experience and privileging women's ideas about the economic possibilities of the future is a theme Harper would return to frequently. In "Enlightened Motherhood," a speech she delivered to the Brooklyn Literary Society on November 15, 1892, Harper spoke about the "rebuilding" work of women and mothers: "The work of the mothers of our race is grandly constructive" she emphasized. "It is for us to build above the wreck and ruin of the past more stately temples of thought and action" (292). Less than a year later, in a speech titled "Woman's Political Future" at the 1893 World's Columbian Exhibition, she drew on the importance of women's rebuilding work again and explicitly articulated advocacy for woman's political voices in national discourse. "Woman's work is grandly constructive," Harper proclaimed. "In her hand are possibilities whose use or abuse must tell upon the political life of the nation, and send their influence for good or evil across the track of unborn ages" (*World's Congress* 433–34). In *Minnie's Sacrifice*, Harper's female characters take center stage: it was women like Minnie, Ellen, and Miriam who had the "grandly constructive" ideas that would effect change.

Building on knowledge she acquires from a classical education, Quaker principles, her mother's lessons around emotion, justice, and action, and lessons from newly freed people, Minnie strategizes a plan for how national reconstruction might work. In a letter to Louis, she outlines this plan, writing, "The South will never be rightly conquered until another army should take the field, and that must be an army of civilizers; the army of the pen, and not the sword. Not the destroyers of towns and cities, but the builders of machines and factories; the organizers of peaceful industry and honorable labor" (*Minnie's Sacrifice* 68). Minnie uses militaristic rhetoric to imagine a world that is conquered and then rebuilt by the forces of peace and honor, creativity, thoughtfulness, and civility. Her vision reflects Harper's own. As Eric Gardner has noted, "Harper's vision of 'reconstruction' thus demanded and valued selective destruction over continued compromise and concealment, and it extended not only to slavery, but to myriad forms of racism, sexism, hate, fear, and greed. For her, these were the issues central to both the War and the national future" ("Return" 611). Minnie imagines a labor force of thinkers, writers, builders, organizers, and laborers working together so that the ideological projects of peace, civility, and honor align with the industrial projects of towns and cities, machines and factories, and industry and labor. Minnie's "army" of civilizers and the pen is one of thinkers, of ideas, doing ideological work with the potential to be "grandly constructive." Commenting on Harper's articulation of a biopolitics of sexual difference, Kyla Schuller similarly notes that in her address at the 1893 World's Columbian Exhibition, Harper "contrasts a masculine world of deterioration, destruction, and death with a feminine politics rooted in productivity, regeneration, and fertility" (69). In *Minnie's Sacrifice*, Harper grounds Minnie's ideological stratagem in a similar kind of biopolitics of sexual difference. In this sense, Harper's characters, especially her women characters, pass on and inherit values that enact economic change. They create a value scheme in service to communal Black economic interests, values that undergird the novel's suggested practices of economic citizenship, the focus of the following section.

ECONOMIC CITIZENSHIP: MONEY, SUFFRAGE, LABOR, AND LAND

In *Minnie's Sacrifice*, Harper is interested in reframing citizenship by offering practices of economic citizenship—that is, citizens' engagement with economic meaning-making—that would carve out a space in postbellum racial capitalism for Black control of Black development, align with the interests of the Black community across class differences, and solidify an economic position for the Black community. Writing about Reconstruction-era activists like Harper, Derrick R. Spires observes, "As state policies and public discourse around citizenship were becoming more racially restrictive, black activists articulated an expansive, practice-based theory of citizenship, not as a common identity as such but rather as a set of common practices" (3). Turning away from state definitions of citizenship that would absorb Black and formerly enslaved subjects into new modalities of racial capitalism, Harper calls on her readers to participate in a "set of common practices" around economic meaning-making. As Spires reminds us, "From the perspective of black theorizing, states do not make citizens—active and involved individuals and collectives create citizens" (16).[18] In the following section, I emphasize three practices of economic citizenship in *Minnie's Sacrifice*: drawing on the multivalent meanings of inheritance and re-historicizing the meaning of money to build institutions and community relations that create social and economic value; organizing for Black economic ownership of Black politics through suffrage and labor rights—especially through Black woman's suffrage and labor; and strategizing access to land ownership. Through Minnie and Louis and a marriage grounded in Black love and purpose, Harper's novel ultimately suggests how a community of people, through individual and collective acts of economic citizenship, can build a communal economic base from which social and political power can flow.

Harper understood that money, far from being a neutral, fungible medium of economic exchange, is deeply infused with social and political meaning.[19] Thus, the first foundational practice is how an individual or community thinks about money, a way of thinking that subtends the other two practices of economic citizenship. Marx describes money as "the absolutely alienable commodity, because it is all other commodities divested of their shape, the product of their universal alienation" (205). In other words, money is the representation of an abstract value that represents an abstract value. But Harper pushes back on money as an "absolutely alienable commodity." By closely following the material conditions of the inheritance's origins and its subsequent circulation, she instead situates money as "icon."[20] In *Minnie's Sacrifice*, money signals the robberies and sin of slavery and the economic and moral necessity for reparations and operates semiotically as a sign with potential meanings that can be actualized by a network of actors or, in Harper's words, a "new community of interests" (74). Ultimately, as icon, money signals that a community's affective and moral attachment to it is actualized in the material conditions in which the money is invested.

When Minnie and Louis invest their inheritance in Black development, the way they think about money re-signifies on its meaning as it was meant to operate under slavery's capitalism. Capitalist societies typically feature "one general-purpose money" (Konings 15). General-purpose money autonomizes itself; it imposes a financial logic that is indifferent to the substance of social life and necessitates a "regulatory capacity that is no longer congruent with the specific, localized qualities of social relations" (15). The economic system of slavery epitomized this "indifference" to an extreme degree, which is what allowed the capitalist accounting practices of enslavers to emerge with as much precision as they did, as chapter 1 discusses. The economic logics of slavery's capitalism and the meanings attached to money under that system were, of course, not contained to the ledger book but were embedded in all aspects of social life. In *Minnie's* Sacrifice, Thomas, Minnie's adopted Quaker father, speaks to this point when he laments, "The system is very strongly rooted and grounded in the institutions of the land, and has entrenched itself in the strongholds of Church and State, fashion, custom, and social life" (Harper, *Minnie's Sacrifice* 30). The economic logics of slavery's capitalism pervaded all parts of society, including institutions people attend (like churches and schools), the clothes they wear, the way they behave, and the money that made all these things possible.

That would have been true also for the money that Louis and Minnie inherit. But, as part of Harper's metaphorical overthrowing of the father-master's economic logics—a reparative device that turns (and returns) white-controlled money accumulated through slavery into Black-controlled money—Minnie and Louis, by circulating their inheritance within the Black community, defy the tendency of capitalist money to operate as a "solvent of social ties" (Konings 15). When asked about his future plans now that he and Minnie are married, Louis responds: "We are going to open a school, and devote our lives to the upbuilding of the future race. I intend entering into some plan to facilitate the freedmen in obtaining homes of their own. I want to see this newly enfranchised race adding its quota to the civilization of the land. I believe there is power and capacity, only let it have room for exercise and development" (73). Minnie and Louis use money to create bonds of social ties rather than the dissolution of them; the substance of social life organizes the operations of their money rather than the other way around. The institutions built by their inheritance generate both physical and ideological structures that invest in Black development. In this sense, how an individual or community thinks about the way money signifies and operates is a practice of economic citizenship in and of itself.

Harper's concern with the way people think about money appeared in her writing before the Civil War. For example, in "Free Labor" (1857), she argues for the moral and economic power that comes with an individual's decision to divest their money from an immoral economy by participating in the free produce movement, the international boycott of goods produced by enslaved labor. And in "Our Greatest Want" she cautions that money, while important, is not the "greatest want" for racial progress.[21] It has its limitations. More important than money, more limitless in its potential to contribute to racial progress, Harper argues, are "earnest, self sacrificing souls" (104). In *Minnie's Sacrifice*, Harper's concern with how one thinks about money and economics shows up again in these ways. But now, after the Civil War and in the midst of the Reconstruction Acts, it shows up additionally as a foundational practice in Harper's articulation of economic citizenship. Thinking about money and economics in this way makes space for organizing Black economic ownership of Black politics, which Harper speaks to in the two scenes discussed below, the first involving Minnie and the second involving Mr. Jackson.

Through Minnie, Harper argues that Black woman's suffrage and economic knowledge are vital aspects of Black politics and foundational to advancing Black economic citizenship for all. Harper, who actively campaigned for African American and woman suffrage in the months between the passing of the Fifteenth Amendment on February 26, 1869, and its ratification on February 3, 1870, addresses the issue in her novel. One night at home, Minnie and

Louis discuss the issue of the ballot, and Minnie argues to Louis that the nation makes a mistake in not extending the vote to women: "'Louis' said Minnie very seriously, 'I think the nation makes one great mistake in settling this question of suffrage. It seems to me that everything gets settled on a partial basis. When they are reconstructing the government why not lay the whole foundation anew, and base the right of suffrage not on the claims of service or sex, but on the broader basis of our common humanity.... Is it not the negro woman's hour also? Has she not as many rights and claims as the negro man?'" (78). Scholars have read this scene as Harper's argument about the need for legal protections for Black women and the ability to protect themselves from oppression (O'Brien, *Race* 144); an echoing of debates about Black suffrage by Wendell Phillips and Parker Pillsbury and Harper's recognition that the claims of "the negro man" did not exist in isolation (Stevenson 232), and an example of Black women's "pragmatic tactical decision to support black (male) suffrage and the Fifteenth Amendment before white audiences but also to argue for woman suffrage inside the black community" (Dudden 185). Famously, Harper put race before sex in her speech at the 1869 American Equal Rights Association meeting. Indeed, Minnie's argument is about all of these things. Additionally, suffrage, being about citizenship, includes questions of economics.

If we consider the economic framework of Harper's novel, and if we center the economic work of her women characters, we can also read the above passage through the lens of economic citizenship. Minnie's question—"when they are reconstructing the government why not lay the whole foundation anew[?]"—calls for a change to everything that led to the nation's situation. Within the scope of the novel, this recalls the economic dynamics of slavery that lead up to the inheritance plot, and especially Miriam's and Ellen's efforts to overhaul those dynamics. Minnie's question about reconstructing the foundation, then, allows Harper to resituate the relationship between slavery and Black women's economic work within the suffrage debates. Black women's work, as the above sections have shown, produces crucial economic knowledge and change. If the nation wants to reconstruct its foundation, it needs that knowledge. When Minnie argues for Black woman's suffrage, when she argues that the "government needs woman's conscience" (78), she evokes all parts of woman's conscience, including that developed by their economic knowledge. This means women like Miriam, Ellen, and Aunt Chloe. And it also means women like Minnie, whose economic knowledge comes not only from her own activist work but also the knowledge inherited from the economic work of women who came before her and laid the foundation on which her reform work builds. In this way, Harper links woman's moral conscience as well as economic consciousness—arising from physical and intellectual labor—to suffrage and suggests that the success of the nation's reconstruction effort hinges not on woman's suffrage but on Black woman's suffrage in particular.

Harper's theorizing of economic citizenship involves individual economic participation by people like Miriam and Minnie as well as collective economic participation. The relationship between individual and collective economic citizenship practices is illustrated through the novel's scene featuring Mr. Jackson. Mr. Jackson, a cobbler who visits the home of Minnie and Louis, is worried about being able to earn enough money to support his family. Before he had the right to vote, he had plenty of work and a steady income. But now that he has the right to vote, no one will hire him. "They wouldn't give me the situation," he explains to Louis and Minnie, "because I had joined the radicals" (76). In addition to being refused work, Mr. Jackson tells the couple, he was offered a $500 bribe for his vote. Taking account of Mr. Jackson's situation, Minnie calculates that $500 to a man "stripped by slavery," "landless and poor, with no assured support for the future," means a "comfortable fire when the blasts of winter are roving around your home; it means bread for the little ones, and medicine for the sick child, and little start in life" (77). In spite of intimidation and starvation tactics by the rebels and the precarious situation of his family, Mr. Jackson refuses the bribe, thus rejecting a model of citizenship that insists he vote against his own interests and "clasp hands politically with his life-long oppressors" (77). Mr. Jackson rejects the false promises of money offered by white bribes, money that would legally and politically, through his vote, reify his own oppression. But now that he has protected the interest and dignity of his vote, he is left without employment or money to feed his family. Serendipitously, Mr. Jackson finds a quarter on the street. And his friends rally their resources and collect an additional seventy-five cents for him. In her history of African American cooperative economic thought and practice, Jessica Gordon Nembhard writes, "African Americans involved in collective economic activities often found that they needed also to engage in political activity to enact public policies or counteract White blocs and racially discriminatory legislation. In addition, African Americans often found it necessary to engage in collective economic practices in order to achieve or maintain the independence they needed to assert themselves politically" (30). Harper illustrates this argument through the dual themes of suffrage and labor in the above scene. With money collected by the Black community, Mr. Jackson is able to provide for himself and his family. His decision to place political interests over much-needed financial resources protects the integrity of his individual vote, but it is a collective economic citizenship, the mutual aid of friends and community, that protects and ultimately makes possible Black ownership of Black politics.

At the time Harper was writing *Minnie's Sacrifice*, national debates about labor had taken center stage. For whites, the abolition of enslaved labor rang the alarm. David R. Roediger emphasizes, "Emancipation removed the ability of white workers to derive satisfaction from defining themselves as 'not slaves' and called into question self-definitions that centered on being 'not Black'" (170). Whiteness reasserted itself in new ways: the nationwide panic of white labor spurred the proliferation of white labor unions, nearly all of which barred Black membership and ignored reconstruction issues (Foner 170, 479). For Blacks, the abolition of enslaved labor was a call to action. In 1869, African Americans established the Colored National Labor Union (CNLU) to organize Black laborers on a national level, and, around the same time as the serialization of *Minnie's Sacrifice*, the *Christian Recorder* was reporting on issues related to the CNLU including the Baltimore Convention of Colored Mechanics.

Black labor and Black union power were clearly on Harper's mind and came out in the pages of her novel and other writing. Early in *Minnie's Sacrifice*, enslaved laborers are seen "wending their way into their lowly huts," and later, through their activist work, Minnie and Louis encounter people holding a range of occupations: cobblers, barbers, businessmen, teachers, soldiers, homemakers, and community organizers (11). Louis attends the political meetings of these newly freed workers "not to array class against class" but because he wants to help facilitate ways their collective vote will express "the new community of interests arising from freedom" (74).

Harper would continue to talk to *Christian Recorder* readers about Black labor power and collective economic efforts that, as Nembhard summarizes, developed "among diverse groups and in diverse settings: in urban and rural areas among farmers, landholders, sharecroppers, day laborers, domestic workers, industrial workers, and the unemployed, as well as small business owners and professionals.... and were sometimes all the stronger because multiple classes were represented" (29). A year after *Minnie's Sacrifice* was published, Harper returned to themes of Black labor power and collective economic efforts more explicitly in an essay titled "Our People" (1870). Focused on the unity of a Black labor force across occupations and the shifting labor market, Harper wrote: "One of the great needs of our people is a greater diversification of our industrial pursuits. The result of overcrowding the labor market in any department of industry is a reduction of the rate of wages" (2). Harper saw the unity of Black labor power across occupations and class divisions as a fundamental practice of economic citizenship. These practices, as Harper advocated in her fiction and nonfiction, would help secure an economic and political position for the Black community. Part of securing that position included securing landownership, the third and final practice of economic citizenship.

For Harper, claiming rights to landownership was both an individual and collective practice. Throughout *Minnie's Sacrifice*, several characters comment on the need to own land.[22] Early in the story, Minnie's adopted Quaker father Thomas, in a conversation with Quaker friends, argues: "One of the most important things for [Black men] to do is to acquire land. He will never gain his full measure of strength until (like Anteus) he touches the earth" (30). In Greek mythology, Anteus, who is of African origin, is overpowered by Hercules only when he is lifted into the air and separated from Mother Earth, the source of all his powers. Thomas, by invoking the story of Anteus, implies landownership as a life source, as having the power of giving continuous life, for the Black community. This is a lesson that Louis continually repeats during his activist work, urging the freedmen, "Be saving and industrious, [and] try to get land under your feet and homes over your heads" (86). As Farah Jasmine Griffin argues about Louis's activism around Black landownership, "Louis, like Harper, . . . knows that political rights mean little without economic independence for the freedmen. Eventually, Harper joined the freedmen in their plea for redistribution of land. For most freedmen, landownership was an integral part of their definition of freedom. In calling for land for the freedmen, Harper and Louis depart from southern mixed-race landowners" (315–16). In addition to cross-class arguments, Black landownership, Harper advises, is not just about owning land, it is also about having something to leave behind. In other words, Harper's landownership argument is also an argument about inheritance.

Harper would continue to press economic arguments about landownership and inheritance to her readers as part of larger arguments around Black development of national resources across multiple industries. In 1870, just a year after the *Recorder* published *Minnie's Sacrifice*, it published Harper's essay "Land and Labor," which opens with a dual argument about Black landownership and resource development. She writes: "There are four sources of national wealth—mining, manufactures, commerce and agriculture. As wealth producers, our chief department has been the agriculture field. . . . Today the agricultural knowledge learned under the old regime of slavery is an element of strength under the new dispensation of freedom. With strong hands and educated muscles, colored men in the South are beginning to draw the land under their feet" (1). Emphasizing Black wealth production before and after the war and claiming inheritance rights to that wealth, Harper's essay argues that agriculture is a primary site for Black development in terms of both landownership and as a laboring industry. Harper does not speak explicitly to cotton or agricultural commodities more broadly in *Minnie's Sacrifice* (which in the case of Louis's inheritance would have been Haitian sugar, coffee, indigo, cacao and/or cotton). But Louis's activist work around landownership can also be read as an argument about leveraging agricultural knowledge and owning the production of agricultural commodities. These are themes Harper addresses more directly in her essay. "Land and Labor" was part of a Black print movement during Reconstruction, on which Katherine Adams has written, that offered "tributes to the heroic productivity of Black cotton labor" (284). These writers, Adams emphasizes, publicized both the enslaved field hand's contributions to global commerce and the freedpeople's productive contributions to the postbellum economy (284). What makes Harper's tributes different, especially those published in the *Christian Recorder*, is that her aim is not only to valorize the agriculture knowledge of the freedman, that unparalleled, intimate knowledge and expertise located in a worker's "educated muscles" and claim ownership of the freedmen's contributions to the U.S. economy, but also to simultaneously offer readers tactical practices to advance Black economic citizenship. In "Land and Labor," Harper admonishes her readers to claim their inheritance of land, to deploy their labor so that their labor remains their own, and to strategically leverage their knowledge of the agricultural industry "not just to get land but to keep it" (1). In other words, land is inheritance to pass on.

Harper's discussion of landownership revolves around both individual and collective economic citizenship practices, a large part of Louis's reform efforts in the novel. Working across class, Louis uses "his influence in teaching them to be saving and industrious, and to turn their attention towards becoming land owners" (74). But in *Minnie's Sacrifice* we rarely get the kind of longer conversations and insights around landownership that we do in Harper's essays. In "Land and Labor," for example, Harper uses three distinct stories to more fully explain how these practices could work. Much like in *Minnie's Sacrifice*, these stories involve a version of how capitalism can work differently in the Black community, because, although Harper was not pro-capitalism, per se, she did recognize pragmatically that she needed to operate within the rapidly developing capitalist economic system. Therefore, if we read Harper's essay as an intertext for the conversations around landownership in her novel, we can more fully distinguish her insights.

In each of the three stories Harper tells in "Land and Labor," she more fully thinks through how the Black community could operate, through landownership, in the nation's capitalist system in ways that would also align with their interests and needs. The first story she tells is about a Reverend Graham, a Black minister from Kentucky with quite some influence, who buys a large plot of land but first makes three promises: first, a plot will go to the church; second, he will not sell to any poor, white man or a man with a bad character; third, if a man dies with his payments unfinished, the land will pass down to his family. The last condition secures Black landownership as a site of inheritance kept in one's family. Graham keeps his promise. He cuts up the plot into tracts and sells them to folks in the Black community, and "in a short time quite a number of new homes began to spring up like wells in the desert dust" (1). The second story she tells is about a man who, while enslaved, established a laundry business with his wife. Through thrift and business savvy, he is able to run a successful enterprise and by the time of emancipation has accumulated quite a bit of money. "When liberty had dawned upon his race," Harper narrates, "with his hoarded savings he was able not only to buy land for himself, but to reach his hand and open the way for quite a number of others to get homes for themselves" (1). The third story shares a common theme with the first two. It is about a blacksmith from Maryland, a successful businessman, who buys land and helps others get a foothold. His real estate investments do so well that he receives a handsome offer for the land. "Preferring to give his own people a chance" (1), he rejects the offer and instead sells seventeen plots within the Black community, giving others the opportunity to become landowners.

The three men in these stories come from vastly different laboring positions as a minister, a formerly enslaved launderer, and a successful businessman. But for Harper the most important trait they have in common is that they all engage an individual (quasi-capitalist) economic citizenship. Each man sells his plots of land at a profit and makes money for himself, though he does not sell those plots for as much as he can. Instead, all three practice an individual economic citizenship practice to communal ends and help fortify a collective economic citizenship.

Harper was interested in people and stories, like the three above and Louis and Minnie's in *Minnie's Sacrifice*, that understood how the dominant economic system worked and looked for ways to make it work for others. She illustrates this point in her novel through the story lines of Louis and Minnie and speaks to it directly in her nonfiction. Toward the end of "Land and Labor," she poses a rhetorical question that asks her readers to consider the role of "combination" in labor and enterprise: "Had we more respect and liking for each other could we not successfully form land clubs, land agencies, and when shut out from white men's shops, organize industries for ourselves, are there not trades and employments that by energy and combination we could introduce among ourselves?" (1).

Harper believed that the "power of combination," a phrase she repeatedly uses in *Minnie's Sacrifice*, could work as a strategy for a political and economic platform. She envisioned a community that created its own economic meaning-making around approaches to money that would create rather than dissolve social ties, around approaches to suffrage that would acknowledge the economic value of Black women's uplift work and protect Black ownership of Black politics, and around approaches to land and labor that insisted on the relationship between the individual and the collective. By seizing the means of economic meaning-making around money, suffrage, land, and labor, Harper in *Minnie's Sacrifice* theorizes ways to develop a communal economic base for the Black community that would offer more stable ground for economic citizenship during the instability of Reconstruction.

CONCLUSION: HARPER'S COMMUNAL ECONOMICS

Through determination and hard work, Louis and Minnie's racial uplift work begins to take root. When their efforts reach a level of success that makes their reform work visible, Louis becomes the target of the white supremacist institutions that the couple's activism threatens: "He began to receive threats and anonymous letters, such as these: 'Louis Lecroix, you are a doomed man.... Beware, the sacred serpent has hissed'" (81). Though Louis receives death threats, it is Minnie who is killed by the Ku Klux Klan. Her death, rather than Louis's, perhaps suggests that the female protagonist, Harper's "pioneer of a new civilization" (67) whose knowledge, insight, and vision engines the couple's reform agenda, posed a serious threat to the dual forces of white supremacy and capitalism. Minnie had ideas so powerful they held the potential to construct—to "pioneer"—a new civilization. Minnie, like Harper herself, envisions the ethos of economic citizenship as grounded in the exchange of interaction between people, not in the exchange of goods between people—a threat to the core of capitalism, which does not allow for the contractual power of human relations to trump the contractual power of market relations. It is this threat, the collective economic work that Louis and Minnie do and their success at it, for which Minnie is murdered.[23]

Minnie's Sacrifice centers on Louis and Minnie, but all of Harper's characters together reframe the meanings of inheritance (as wealth, people, and values) and rewrite practices of citizenship (labor, suffrage, and landownership) in a racist postbellum economy that allowed for a degree of racial progress only when that progress aligned with the interests of whites. It is a collective effort that creates the communal economic base from which Black development can advance, from the sacrifices that Miriam and Ellen make when they redirect their children's and grandchildren's futures in ways that reconstruct the antebellum economic foundation, to Louis and Minnie's postbellum uplift work that reconstructs and builds on the foundation laid out by their foremothers, to Mr. Jackson and the "new" community's commitment to cross-class political and economic solidarity. Bringing this host of characters together, Harper was very much working within the capitalist system as it existed but was theorizing economic citizenship practices for racial equality outside of white capitalist interest.

Frances Harper used the novel form to encourage her Black readers to understand their economic fate as linked and to claim their economic destiny through community-based economic action. She laid the foundation for this claim by reaching back into the eighteenth century and weaving together a wide range of economic issues in *Minnie's Sacrifice*. This tapestry included the triangulation of Haiti, Louisiana, and the North in the transnational slave trade; the alignment of the historical moments of the Haitian Revolution and U.S. Civil War; the operations of inheritance and reparations; the relationship between marriage and community; Black mutual aid and cross-class alliances; physical and ideological structures for education, labor, suffrage, and land ownership; and practices of economic citizenship amid the intensification of white violence. Put more succinctly, in *Minnie's Sacrifice* a remarkable number of issues around gender, race, and economics come together within a narrative framework produced at the intersection of slavery's aftermath and Reconstruction-- era capitalism. Thus, it was in fiction that Harper could more deliberately probe the interplay of race, gender, and Black economic possibility. By rewriting the very idea of economic value in relation to inheritance and citizenship, Harper's novel offers the kind of insight generated by women's economic meaning-- making that is often overlooked in histories of slavery and capitalism.

EPILOGUE

Women's Literature as Economic Theory

THROUGHOUT *Slavery, Capitalism, and Women's Literature*, I have argued that centering nineteenth-century women writers as economic critics and theorists provides crucial, previously unconsidered insights into the relationship between U.S. slavery and capitalism. Because the four women studied here write from particular gendered and racialized positions under slavery's capitalism, they offer a range of economic insights and perspectives different from those offered by the dominant white and masculine-coded discourses of histories of capitalism. I traced these insights using an analytic reversal of nineteenth-century economic rhetoric, emphasizing how women writers used the language of capitalism to critique slavery rather than using the language of slavery to critique capitalism. When we center these insights, we see what has been there all along: women writers participating in, and creating, economic discourse.

The aim of this book has been twofold. First, it reinstates nineteenth-century women writers as economic thinkers, critics, and theorists and argues for the value in reading women's literature as economic theory. Slavery's capitalism, as a social, political, and economic system, was the structuring force of the period before the Civil War, as its codified aftermath was in the postbellum period. Reading some of the nineteenth century's best-known women writers—Stowe, Larcom, Jacobs, and Harper—through this lens demonstrates how their writing, all of which engages the instruments, practices, and logics of slavery's capitalism, is anchored by economic acuity. They modeled formulations of economic thinking around some of the linchpins of slavery's capitalism—accounting and sentimentality (Stowe), cotton and women's labor (Larcom), property and freedom (Jacobs), and inheritance and reparations (Harper)—that could influence, inform, or underwrite economic thought, then and now. As the preceding chapters have shown, this literature contributes new possibilities for economic meaning-making outside of those we typically find in economics and economic histories and shows "economics" as something of a fiction—its own kind of narrative.

The second aim of this book has been to illuminate what gets lost when we do not include nineteenth-century women's literary voices in contemporary conversations about slavery's capitalism. Beyond their pointed and explicit critiques, women writers offer unique economic insights to the slavery-capitalism conversation that can only be accessed through their creative and imaginative writing. Because their texts take the material-historical connection of slavery and capitalism as a starting point, they can be read for the more speculative extensions of that connection. These speculative extensions lead to insights about slavery's capitalism that are not possible to discover on a material-historical level. In this way, literary analysis of such literature as economic discourse brings to the surface how slavery's capitalism showed up in women's everyday lives—in their engagement with sentimental accounting, technologies of labor, objects or property, and forms of inheritance—and how their writing generated economic insights from these interactions. In other words, this body of literature allows us to access a more intimate sense of how slavery's capitalism appears in not just the text but also the texture of nineteenth-century culture, to reach those sensations and sensibilities that lie beyond surface touch. The result brings us closer to a more complete picture of slavery's capitalism.

The recent explosion of scholarship in the histories of U.S. slavery and the histories of U.S. capitalism, to which this book responds, expresses an interest in understanding the role of capitalism in shaping not just U.S. history but also the current moment. As many others also point out, these histories hold immense explanatory power for a number of reasons. First, capitalism is an incredibly powerful and adaptive system that seeps into every aspect of life and leaves no individual, community, or institution untouched. Second, the precise role that slavery played in its development is still being uncovered by scholars from a wide range of disciplines. And last, our nation has yet to fully reckon with its history of slavery, the system that engined and engineered U.S. capitalism before the Civil War and continues to shape it today.

Nineteenth-century women's literary scholarship speaks to each of these issues. The fact that women's literary texts are permeated with economic concerns but rarely included in the canon of economic writing raises important questions for scholars: Who gets to author economic writing? And who gets to create or authorize economic meaning-making? To think through these questions and to make a final case for reading nineteenth-century women writers as economic critics and theorists, I turn briefly to a history of the relationship between the fields of economics and nineteenth-century women's literature.

Before the eighteenth century, "economics" had more in common with humanities disciplines like philosophy, history, and literature than it did with science disciplines like physics and mathematics.[1] Economics was speculative and imaginative rather than prescriptive or predictive. It was only in the eighteenth century, with the work in the Anglophone world of people like David Hume, Adam Smith, and David Ricardo, that the idea of "the economy" became itself an object of study. In the last few decades, literary scholars, economists, and economic historians have contributed to the subfield of literary-economic criticism, historicizing the relationship between the two fields and highlighting certain affinities between them.[2]

The previously shared discursive field of economics and the humanities became somewhat obscured as various social and political factors forged a disciplinary split between them. The nineteenth century, for example, saw further separation of these disciplines, facilitated in large part by the operations of the university system, the institutionalization of the production of knowledge, and the rise of disciplinary boundaries.[3] Economics increasingly modeled itself on the natural sciences and engineering, which in the nineteenth century meant moving into a more masculinist and elite sphere.[4]

This disciplinary split, I argue, was crucial to the emergence of women writers as economic critics and theorists. There were, of course, nineteenth-century women economists, but, generally, women interested in economic issues were left to explore those issues in literature.[5] Confined to imaginative and creative writing, women economic theorists had the advantage that the conventions of their literary forms (like the novels, poetry, and narrative studied here) allowed, invited, even demanded different ways of thinking: metaphorical bridging, phenomenological explorations, the problematizing of subjectivity's interaction with historical setting through character development, et cetera. This disciplinary split, I argue, gave rise not to the exclusion of women from the economic writing but rather to a proliferation of women's economic critique and theorization in their imaginative and creative works. These writers, as women, were central to the economy but marginal to economic management, economic policy making, and academic economic theorization. This triad—the conventions of literary form, women's centrality to the market, and women's marked distance from its management, policy making, and theorization—gave women writers a unique vantage point from which to critique the U.S. economic system. Thus, if we really want to appreciate an economic theorization of the nineteenth century at the crucial moment of thinking through slavery's capitalism, we have to go not to the mainstream economic theorists for the relationship between slavery and capitalism but to the women writers of that century.

To illustrate, I turn to a sampling of nineteenth-century women writers and read their work through the lens of slavery's capitalism. Because the preceding chapters focused on some of the most canonical women writing in the middle decades of the nineteenth century, here I briefly survey both well-known and lesser-known writers from before the Civil War to the turn of the century. Like many women writers of the period and like the women featured in this book, the writers surveyed below knew that slavery and capitalism were intimately connected systems. They penned their texts from this starting point. Granting them this economic knowledge at the outset makes their economic acuity and insights around slavery's capitalism, whether explicitly stated or as speculative extensions, all the more visible. And it allows for sharper analysis of how women writers participated in nineteenth-century economic discourse around slavery and capitalism. To highlight just some of the insights, meaning-making, and theorization read through this lens, I offer an eclectic sampling of women writers and texts across a variety of forms, genres, and economic issues.

The *Narrative of Sojourner Truth* (1850), for example, is an incredibly rich and underutilized resource for such a study. Truth, an enslaved worker and later a waged worker, was particularly attentive to issues of labor and gender, as previous scholars have noted, and also the larger economic systems that structured her labor. While working in the free North, she located the economic overlap of slavery and capitalism in her own laboring position, commenting that she was part of "one great system of robbery and wrong... [where] 'the rich rob the poor, and the poor rob one another'" (78). While her own labor is often taken up in scholarly conversation, her work in organizations and businesses is less so. Yet Truth participated in a number of organized businesses. She joined the utopian community established by the Northampton Association of Education and Industry, which communally owned and operated a silk mill; she witnessed the economic mismanagement of religious movements like the Kingdom of Matthias; and she participated in the business of the antislavery lecture circuit. Her *Narrative*, then, can be read not just for her economic insights into slavery's capitalism from her own laboring position but also with an eye toward her participation in a utopian community with a business model that attempted to operate outside of slavery's capitalism, her observations on the relationship between religion and economics, and her participation in the antislavery lyceum, a business itself.[6]

Similar to Truth, Eliza Potter, a free-born Black hairdresser, located the economic overlap of slavery and capitalism in her own laboring position. In her memoir, *A Hairdresser's Experience in the High Life* (1859), Potter chronicles her travels around the United States and Europe as she dresses the hair of wealthy, white women, many of whom are enslavers. Through this hairdressing work, she, like Truth, documents the continuities between slavery and capitalism. Potter comes to view the U.S. economy, in Xiomara Santamarina's words, "as a system that renders even free workers who are not slaveowners dependent on the enslaved" ("So you can see" 184). But as a successful businesswoman who was highly skilled and sought after and highly mobile and well-traveled, Potter's economic insights went beyond the everyday. She placed the nation's politics around slavery in a broader context of international relations to criticize the way money circulates in a global political economy. An example is found in her description of the regent-president of the Kingdom of Hungary's visit to the United States in 1851–1852 to rally for the cause of a free and democratic Hungary. When one of Potter's wealthy clients asks her whether she will donate money to his cause, she replies that she will not. She argues, "We have millions of slaves to look to in our country, which is a curse to it; and before we go abroad to pluck the mote out of our brethren's eye, let us pick the beam out of our own eye" (127). Through this scene, Potter documents the role of wealthy, white elite American foreign philanthropy within the economy of slavery's capitalism. She marks it as a specific practice of hypocritical economic justice that allows a moral catharsis driven by economic agency. It justifies lack of attention to economic oppression and exploitation in the nation and absolves individual responsibility, thus licensing a broader reinforcement of that oppression and exploitation. Because Potter's economic knowledge arises from her laboring position, one that she herself locates at the intersections of slavery and capitalism, her analysis and insights of interlocking regional, domestic, and international economics also arise from this lens.

Elizabeth Keckley, who is best known as Mary Todd Lincoln's modiste, and her narrative *Behind the Scenes* (1868) move women's critique and theorization of slavery's capitalism to a national stage. Keckley's text, as with Truth's and Potter's, can be read for explicit economic insights that arise from Keckley's laboring position. Additionally, however, we can read her text for more implicit theories of economic meaning-making around one's entrepreneurial labor within slavery's capitalism. For example, Keckley opens her autobiography by situating the reader between the event of her birth and the present moment. Significantly, she marks these two periods of her life by the activity of thought. She writes: "I was born a slave ... therefore I came upon the earth free in God-like thought, but fettered in action. ... I am now on the shady side of forty, and as

I sit alone in my room the brain is busy" (1). Mental activity, Keckley tells us from the start, is the engine of her life. If we read meanings of labor through Keckley's own lived experience and outside of those meanings prescribed by the logics of slavery's capitalism, we can extend the definition of Keckley's labor beyond the value and products of her work and argue that it is her incredibly dynamic mental activity—the thought work she does around her labor—rather than the labor itself that defines her subjectivity. Such a focus shifts from understandings of one's ownership of oneself or one's labor as defined by the logics of slavery's capitalism to ownership of one's thoughts as defined by oneself. That is to say, Keckley's more revealing work, when read against the lens of slavery's capitalism, is her entrepreneurial thought—the activity of what she calls her "busy" brain. Tracing Keckley's economic mind at work reveals her refusal of capitalism's attempt to alienate her from her work across the span of her career, first as an enslaved seamstress and later as a wage-earning modiste in the burgeoning fashion industry of antebellum Washington, D.C. Analysis of her economic mind at work highlights her trajectory to own her thoughts, ultimately manifested through her ingenuity and design work as a modiste, an expert in creative thinking on fashion design. In other words, Keckley's mental work is creative and shows ingenuity in determining what the fashion industry or system should produce rather than allowing her thought-work or labor to be defined by the demands of the system. In this sense, Keckley's text can be read both for the way she takes the material-historical connection of slavery and capitalism as a starting point for her narrative as well as for the more speculative extensions of that connection.

Publishing around the same time as Keckley, Rebecca Harding Davis, who wrote with a regionalist approach to slavery and capitalism discourse, stands in marked contrast to Keckley, who wrote from the nation's capital. Davis, who wrote from the North-South borderlands of Wheeling, West Virginia, was intent on giving readers a sense of the time at close range. Her novel *Waiting for the Verdict* (1868) takes a local approach, "reports" on the war and its economic aftermath in a realistic, journalistic style, and helps introduce the role of realism into conversations around slavery's capitalism. As its title implies, the novel questions whether the United States will take responsibility for its crimes of slavery, and the story really is a story about waiting. Davis's use of realism—what Sharon Harris describes as Davis's intention to give her readers "an illusion of actual experience" (*Realism* 6)—largely tells this story. In this sense, the novel's illusion of the "actual experience" of the nation's inability to reach a verdict theorizes the high economic and social cost of stagnation to the nation. It lingers on postbellum anxieties about the future, quotidian feelings of uncertainty and doubt, and a stifled optimism for what postwar reconstruction might present the nation. Conversations and scenes framed by economic concerns—including inheritance, economic and land retribution, government funding for Black education, and the responsibility of white Americans—unfold in what feels like real time. We hear the economic voices of abolitionist northerners, converted southern enslavers, and formerly enslaved workers who claim the fruits of their labor, the land they tilled, the houses they built, and the wages they earned but were not paid. These scenes have no resolution. They are, like the larger story they are a part of, conversations about waiting. True to the realist mode in which Davis crafted her novel, at the novel's conclusion, Davis's characters are left waiting for the nation's verdict. Davis would continue to think through the economic and social cost of stagnation and the price the nation would pay for not confronting its past in her later writing. In a chapter titled "The Civil War" in her autobiographical reflections *Bits of Gossip* (1904), Davis comments on the economic continuities of slavery and postbellum U.S. capitalism. She writes: "The abolition of slavery is the only result of this great war which we recognize. But there were other consequences almost as momentous. The first huge fortunes in this country were made by army contractors in the North during the war. The birth of the millionaire among us, and the disease of money-getting with which he has infected the nation, is not usually reckoned among the results of the great struggle. But it was a result, and is quite as important a factor in our history as is the liberation of the negro" (137–38). More than three decades after her postbellum novel, Davis drew on her wartime observations and noted how slavery, abolition, the war, and the nation's unwillingness to confront and take responsibility for its crime of slavery ushered in the next phase of U.S. capitalism, a phase rooted in the nation's unresolved race relations that Davis documented in *Waiting for the Verdict*.

Rebecca Harding Davis was one of many women writers who marked the long shadow of slavery's economics years and decades after the Civil War. This economic through line pervades women's literature. Women's economic analysis of slavery's capitalism and its aftermath continued to appear in late nineteenth-century women's writing and through to the turn of the century. Women writers at the end of the century, after all, inherited this economic discourse and critique from the women writers who came before them, like Stowe, Larcom, Jacobs, and Harper, just as these four women had inherited economic discourse from women writing in the early decades of the nineteenth century, like Lydia Maria Child. Late nineteenth-century and turn-of-the-century women writers would build on that inherited discourse and offer economic insights on the relationship between slavery and capitalism that were unique to their own time, now with the advantage of time and distance, retrospection and hindsight.

Take, for example, a pair of women writers, like abolitionist Elizabeth Buffum Chace, the wife of a successful manufacturer, and her daughter Lillie Buffum Chace Wyman, a postbellum writer who would later become known for her labor reform literature, activist work, and critique of capitalism. In Wyman's writing are traces of the economic and theoretical thought she inherits from her mother's abolitionist work, showing how women's economic insights were passed down and also showing how such insights arise in the transitional spaces of women's political and social movements. Elizabeth Buffum Chace's antebellum Rhode Island home was a "side track" on the Underground Railroad shepherding fugitives to safety (Stevens 54) and hosting antislavery lecturers, including Sojourner Truth, William Lloyd Garrison, Lucy Stone, and William Wells Brown. It was in this setting that her daughter Lillie Buffum Chace Wyman came of age (50). In her own childhood memoirs, published in 1889, Wyman reflected on the end of the antislavery movement that came with the Civil War, writing that abolitionist children like her were "trained for a conflict in which they were not permitted to fight" (quoted in Stevens 77). Wyman, who felt called to activist work and petitioned the Rhode Island state legislature for workers' rights against her own class interest, would later become known for her late nineteenth-century labor reform fiction.[7] In Francis Willard's *American Women: Fifteen Hundred Biographies with over 1,400 Portraits*, Wyman is described as one who "looks to socialism" (806) for solutions. Pairing these two activist women writers allows us to consider the ways their writing represents a larger transitional phase in nineteenth-century U.S. woman's activism, a phase that reveals continuities in the capitalist critique that took place between antebellum women's abolitionist literature and postbellum women's labor reform literature. But Chace and Wyman are a particularly interesting pair for a study on women writers and the slavery-capitalism debates for another reason. Elizabeth Buffum Chace was married to Samuel Chace, a successful businessman and manufacturer who owned textile mills across Rhode Island and Massachusetts. Samuel Chace owned a cotton manufacturing firm called Valley Falls Company, which imported its raw materials from the South and employed hundreds of factory workers, placing it at the intersections of slavery, manufacturing, and the cotton market, precisely the intersections that his wife and daughter wrote about.[8] Samuel Chace's company is also the corporate antecedent of Berkshire Hathaway, the company owned by Warren Buffet, one of the wealthiest individuals in the world. So here we find Chace and her daughter Wyman at the very intersection of abolition, enslaved labor, factory labor, and capitalism in ways that remind us that the economics of the nineteenth century, and the women who wrote about them, are not as far away as they might seem.

A final example, one that also attends to the long shadow of slavery's capitalism, is found in socialist activist and writer Celia B. Whitehead. Whitehead's late nineteenth-century and early twentieth-century work appeared in mainstream newspapers across the country as well in radical anarchist and socialist publications like *Free Society: A Periodical of Anarchist Thought, Work, and Literature* and the *Alliance of the Rockies*, a monthly newspaper published by the Farmers' Alliance and Industrial Union. Born in 1844 to a New England abolitionist family, Whitehead developed an interest in reform as she came of age during the Civil War. Her public activist career began with the postbellum woman's movement. She is perhaps best known for adopting the pen name Henrietta James and writing a short story titled "Another Chapter of *The Bostonians*" (1887), which protests the portrayal of women activists in Henry James's novel (Petty 398–402). Much of Whitehead's late nineteenth-century writing, which frequently references the abolitionist and woman's movements, takes the form of capitalist critique, analyzing "the quick rise of American plutocracy" after the Civil War ("Pessimism" 799) and the operations of "monster combinations of the capitalists" ("God's Will" 638), for example, and also criticizing U.S. imperialism and foreign policy, and promoting socialism. In this last regard, Whitehead's promotion of socialism recalls the socialist implications and references of Lydia Maria Child's *Appeal* noted in the introduction to this book. This line of socialist thought extends women writers' economic critique of slavery to before and after the war since, as one proslavery analysis put it after weighing the threat of the abolitionist North: the "socialist is the true abolitionist, and he only fully understands his mission."[9] The work of abolitionist-socialist women writers like Whitehead who published in smaller, radical venues moves exploration of the role of women's literature in debates about slavery and capitalism to an exploration of its role in economic debates about slavery and socialism.

Slavery's capitalism was the historical and economic context from which these women wrote and it was the structuring force for the kind of labor, dialogue, relationships, and experiences in which their characters engaged. When we read women's writing through this lens, we see more clearly, as the above survey highlights, pointed critique of links between slavery and capitalism, women's economic meaning-making around different types of labor, the contribution of genre to women's economic insights, theoretical and economic continuities in women's capitalist critique across abolitionist and labor reform writing, and the related, emerging conversation around slavery, abolition, and socialism.

To conclude, I want to return to the questions that opened the above section: Who gets to author economic writing? And who gets to create or authorize economic meaning-making? While these questions arise from an exploration of nineteenth-century women's literature, they have implications beyond that time and beyond that canon. Those implications take the form of a third question: what are the stakes involved in economic meaning-making? As Stowe understood, those who create the accepted economic narrative hold the power. And, as Frances Ellen Watkins Harper foresaw in the early years of Reconstruction, the narrative of slavery's capitalism would not end with the constitutional abolition of slavery but would cast a long shadow, one that continues to shape contemporary American life. We have seen this most recently in the racial disparities in managing national and community resources during the COVID-19 pandemic that began in 2020, which, as Frances Ellen Watkins Harper might have put it, "[brought] to the surface the poison of slavery which still lingers in the body politic" ("National Salvation" 8). The COVID-19 pandemic placed front and center U.S. policies of managing relations between people and resources that are rooted in economic ideologies of slavery's capitalism.[10] The scourge of inequities shaped by racial capitalism that have long been part of the nation's history—inequities in health care, education, housing, worker protection, food systems, and too many other categories to list here—appeared in new forms alongside the scourge of the virus. Black communities and other communities of color across the country were hit harder by the virus, in greater numbers, and with fewer resources available to them than white communities. In this context, it is worth stating bluntly that economic narratives, and their influence on economic policy, are not merely a theoretical site of political struggle. They are an everyday matter of life and death. To trace the question—who gets to author and authorize economic writing—is to make urgent, for literary scholars, the task of recovering and contributing to more complete narratives of our nation's economic history.

National economic narratives can be and need to be rewritten, in part by literary scholars, especially women's literary scholars, using the expansive archive of primary sources left behind by nineteenth-century women writers. Because the nineteenth-century U.S. economic system necessitated a wide spectrum of female disempowerment across racial, geographical, and class lines to keep it going, the literature written by women offers a wide range of responses, analyses, challenges, and revisions to that system. Approaching this archive with intersectional feminist methodologies that include economic analysis and criticism along with the field's ethical concern for social justice can make visible the insights of women's economic writing. The combination of nineteenth-century women's literature and intersectional literary analysis lends crucial new dimensions to how economic meaning-making could and did change over time. In this sense, what I am advocating is a shift in method that reads the powerful nineteenth-century conjunction of abolition, feminism, sentimentality, and realism through the economic lens of slavery's capitalism. I have argued, to that end, that nineteenth-century women's literature helps construct a more accurate narrative of the economic operations of slavery's capitalism. The more complete the national narrative of slavery's capitalism is and the more fully we understand how it shows up in all its economic and cultural forms—including in women's lives and literature—the more complete a responding national narrative of reparatory justice can be.

Getting these economic narratives right is crucial because economic and legal policies rely on them. And while I do not claim that literary scholarship itself might change economic or legal policies, I do believe it can begin to change the national economic narratives our nation tells itself and on which those policies are built. In a time marked by inequality and injustices, many of which reproduce or continue the inequalities and injustices of the nineteenth century, this is an urgent task. What I have aimed to show here, then, are the roles that nineteenth-century literary scholars can play in telling a more accurate national economic narrative.[11]

Ultimately, the value of this study lies in its potential to expand the canon of contemporary critiques of capitalism by adding the unique insights of nineteenth-century women writers. Today's critical economic analysis calls for an urgent focus on capitalism, slavery, race, and gender. Nineteenth-century women writers were attending to this call. These are central, ever-present issues in nineteenth-century women's writing and nineteenth-century women's literary studies. When we read this body of work through the lens of slavery's capitalism, we ensure that the relationship between gender, race, and economics is always already centered, which in turn allows us to better hear women's economic voices and learn from their economic insights, which were there all along.

NOTES

INTRODUCTION: Nineteenth-Century Women Writers and the Slavery and Capitalism Debates

1. For analysis of Child's economic discourse in another of her works, see Tara Robbins Fee, "The Real Housewives of New England: Poverty and Epistemology in Lydia Maria Child's *The American Frugal Housewife*," *ESQ: A Journal of Nineteenth-Century American Literature and Culture* 65, 1 (2019): 1–32.

2. The fact that Child understood the continuities between slavery and capitalism was not in itself remarkable. As Beckert and Rockman write, "Nineteenth-century Americans had little difficulty grasping slavery's capitalism. Advocates of national economic development presumed the reciprocal relationship of the slaveholding and nonslaveholding states, as well as the mutual interests of the slaveholder, manufacturer, and merchant" (*Slavery's Capitalism* 2). Throughout nineteenth-century written discourse, abolitionists and proslavery advocates alike referenced the symbiotic relationship of the North and the South in their speeches and writing, what Charles Sumner summarized in a concise parallelism as the "lords of the lash and lords of the loom" (233). And others before Child had studied the history of the slave trade, placed it in a global history, highlighted the North's complacent and advantageous relationship with southern slavery, and argued on behalf of enslaved mothers. Child's *Appeal*, in this last regard, drew from the British antislavery movement, Quaker activists like Elizabeth Margaret Chandler, and Black women writers including Maria Stewart, Sarah Douglass, and Sarah Forten (Karcher 186). This accepted knowledge in the nineteenth century is part of the reason that it is so generative to turn to women writers as participants in the slavery and capitalism debates. Because women writers already understood the continuities between slavery and capitalism, we can more intentionally probe their writing for how those continuities appear.

3. This scholarship includes histories and overviews of the slavery and capitalism debates, as well as critiques of those histories and overviews, which have become their own genre. For example, see Nan Enstad, "The 'Sonorous Summons' of the New History of Capitalism, Or, What Are We Talking about When We Talk about Economy?," *Modern American History* 2, 1 (2019): 83–95; Robert William Fogel, *The Slavery Debates, 1952–1990: A Retrospective* (Louisiana State University Press, 2003); Hartigan-O'Connor, "Gender's Value in the History of Capitalism"; Guy Emerson Mount, "Capitalism and Slavery: Reflections on the Williams Thesis," *Black Perspectives* (African American Intellectual History Society), November 21, 2015, https://www.aaihs.org/capitalism-and-slavery-reflections-on-the-williams-thesis; James Oakes, "Capitalism and Slavery and the Civil War," *International Labor and Working-Class History* 89 (2016): 195–220; Mark M. Smith, *Debating Slavery: Economy and Society in the Antebellum*

American South (Cambridge University Press, 1998); and Stanley, "Histories of Capitalism and Sex Difference."

4. Recent scholarship has looked more closely at Du Bois as an economist. See, for example, Lynn C. Burbridge, "W. E. B. Du Bois as Economic Analyst: Reflections on the 100th Anniversary of *The Philadelphia Negro*," *Review of Black Political Economy* 26, 3 (1998): 13–31; Andrew J. Douglas, *W. E. B. Du Bois and the Critique of the Competitive Society* (University of Georgia Press, 2019); and Paget Henry and George Danns, "W. E. B. Du Bois, Racial Capitalism and Black Economic Development in the United States," *CLR James Journal* 26, 1/2 (2020), 267–91.

5. For more on Sadie Alexander, see Sadie Tanner Mossell Alexander and Nina Banks, *Democracy, Race, and Justice: The Speeches and Writings of Sadie T. M. Alexander*, edited by Nina Banks (Yale University Press, 2021).

6. U. B. Phillips is generally credited with producing the first study of this kind with "The Economic Cost of Slaveholding in the Cotton Belt," *Political Science Quarterly* 20, 2 (1905): 257–75. Other significant early studies include U. B. Phillips, *American Negro Slavery: A Survey of the Supply, Employment and Control of Negro Labor as Determined by the Plantation Régime* (D. Appleton, 1918); Alfred H. Conrad and John R. Meyer, *The Economics of Slavery and Other Studies in Econometric History* (Transaction Publishers, 1964); and Laurence J. Kotlikoff, "The Structure of Slave Prices in New Orleans, 1804–1862," *Economic Inquiry* 17, 4 (1979): 496–518.

7. Sources that speak directly to the issues of definition include John Clegg, "A Theory of Capitalist Slavery," *Journal of Historical Sociology* 33, 1 (2020): 74–98; Julian Go, "Three Tensions in the Theory of Racial Capitalism," *Sociological Theory* 39, 1 (2021): 38–47; Huston, "Slavery, Capitalism, and the Interpretations of the Antebellum United States"; Robin D. G. Kelley, "What Did Cedric Robinson Mean by Racial Capitalism?," *Boston Review*, January 12, 2017, https://www.bostonreview.net/articles/robin-d-g-kelley-introduction-race-capitalism-justice; Nancy Leong, "Racial Capitalism," *Harvard Law Review* 126, 8 (2013): 2151–226; Scott Reynolds Nelson, "Who Put Their Capitalism in My Slavery?," *Journal of the Civil War Era* 5.2 (2015): 289–310; Michael Ralph and Maya Singhal, "Racial Capitalism," *Theory and Society* 48, 6 (2019): 851–81; Caitlin Rosenthal, "Capitalism When Labor Was Capital: Slavery, Power, and Price in Antebellum America," *Capitalism: A Journal of History and Economics* 1, 2 (2020): 296–337; Smallwood, "What Slavery Tells Us about Marx"; and Dale Tomich, "The Second Slavery and World Capitalism: A Perspective for Historical Inquiry," *International Review of Social History* 63, 3 (2018): 477–501.

8. See also, for example, Wendy Gamber, *The Female Economy: The Millinery and Dressmaking Trades, 1860–1930* (University of Illinois Press, 1997); Claudia Goldin, *Understanding the Gender Gap: An Economic History of American Women* (Oxford University Press, 1990); Alice Kessler-Harris, *Out to Work: A History of Wage-Earning Women in the United States* (Oxford University Press, 1982); and Alice Kessler-Harris, *Women Have Always Worked: A Historical Overview* (Feminist Press, 1981).

9. Here I am referencing recent histories of slavery and capitalism, including Baptist, *The Half Has Never Been Told*; Edward E. Baptist and Stephanie M. H. Camp, eds., *New Studies in the History of American Slavery* (University of Georgia Press, 2006); Baucom, *Specters of the Atlantic*; Beckert, *Empire of Cotton: A Global History*; Beckert and Desan, eds., *Amer-*

ican Capitalism; Beckert and Rockman, eds., *Slavery's Capitalism*; David Brion Davis, *The Problem of Slavery in the Age of Emancipation* (Knopf, 2014); Huston, *Calculating the Value of the Union*; Hyman and Baptist, eds., *American Capitalism*; Johnson, *River of Dark Dreams*; Brian P. Luskey and Wendy A. Woloson, eds., *Capitalism by Gaslight: Illuminating the Economy of Nineteenth-Century America* (University of Pennsylvania Press, 2015); David Roediger and Martin H. Blatt, *The Meaning of Slavery in the North* (Garland Publishing, 1998); Caitlin Rosenthal, *Accounting for Slavery*; Adam Rothman, *Slave Country: American Expansion and the Origins of the Deep South* (Harvard University Press, 2005); Joshua D. Rothman, *Flush Times and Fever Dreams: A Story of Capitalism and Slavery in the Age of Jackson* (University of Georgia Press, 2012); Calvin Schermerhorn, *The Business of Slavery and the Rise of American Capitalism, 1815–1860* (Yale University Press, 2015); Gavin Wright, *Slavery and American Economic Development* (Louisiana State University Press, 2006); and Michael Zakim and Gary J. Kornblith, eds., *Capitalism Takes Command: The Social Transformation of Nineteenth-Century America* (University of Chicago Press, 2012).

10. See Adrienne D. Davis and the BSE Collective, eds., *Black Sexual Economies: Race and Sex in a Culture of Capital* (University of Illinois Press, 2019); Berry, *The Price for Their Pound of Flesh*; Finley, *An Intimate Economy*; Glymph, *Out of the House of Bondage*; Nembhard, *Collective Courage*; Ellen Hartigan-O'Connor, *The Ties That Buy: Women and Commerce in Revolutionary America* (University of Pennsylvania Press, 2009); J. Jones, *Labor of Love, Labor of Sorrow*; Jones-Rogers, *They Were Her Property*; Jennifer L. Morgan, *Reckoning with Slavery: Gender, Kinship, and Capitalism in the Early Black Atlantic* (Duke University Press, 2021); Jessica Marie Johnson, *Wicked Flesh: Black Women, Intimacy, and Freedom in the Atlantic World* (University of Pennsylvania Press, 2020); Daina Ramey Berry and Leslie M. Harris, eds., *Sexuality and Slavery: Reclaiming Intimate Histories in the Americas* (University of Georgia Press, 2018); Alys Eve Weinbaum, *The Afterlife of Reproductive Slavery: Biocapitalism and Black Feminism's Philosophy of History* (Duke University Press, 2019).

11. The following list is not meant to be exhaustive but to highlight the range of scholarly approaches to the relationship between gender, labor, and economic culture in nineteenth-century women's literature and nineteenth-century American literature more broadly: David Anthony, *Paper Money Men: Commerce, Manhood, and the Sensational Public Sphere in Antebellum America* (Ohio State University Press, 2009); Anne E. Boyd, *Writing for Immortality: Women and the Emergence of High Literary Culture in America* (Johns Hopkins University Press, 2004); Cook, *Working Women, Literary Ladies*; Cope, "I Verily Believed Myself to Be a Free Woman"; Susan Coultrap-McQuin, *Doing Literary Business: American Women Writers in the Nineteenth Century* (University of North Carolina Press, 1990); David Dowling, *Capital Letters: Authorship in the Antebellum Literary Market* (University of Iowa Press, 2009); John Ernest, "Economies of Identity: Harriet E. Wilson's 'Our Nig,'" *PMLA* 109, 3 (1994), 424–38; Joseph Fichtelberg, *Critical Fictions: Sentiment and the American Market, 1780–1870* (University of Georgia Press, 2003); Michael Germana, *Standards of Value: Money, Race, and Literature in America* (University of Iowa Press, 2009); Susan K. Harris, *19th-Century American Women's Novels: Interpretive Strategies* (Cambridge University Press, 1990); Hildegard Hoeller, *From Gift to Commodity: Capitalism and Sacrifice in Nineteenth-Century American Fiction* (University of New Hampshire Press, 2012); Leon Jackson, *The Business of Letters: Autho-*

rial Economies in Antebellum America (Stanford University Press, 2008); Amy Schrager Lang, *The Syntax of Class: Writing Inequality in Nineteenth-Century America* (Princeton University Press, 2003); Merish, *Sentimental Materialism*; Walter Benn Michaels, *The Gold Standard and the Logic of Naturalism: American Literature at the Turn of the Century* (University of California Press, 1987); Peterson, "Capitalism, Black (Under)development, and the Production of the African-American Novel in the 1850s"; Lora Romero, *Home Fronts: Domesticity and Its Critics in the Antebellum United States* (Duke University Press, 1997); María Carla Sánchez, *Reforming the World: Social Activism and the Problem of Fiction in Nineteenth-Century America* (University of Iowa Press, 2008); Lyde Cullen Sizer, *The Political Work of Northern Women Writers and the Civil War, 1850–1872* (University of North Carolina Press, 2000); Carolyn Sorisio, "Unmasking the Genteel Performer: Elizabeth Keckley's *Behind the Scenes* and the Politics of Public Wrath," *African American Review* 34, 1 (2000): 19–38; Mary Templin, *Panic Fiction: Women and Antebellum Economic Crisis* (University Alabama Press, 2014); Joyce W. Warren, "Fracturing Gender: Woman's Economic Independence," *Nineteenth-Century American Women Writers: A Critical Reader*, edited by Karen L. Kilcup, (Blackwell, 1998): 146–163; Joyce W. Warren, *Women, Money, and the Law: Nineteenth-Century Fiction, Gender, and the Courts* (University of Iowa Press, 2005).

12. In light of the more recent historical scholarship and attention to slavery and capitalism, literary scholars are reading nineteenth-century literature specifically at these intersections. Xiomara Santamarina's *Belabored Professions* (2005), which explores texts by Sojourner Truth, Harriet Wilson, Eliza Potter, and Elizabeth Keckley, is an early example of nineteenth-century women's literary scholarship that locates its analysis at the intersection of slavery and capitalism. More recently, in *Fugitive Testimony* (2017), Janet Neary argues that "Jacobs appropriates the language of debt and inheritance to reveal the arbitrary and destructive workings of racial capitalism under slavery" (159), and Ingrid Diran argues in "Scenes of Speculation: Harriet Jacobs and the Biopolitics of Human Capital" that Jacobs "develops a counterlogic of finance" that she leverages to facilitate her escape from enslavement (697). In *Cavaliers and Economists*, Katharine Burnett offers literary and economic analysis of southern literature, including proslavery southern women. Sylvia Jenkins Cook in *Clothed in Meaning* reads the laboring voices of mill workers and formerly enslaved people against the parallel rising histories of the empire of cotton and the empire of fashion in the nineteenth century. And in "Stowe's Slavery and Stowe's Capitalism: Forced Reproductive Labor in *Uncle Tom's Cabin*" (2022), Andrew Donnelly situates Stowe's fictional representations of Black women's enforced reproduction in the context of slavery and capitalism.

13. For more on the theorization of difference in the history of women, see Elsa Barkley Brown, "'What Has Happened Here': The Politics of Difference in Women's History and Feminist Politics," *Feminist Studies* 18, 2 (1992): 295–312.

14. Women's historians of capitalism have noted that economic meaning-making and the women who contribute to it have been a blind spot for scholars of pre-1900 U.S. capitalism. For example, historian Ellen Hartigan O'Connor has argued that many recent studies of "pricing, exchange, and accumulation of goods, labor, and bodies" have "overlook[ed] how the very idea of economic value was undergoing a transformation" (Hartigan-O'Connor 614). This book poses Stowe, Larcom, Jacobs, and Harper as writers who were not just aware of raw eco-

nomics but also challenged and contributed to what O'Connor calls the "transformation" of economic value.

15. As bell hooks reminds us, "To be truly visionary we have to root our imagination in our concrete reality while simultaneously imagining possibilities beyond that reality" (*Feminism Is for Everybody* 110).

16. For example, Burnett argues in *Cavaliers and Economists* that McIntosh wrote in a language that was both a "defense of slavery" and a critique of the "southern economy," thus allowing the author to use "the language of economic progress and reform" to reframe slavery as "an economic problem" rather than a "question of morality" (134–37).

17. See, for example: Gerald Horne, *The Apocalypse of Settler Colonialism: The Roots of Slavery, White Supremacy, and Capitalism in Seventeenth-Century North America and the Caribbean* (New York University Press, 2017); Moon-Ho Jung, *Coolies and Cane: Race, Labor, and Sugar in the Age of Emancipation* (Johns Hopkins University Press, 2006); Tiffany King, *The Black Shoals: Offshore Formations of Black and Native Studies* (Duke University Press, 2019); Quynh Nhu Le, *Unsettled Solidarities: Asian and Indigenous Cross-Representations in the Américas* (Temple University Press, 2019); Stephanie E. Smallwood, "Reflections on Settler Colonialism, the Hemispheric Americas, and Chattel Slavery," *William and Mary Quarterly* 76, 3 (2019), 407–16.

CHAPTER 1. Accounting for Harriet Beecher Stowe's
Uncle Tom's Cabin

1. For another reading of Stowe's opening scene in the context of capital and the law, see Alfred L. Brophy, "The Market, Utility, and Slavery in Southern Legal Thought," *Slavery's Capitalism: A New History of American Economic Development*, ed. Sven Beckert and Seth Rockman (University of Pennsylvania Press, 2016), 262–76.

2. Scholars of slavery and capitalism have used accounting and accounting rhetoric to make sense of the logics of slavery and its costs to the nation, both to financial and moral ends. See, for example, Berry, *The Price for Their Pound of Flesh*; Jones-Rogers, *They Were Her Property*; Jennifer L. Morgan, *Reckoning with Slavery: Gender, Kinship, and Capitalism in the Early Black Atlantic* (Duke University Press, 2021); Painter, "Soul Murder and Slavery"; Stephanie E. Smallwood, *Saltwater Slavery: A Middle Passage from Africa to American Diaspora* (Cambridge: Harvard University Press, 2007); Hortense J. Spillers, "Mama's Baby, Papa's Maybe: An American Grammar Book," *Diacritics* 17, 2 (1987): 65–81; C. Rosenthal, *Accounting for Slavery*.

3. For a reversal of this approach (i.e., an argument about sentimental fiction's influence on real-life accounting practices), see Lisa Evans and Jacqueline Pierpoint, "Framing the Magdalen: Sentimental Narratives and Impression Management in Charity Annual Reporting," *Accounting and Business Research* 45, nos. 6–7 (2015): 661–90.

4. For an overview of the scholarship that reads these two texts together and attempts to reconcile what is referred to as "Das Adam Smith Problem," see Leonidas Montes, "*Das Adam Smith Problem*: Its Origins, the Stages of the Current Debate, and One Implication for Our Understanding of Sympathy," *Journal of the History of Economic Thought* 25, 1 (2003): 63–90.

5. For an overview of the influence of the Scottish philosophers, like Adam Smith, on

Stowe and her writing of *Uncle Tom's Cabin*, see Camfield, "The Moral Aesthetics of Sentimentality," 323–27.

6. For definitions of and debates around Stowe's liberal sentimentalism and for previous scholarship on the relationship between sentimentality and/or domesticity and the market in American literature, see, for example, Lauren Berlant, *The Female Complaint: The Unfinished Business of Sentimentality in American Culture* (Duke University Press, 2008); Berlant, "Poor Eliza"; G. Brown, *Domestic Individualism*; Bruce Burgett, *Sentimental Bodies: Sex, Gender, and Citizenship in the Early Republic* (Princeton University Press, 1998); Douglas, *The Feminization of American Culture*; Foreman, *Activist Sentiments*; Halpern, *Sentimental Readers*; Glenn Hendler, *Public Sentiments: Structures of Feeling in Nineteenth-Century American Literature* (University of North Carolina Press, 2001); Christine Levecq, *Slavery and Sentiment: The Politics of Feeling in Black Atlantic Antislavery Writing, 1770–1850* (University of New Hampshire Press, 2008); Marianne Noble, *The Masochistic Pleasures of Sentimental Literature* (Princeton University Press, 2000); Scott M. Reznick, "'The Sense of Liberty': Rethinking Liberalism and Sentimentality in Harriet Beecher Stowe's Antislavery Fiction," *ESQ: A Journal of Nineteenth-Century American Literature and Culture* 65, 4 (2019): 602–41; Lora Romero, *Home Fronts: Domesticity and Its Critics in the Antebellum United States* (Duke University Press, 1997); Shirley Samuels, ed., *The Culture of Sentiment: Race, Gender, and Sentimentality in Nineteenth-Century America* (Oxford University Press, 1992); Schuller, *The Biopolitics of Feeling*; Tompkins, *Sensational Designs*; and Weinstein, *Family, Kinship, and Sympathy in Nineteenth-Century American Literature*.

7. Economist Richard Edwards terms the fundamental conflict cited above "contested terrain" (14–17). As Edwards theorizes, "unlike other commodities in production, labor power is always embodied in people, who have their own interests and needs and who retain their power to resist being treated like a commodity" (14). Those human interests, needs, and individual and collective power make the laborer an indeterminate component of the labor process. Thus, control systems are used to organize the labor process and reduce conflict engendered by the indeterminacy of human nature. But because the conflict and indeterminacy can never be resolved, new mechanisms of control are constantly introduced (16). In addition to Edwards, early definitions of accounting controls are generally also credited to business historian Robert Simons. Simons defines management control systems as made up of constraint and monitoring devices as well as formalized procedures and systems, such as planning, budgeting, environmental scanning, competitor analyses, performance reporting and evaluation, resource allocation, and employee rewards that use information to maintain or alter patterns in organizational activity (Simons 128). Though these terms are typically discussed in industrial work environments, their definitions are useful when considering the accounting control systems that appear in Stowe's depiction of slavery. See also Beniger, *The Control Revolution*; Ritzenberg, *The Sentimental Touch*; and Yates, *Control through Communication*.

8. For further discussion on the oppressive and liberatory effects of accounting, see Cooper, "On the Intellectual Roots of Critical Accounting"; and Modell, "Critical Realist Accounting Research."

9. Even if enslavers or their managers or overseers had no formal accounting training, they may have encountered its practices since bookkeeping was a part of the elementary education

in the first half of the nineteenth century. According to Harry C. Bentley and Ruth S. Leonard's *Bibliography of Works on Accounting by American Authors*, at least twenty-five arithmetic textbooks by American authors published before 1850 included instructions for bookkeeping (Densmore 89). And because instructions for bookkeeping were often included in arithmetic texts, "a rudimentary knowledge of accounting methods was within the grasp of anyone with a common school education or an understanding of simple arithmetic" (Densmore 78).

10. Accounting historians Fleischman and Tyson have written on the relationship between slavery, accounting, and the law. On this relationship, they write: "Against the backdrop of racist legal codes that defined race relations in every southern state, accounting served to facilitate slave exchanges, systematize slave transactions, value slaveholder estates, and monitor slave productivity" (379–80).

11. Part of what I want to highlight here, in Stowe's discussion, is what historian John Clegg marks as the different conversations between *how* the labor-power of enslaved and wage laborers is bought and sold; in both cases, labor-power is bought and sold. It is the fact of the sale of "labor-power" as distinct, for example, "from the labor of peasants, serfs, or members of the family or tribe," and the fact that such labor is commodified, he argues, that "makes them suitable to capitalist accumulation" (83). It is here, in this link, that Clegg, in large part, draws the relationship between slavery and capitalism. Because labor can be exchanged in both cases, he argues, capitalists are then allowed "to expand production within a given sector (often by bidding labor away from competitors) and to thereby take advantage of the economies of scale which can fund such an expansion" (83). If we ground the St. Clare-Ophelia scene in terms of commodified labor-power, we can locate in the discussion of enslaved versus waged labor another possible suspicion of Stowe's around the relationship between slavery and capitalism.

12. There are, according to James L. Huston, four lines of thought related to the debate about the relationship between abolition and capitalism. I paraphrase these four lines from Huston's "Abolitionists, Political Economists, and Capitalism": 1) in their advocacy for waged labor, the abolitionists "wittingly or not" paved the way for industrial capitalism and the oppression of the working classes; 2) the abolitionists, because they emphasized republicanism, were anticapitalists because they rejected the role of self-interest that lay at the core of capitalist thought and behavior; 3) the abolitionists were religious moralists, opposed to capitalism either because morality superseded the economic process or because they would not place money worship above worship of God almighty; and 4) human sensitivity, according to Thomas Haskell, originated in market transactions because individuals in a commercial economy learned to obey their promises when written down in legal contracts; they learned to deal with others without resorting to physical coercion, thereby inculcating a humanitarian sensibility (487). Additionally, while this chapter deals with literary representations of accounting as a specifically white, capitalist logic that gets taken up by enslavers, it is significant to note that a similar logic is also taken up by white abolitionists, as Teresa Goddu argues in *Selling Antislavery*. Goddu shows how the American Anti-Slavery Society practiced the business of antislavery by framing its media as cultural commodities, thus ushering in a new culture industry. Almost immediately after its publication, *Uncle Tom's Cabin* came to play a featured role in this industry.

13. David Reynolds, in *Mightier than the Sword*, postulates that Stowe's husband Calvin, a "foreign language expert," could well have read Marx to her (23).

14. Degree of control, which drives the logic of accounting, was a predominant theme in the economic discourse of both abolitionists and classical economists. Historian James L. Huston has argued, "This common ground [of noncoercion] produced a host of similarities between capitalist economics and abolitionist ideals that easily could be interpreted as identical. Their commitment to noncoercion in economic life pushed abolitionists and political economists to advocate similar institutions and policies. But an enormous gap between them appeared when it came to explaining the reasons behind their commitments" ("Abolitionists" 488). The notion of morality, as related to coercion, best explains that gap: for abolitionists, noncoercion was defined by biblical morality, while for economists noncoercion was defined by market mechanics (489).

15. For another reading of Stowe's treatment of George Harris in this regard, see Ammons, 239–238.

16. The domestic sphere is not simply vulnerable to market forces, as the narrative of sentimentalism would have it. Rather, the logics of accounting that structure slavery and capitalism also structure the domestic sphere and the relationships within it. This is evinced through Topsy's early scenes in which the plantation household economy frames her introduction and storyline. These scenes are typically read to show the innate racism of the northern Ophelia, who "always had a prejudice against negroes" (Stowe 291), as the critical target of the scene. But if we take plantation accounting as the starting point for analysis, then observing Ophelia as a domestic manager in the southern home makes all the more clear how the logics of racial capitalist accounting—Topsy, according to Ophelia, is a "wasteful child"—were not just a "contagion" that infected the domestic sphere (G. Brown, "Getting in the Kitchen" 505) but also one that fundamentally structured it.

17. For additional readings of Topsy in Stowe's economy, see, for example, Tavia Nyong'o, "Racial Kitsch and Black Performance," *Yale Journal of Criticism*, 15, 2 (2002): 371–91; and Alexandra Urakova, "*I* Do Not Want Her, I Am Sure": Commodities, Gifts, and Poisonous Gifts in Uncle Tom's Cabin," *Nineteenth-Century Literature* 74, 4 (2020): 448–72.

18. Similar to my own argument, which specifically locates Stowe's sentimental accounting within the slavery and capitalism debates, Elizabeth Ammons comes to a similar conclusion previously writing that "the book's most lasting importance may lie in its brilliantly typical but instructive failure to recognize the impossibility of arguing against slavery but for colonialism, racism, missionary Christianity, and world capitalism" (244).

CHAPTER 2. Slavery's Cotton Market in Lucy Larcom's "Weaving"

1. "Weaving" was first published in Larcom's 1868 collection entitled *Poems*, but it was likely penned during the Civil War, possibly around 1862–63. Located in the "War-Memories" section of *Poems*, "Weaving" has no date but is situated between two poems that are dated: "The Sinking of the Merrimack," dated May 1862, and "Waiting for News," dated July 1863 (134).

2. By pushing the labor of working-class female factory workers and enslaved women field workers into a larger women's literary culture, Larcom ensures that her literary representations of their labor become part of what Lori Merish calls the "discursive processes through which middle-class consumption was *produced* in tandem with a new ideal of domestic womanhood"

(*Sentimental Materialism* 2). Larcom refuses to render invisible the relation of their labor to these discursive processes. In other words, these two types of women workers performed labor that produced the kinds of commodities, like fashionable clothing, accessories, and furnishings, integral to the production of a material culture that would make possible the emergence of what Merish references as the "'feminization' of middle-class consumerism" (2) as well as what she describes as the "affiliated emergence of an ethic of feminine consumption and the literary genre of domestic fiction" (2), which we can also see through the explosive cultural and commercial phenomenon of Stowe's *Uncle Tom's Cabin*.

3. For a reading of the ways women mill workers used their poetry to position themselves in a "wider tradition of female poetic authorship" (157), a different kind of "world of women" than the one I discuss here, see Putzi, "Poets of the Loom, Spinners of Verse."

4. Lived experience or the lived body is one's opening onto the world. It is in and through the body, Merleau-Ponty argues, that one perceives the world. Merleau-Ponty, who argues "I am my body" (*Phenomenology* 206), rejected mind-body dualism and instead viewed the mind as always inseparable from one's physiological and situated condition, so that even abstract thinking is embodied. The lived body, for Merleau-Ponty, stands in contrast to the objective body—the body as object among other objects. It stands for the body that carries one through the world and, endowed with the ability to think and perceive, is the seat of subjectivity. While Merleau-Ponty's theories of phenomenology offer useful ways to discuss Larcom's poem, it is critical to note that when Merleau-Ponty discusses the "body" he discusses bodies as bodies. Missing from consideration are the ways in which all bodies are not the same; that is, bodies have race and gender. My discussion of "Weaving" makes use of Merleau-Pontian phenomenology and adds to it by giving explicit attention to the ways different bodies are racialized and gendered.

5. For example, historian David R. Roediger's seminal *The Wages of Whiteness* argues that whiteness can be read as a response to a fear of dependency on wage labor in a slaveholding republic (13). For analysis more specific to *The Lowell Offering* and the ways in which factory girls used the periodical "to produce a complex, often racialized as well as gendered and class-sensitive, subjectivity" (150), see Alves, "Lowell's Female Factory Workers."

6. Studies in the gendered division of enslaved laborers have found that division based on gender did not influence field work. For example, Richard H. Steckel reported on an examination of the "distribution of skills reported on the mortality schedule of the 1860 census for certain counties in Georgia, Mississippi, and South Carolina" (45). He writes that, after "adjustments for the age distribution of deaths, these data suggest that 77 to 91 percent of the males and 63 to 77 percent of the females were field hands" (45).

7. Shirley Marchalonis offers a comprehensive biography of Lucy Larcom in *The Worlds of Lucy Larcom, 1824–1893*, which I briefly summarize here. Marchalonis recounts that Larcom's mother moved the family to Lowell to take a position as a boardinghouse mother after her husband's death. Larcom was initiated into the world of factory work at the age of eleven and would spend the next ten years in the Lowell mills. While at Lowell, Larcom joined the women's "improvement circles," self-guided reading and writing communities formed by factory women after working hours and aimed at self-edification. She also wrote for the *Lowell Offering*, the first working-class literary periodical in the United States, written and edited by

women. Many of the young women involved in Lowell's early improvement circles were aspiring writers who lent their literary talents to *The Lowell Offering*. Larcom was one of the most successful writers of the group. By the time "Weaving" was published, she had already received recognition on the national stage, and she remained part of the national literary scene as poet, editor, and freelance writer until her death in 1893. Regardless of how far beyond the Lowell mills her career would take her, Marchalonis writes, Larcom's life—and much of her writing—was marked by her time in the mills.

8. While Larcom was the best-known poet to come out of Lowell, she was not the only factory worker who took up the issue of slavery in verse or the first. Decades before the publication of "Weaving," working-class women, in the pages of the labor reform paper the *Voice of Industry*, used their writing to document economic insights that arose from their own gendered, racialized, and laboring positions. The 1840s saw a considerable number of poems published on this theme. For instance, the anonymous poem "There Must Be Something Wrong" critiques slavery's economics by discussing its exploitation of the earth's resources, including human beings, and linking "fruitful soil" with "human toil." In "The Slave's Revenge" by Sarah W., the poem's narrator discusses family separation, a staple of sentimental abolitionist literature, but with a novel and graphic twist, foregrounding a father's (rather than mother's) perspective as father, husband, and worker. Another anonymous poem, "North and South," reminded its readers that "that wrong is here [in the North]." For a discussion of the poetic voice of white working-class women in antislavery poetry, see Alves, "My Sisters Toil."

9. "Weaving" was not the only poem in which Larcom documented her thoughts about working on the cotton produced by enslaved workers. In *An Idyl of Work*, Larcom's 1875 book-length narrative poem, she wrote:

> When I have thought what soil the cotton plant
> We weave is rooted in, what waters it—
> The blood of souls in bondage—I have felt
> That I was sinning against light, to stay
> And turn the accursèd fibre into cloth
> For human wearing. I have hailed one name—
> You know it—'Garrison'—as a soul might hail
> His soul's deliverer. (*Idyl* 136)

The thirteen-year span between the penning of "Weaving" circa 1862–63 and *Idyl* in 1875 calls our attention to the length of time over which Larcom grappled, at least in print, with conflicted feelings about her participation in the cotton market and calls attention to the insufficiency of "antebellum" and "postbellum" as historical demarcations for discussing slavery's capitalism. For more on *An Idyl of Work*, see Sylvia Jenkins Cook, "The Working Woman's Bard: Lucy Larcom and the Factory Epic," in *Working Women*, 158–87.

10. Shirley Marchalonis describes Larcom's spatial positioning on the factory floor. She writes, "[Larcom's] spinning frames faced the window, and at slack periods she could turn her back on the roomful of girls and machines to look out at the Merrimack, or think, or tend her plants, or read the poems that she, like other girls, had cut out and pasted on her part of the wall—poems by Mrs. Hemans, Miss Landon, George Herbert, William Cullen Bryant, and others, all chosen to inspire the mind and spirit" (31).

11. Iris Marion Young further explains, "The idea of the lived body recognizes that a person's subjectivity is conditioned by sociocultural facts and the behavior and expectations of others in ways that she has not chosen. At the same time, the theory of the lived body says that each person takes up and acts in relation to these unchosen facts in her own way" (18).

12. For a bodily reading of white female workers' vulnerability, see *Archives of Labor*, in which Lori Merish examines Lowell women's body discourse as an early instance of what Michael Denning and Tim Libretti call the "proletarian grotesque" and argues that Lowell women's discourse of the body was a "materialist strategy" that "disrupted the distance and repose of the bourgeois aesthetic" and instead made visible the vulnerability of the working-class female laboring body, "revealing the bodily injuries of class" such as physical harm, starvation, disfigurement, and violation (84).

13. Merleau-Ponty terms this dynamic the "intentional arc." The "intentional arc" represents an interconnected unity of consciousness, embodiment, and the world, which forms a feed-back loop and informs every aspect of our experience. In *Phenomenology of Perception* he writes: "Let us therefore say ... that the life of consciousness—cognitive life, the life of desire or perceptual life—is subtended by an 'intentional arc' which projects round about us our past, our future, our human setting, our physical, ideological and moral situation, or rather results in our being situated in all these respects. It is this intentional arc which brings about the unity of the senses, of intelligence, of sensibility and motility" (136). According to Merleau-Ponty's conception of the intentional arc, knowledge is not found in oneself or in one's mind, but rather in the outputs of this unity that are routed back as inputs.

14. As explored in this analysis, Larcom's "Weaving" embodies the concept of Merleau-Ponty's "intentional arc" but with critical attention to "the body" as one that is gendered as feminine and racialized as white.

15. Gender, labor, race, and class analyses of slavery's capitalism often privilege examinations of the subject's status in the system over a focus on the effect produced by it on the individual person. This analysis foregrounds effect. It reads moments that describe the effect of the nineteenth-century U.S. economy on human subjects in order to privilege the subjective experience of what Linda Martín Alcoff calls the "everydayness of racial experience" and the "microinteractions" of the everyday in which "racialization operates, is reproduced, and is sometimes resignified." In contrast to objective critical approaches that define race "by invoking metanarratives of historical experience, cultural traditions, or processes of colonization," subjective approaches, as this chapter illustrates, that rely on "the lived experience of racialization can reveal how race is constitutive of bodily experience, subjectivity, judgment, and epistemic relationships" (182–83).

16. For a reading of the linguistic configurations of whiteness in antislavery poetry by factory workers, see Alves, "My Sisters Toil." Alves argues that the "racial position of white female factory poets influences their depiction of enslaved black men and women as other, while producing their own racial identity, their whiteness, as an unwritten norm transcribed on the text" (141).

17. As defined by Alcoff, "disjuncture" is a tension that manifests in "the very postural model of the body" and names "that nonlinguistic imaginary position of the body in the world and its imagined relation to its environment and to other bodies" (186).

18. Larcom considered herself an abolitionist, and it was in her writing, rather than on the

front lines of the movement, that one can find her most passionate antislavery sentiments. In her private correspondence, Larcom often mused about various forms of activism and confided her frustration that she was not doing enough. For example, in a letter to her friend Elizabeth, she wrote: "What are we to do about Kansas? I verily feel as if I would fly out of myself with shame and indignation, sometimes. Alas! If I should even convert one after I get there, I think I could not stay away" (quoted in Marchalonis, *Worlds* 104). And in a June 2, 1856, letter to Whittier, Larcom writes: "We are indeed living in a revolution. It makes me ache to think I am doing nothing for the right, for *the holy cause*. What can one do? It is not very agreeable to sit still and blush to be called an American woman" (Shepard and Larcom 506). But she also looked to the literary form as the type of activism that best suited her skills. In a letter to her friend Becky, Larcom compares her literary visions to Stowe's *Uncle Tom's Cabin* and concludes that she is best suited to poetry of the everyday. She wrote: "I don't feel as if any great American story has been written except *Uncle Tom*.... Mrs. Stowe has just issued a new edition of the 'Mayflower,' which contains some capital things.... If I attempt to write a book, I should not dream of anything great; I should only attempt some sketches of American life, as I have seen it" (quoted in Marchalonis, *Worlds* 97).

19. Merleau-Ponty's use of "fabric" as a metaphor of the visible world—"the visible is one continuous fabric" (*Visible* 138)—presupposes an invisible world.

20. Merleau-Ponty's metaphor of weaving "the fabric of one sole Being" is useful in thinking through the weaver's understanding of her "perceived world" as made up of people and things. He explains the metaphor, in part, by writing that "the body, by withdrawing from the objective world, will carry with it the intentional threads that unite it to its surroundings and ... in the end, will reveal to us the perceiving subject as well as the perceived world" (*Phenomenology* 74).

21. See also Susan Alves's suggestion of a "racist canceling-out," in poems by women factory workers, of the working African American men and women who were part of Lowell's economy ("My Sister's Toil" 140–41).

CHAPTER 3. The Property Knowledge of
Harriet Jacobs in *Incidents in the Life of a Slave Girl*

1. Because a main component of this book's goal is to read women's literature in ways that make visible economic arguments that are not otherwise accessible, I read Linda primarily as a literary figure that allows Jacobs to probe the interplay of race, gender, and property ownership more deliberately than she could in real life. When I reference Jacobs in the chapter, I am referring to Harriet Jacobs as the author of *Incidents* and as a historical actor who, like the other writers in this book, was engaged in the political and economic debates of her time and used her writing to participate in those debates.

2. See also Carole Shammas, "Re-Assessing the Married Women's Property Acts," *Journal of Women's History* 6, 11 (1994): 9–30; Reva B. Siegel, "Home as Work: The First Woman's Rights Claims Concerning Wives' Household Labor, 1850–80," *Yale Law Journal* 103, 5 (1994): 1073–217; and Amy Dru Stanley, *From Bondage to Contract*.

3. For more on the economy of property ownership in the enslaved community, see Penningroth, *Claims of Kinfolk*, especially 46–51, 79–87, 107–9, and 136–41. See also Margalynne

J. Armstrong, "African Americans and Property Ownership: Creating Our Own Meanings, Redefining Our Relationships," *African-American Law and Policy Report* 1, 79 (1994): 79–88; Nembhard, *Collective Courage* ; Schweninger, *Black Property Owners in the South*; and Betty Wood, *Women's Work, Men's Work: The Informal Slave Economies of Lowcountry Georgia* (University of Georgia Press, 1995).

4. In Greek, where properties (characteristics) are first taken up philosophically, the term *sumbebekos* means roughly "what is carried along with or by," and this is the term used to discuss property in the sense of possession.

5. Though this chapter is less concerned with whiteness, Linda also shows how property and race—cotton and whiteness—shape one another here and in an earlier scene with cotton. When Mr. Flint shows a northern visitor around his plantation, the focus of the visit is on cotton as the final product. Linda narrates that the "cotton crop was all they thought of" and notes the violent dimension of white definitions of property. She says: "Their talk is of blighted cotton crops—not of the blight on their children's souls" (52). This grammatical equivalency between cotton crops and children's souls highlights how a generational legacy of violent, white definitions of property is passed down genealogically by white fathers who are "cruel and sensual," to sons who are "violent and licentious" and to contaminated daughters and "wretched" wives (52).

6. For more on "negro cloth" and the clothing of enslaved people, see also Finley, *An Intimate Economy*, 54–56, 142n19.

7. For more on sailing and sailors in slavery and emancipation, see David S. Cecelski, *The Waterman's Song: Slavery and Freedom in Maritime North Carolina* (University of North Carolina Press, 2001); and Timothy D. Walker, ed., *Sailing to Freedom: Maritime Dimensions of the Underground Railroad* (University of Massachusetts Press, 2021).

8. For discussion of enslaved people's ability to legally bequeath inheritances (property) to their descendants in *Incidents*, see Molly Ball, "On Making the Present Past: Nongenerational Temporality in *Incidents in the Life of a Slave Girl*," *ESQ: A Journal of Nineteenth-Century American Literature and Culture*, 62, 3 (2016): 419–42.

9. Though not a phenomenological analysis, noteworthy here is Lloyd Pratt's discussion of time in *Archives of American Time* where he articulates a competition among linear time and what he calls "laboring time and spirit time . . . nonlinear modes of being in time [that] characterize African American life writing as much as or more than linear progress did" (158).

10. Thanks to Brigitte Fielder for her conversation on this point.

11. Though Linda's "playthings" appear to be made mostly from cotton, toys were crafted from a wide range of material, as Wilma King has documented. King writes that "young slaves fashioned their own toys from whatever was available, and they used their imaginations freely" (45) and offers examples from testimonies like that of Candis Goodwin, who recounts gathering brown pine needles to build a house and using green needles for the grass around it (45). King explains further: "Children molded marbles from clay and baked them in the sun, while rags and string were basic materials for making balls and dolls. Acorns became tiny cups and saucers. The South Carolinian Anderson Bates remembered children playing with cane whistles which they or someone else made. Children also crafted 'horses' from branches and small tree limbs" (45).

12. See also Diran, "Scenes of Speculation," for a reading of the larger narrative through the language of finance and speculation.

13. Ideological properties of property are determinable, which means that the same objects to which Linda granted liberatory properties could hold oppressive properties. An example of this occurs when Linda narrates her relation to her mother's wedding ring and silver thimble. When Mrs. Flint enters Martha's house and accuses Linda concerning her husband, Aunt Martha believes Mrs. Flint's accusations. We can read the grandmother's reaction through the lens of property. Linda narrates, "My grandmother, whose suspicions had been previously awakened, believed what [Mrs. Flint] said. She exclaimed, 'O Linda! has it come to this? I had rather see you dead than to see you as you now are. You are a disgrace to your dead mother.' She tore from my fingers my mother's wedding ring and her silver thimble" (56). Reacting to Mrs. Flint's accusations, Aunt Martha dispossesses Jacobs of two types of property: a family heirloom and access to her home. Believing that Linda has behaved in ways that disgrace the memory of her mother and the reputation of her family, Martha tears the ring and thimble from her granddaughter's fingers and banishes her from the house, "order[ing her] to go, and never to come there again" (57). The feeling of dispossession is marked by her awareness of the different and newly audible sound of the gate closing behind her as she leaves her grandmother's house: "With what feelings did I now close that little gate, which I used to open with such an eager hand in my childhood! It closed upon me with a sound I never heard before" (57). Her mother's ring and thimble and her grandmother's house and gate had previously offered comfort and protection, spiritually and physically, but now their present absences represent an "agonizing suspense" as to her future condition (57).

14. Thanks to Brigitte Fielder for bringing to my attention that Jacobs's doll may have been the model for one of American Girl's first Black girl dolls. This commodification is ironic in a chapter about Jacobs's creation of objects and their meaning outside of the legal and market forces of slavery and capitalism. According to the company's website, Addy's Ida Bean Doll was introduced in 1993 and retired in 2013 and sold for between $14 and $18. The company's description of Ida Bean reads: "Black cotton doll with yarn hair. Red yarn ribbon in hair. Embroidered white eyes and red mouth. Attached ¼" diameter gold metal hoops for earrings. Non-removable purple print long sleeved dress and white pantaloons. Filled with polyfil beads to simulate the feel of 'beans.'" A fictional story, set in antebellum North Carolina, accompanies the purchase of the doll. In the story, an enslaved mother named Ruth Walker crafts a doll named Ida Bean for her daughter Addy (who is also represented by a doll in the company's line). Ruth, who is described as "a skilled seamstress," believes that "Master Stevens" would not break up her family, partially because of her seamstress skills and the value it brings to his plantation. But after Stevens sells her husband and son, Ruth plans to escape in order to protect Addy. The Ida Bean doll raises several questions. What happens when Jacobs's doll, albeit in model form, which is specifically not made for the market, is produced for the market? What does it mean for children other than Jacobs's children to play with and touch the doll that was crafted specifically for Jacobs's children as a way to mother when she had such limited options? And what happens to the properties of the doll—Jacobs's specific form of mothering—when they are detached from the primary purpose of the object? For more on the American Girl his-

torical fiction series and nineteenth-century American literature, see Brigitte Fielder, "Black Girls, White Girls, American Girls: Slavery and Racialized Perspectives in Abolitionist and Neoabolitionist Children's Literature," *Tulsa Studies in Women's Literature*, 36, 2 (2017): 323–52.

15. These readings are informed in part by Bethany Berger, "Property to Race/Race to Property," SSRN, https://ssrn.com/abstract=3825124.

16. In *The Intimacy of Paper*, Jonathan Senchyne notes that roughly between 1690 and 1867 "paper was made from shredded and pulped linen, hempen, and cotton rags, many of which were collected from homes and recycled into paper" (3). He adds: "Rag paper signifies from the rags embedded within it, as well as from the ink printed or written on it" (3). Ads for businesses that turned rags into paper abounded in early American print culture. To "read a newspaper in the eighteenth and nineteenth centuries," as Jacobs does throughout her narrative and especially in the attic scenes, "was to be constantly confronted with calls for rags" from papermakers (70–71). The cotton rags that originated as seeds on southern plantation fields and would later be turned into paper held, embedded in its fibers, the forced racialized and gendered labor relations of slavery's cotton. Additionally, considering again that nineteenth-century paper was often made from cotton rags, such rags may have comprised the paper on which she wrote her letters to Dr. Flint, the letters that redirected him away from her hiding place and ultimately aided her escape from him.

17. In *Haunted Property*, Sarah Gilbreath Ford makes a noteworthy connection between the supposed ownership of Tom and his "cabin," as referenced in the title of in Stowe's novel *Uncle Tom's Cabin* and Jacobs's ownership of her own domestic sphere at the end of *Incidents* (29–32). Ford writes that the "charm radiating from [Tom's] cabin certainly derives from Tom and Chloe's homemaking, but the cabin is not his" (29). Ford argues that Stowe underscores the point that Tom cannot own property because he is property "by later titling the chapter of Tom's departure 'The Property Is Carried Off.'" It is this "disparity" in Stowe's narrative, Ford concludes, between the supposed possession of property by Tom in the novel's title and the possession of Tom as property that Jacobs targets in her own narrative (30). Ford argues that by "owning" her narrative, Jacobs is able "to repossess and claim the property" of her own life, thus "creating [her] own 'cabin'" (32).

18. Sylvia Jenkins Cook also emphasizes this interconnection. She writes: "Fabrication is both the making of cloth and the making of ideas. In the nineteenth century, the link between the two arose from a tangible chain of associations leading from cloth (especially cotton) to the paper that was made from rags of clothing, and thence to the thoughts that were physically committed to that paper by writers" (*Clothed* 8).

CHAPTER 4. Reconstruction's Inheritance in
Frances E. W. Harper's *Minnie's Sacrifice*

1. *Minnie's Sacrifice* was published serially in the *Christian Recorder* between March 20, 1869, and September 25, 1869. Frances Smith Foster rediscovered *Minnie's Sacrifice* along with Harper's two other postbellum novels, *Sowing and Reaping* (1876–77) and *Trial and Tri-*

umph (1888–89), and published them in her 1994 collection. Some installments and chapters of *Minnie's Sacrifice* have yet to be recovered, including an installment at the end of chapter 8, all of chapters 10 and 15, and an installment at the end of chapter 11. For more context on the nineteenth-century print culture in which it appeared, and for a remarkable and comprehensive cultural and material history of the *Christian Recorder* and Black print culture, see Eric Gardner's *Black Print Unbound*.

2. Reconstruction was a pivotal moment in the history of U.S. capitalism. Eric Foner describes Reconstruction as a "period of unprecedented economic expansion presided over by a triumphant industrial bourgeoisie" (460). For his full description, see *Reconstruction*, 460–69.

3. For an account of Harper's Reconstruction politics and reform work that analyzes the pedagogical rhetoric of her writing and oratory, see Stancliff, *Frances Ellen Watkins Harper*, 51–80.

4. My understanding of Harper's call for economic incursion is influenced by two main sources. First, Robin D. G. Kelley's writes in his 2021 foreword to Cedric Robinson's *Black Marxism* that what most people get wrong about Robinson's landmark book is that it was more about Black revolt than racial capitalism. Part of the Black Radical Tradition, Kelley explains, *Black Marxism*'s project was to defy "racial capitalism's efforts to re-make African social life and generate new categories of human experience stripped bare of the historical consciousness embedded in culture" (Kelley xvii–xviii). Harper, I would argue, historicizes the novel's inheritance plot to this end. A second source of understanding is what I read as Harper's disruption of the "accommodation clause" of Derrick Bell's interest-convergence theory, which states that the "interests of blacks in achieving racial equality will be accommodated only when it converges with the interests of whites" (523).

5. As scholars have discussed, the trope of the "tragic mulatta" is common but has multiple variations, some of which are not so tragic. For an overview of variations of the trope in nineteenth-century American literature, see William L. Andrews and Mitchell A. Kachun's introduction to Julia C. Collins, *The Curse of Caste; or The Slave Bride: A Rediscovered African American Novel* (Oxford University Press, 2006). Andrews and Kachun write: "Before 1865 most mulattas in American fiction must endure a stint in slavery and withstand intimidation by lascivious slave owners and brutal overseers, but more often than not these women eventually encounter a northerner or a European on whose love they can rely. Only in *post-*-Civil War American fiction does mixed-race beauty become, with increasing inevitability, the stamp of tragedy. Only in post-slavery America, with its hardening lines of racial separation and its mounting hysteria over white supremacy, does the mulatta/mulatto become a byword for the fear of racial pollution that many prominent white American writers pandered to or (sometimes) interrogated" (xliii). For a discussion of a "discourse of mixed-race heroines running counter to the figure of the tragic mulatta," see Eric Gardner, "Coloring History and Mixing Race in Levina Urbino's *Sunshine in the Palace and Cottage* and Louise Heaven's *In Bonds*," *Legacy: A Journal of American Women Writers* 24, 2 (June 2007): 187–206. According to Gardner, this counter-discourse is "one in which the mixed-race heroine not only avoids a tragic end but actually embraces her genealogy, uses her visual racial indeterminacy to aid nation-building and self-empowerment, and finds fulfillment in a multi-racial family housed within the larger Black community" (188).

6. *Minnie's Sacrifice*, along with *Sowing and Reaping* and *Trial and Triumph*, speaks to the Black community about those issues Harper found most relevant to the Black community in the decades following the Civil War. Carla L. Peterson argues that "discipline itself is at the center of *Sowing and Reaping* as intemperance is perceived as a breakdown of discipline that pervades the nation" ("Reconstructing" 316). In "Sowing and Reaping: A 'New' Chapter from Frances Ellen Watkins Harper's Second Novel," Eric Gardner, with his rediscovery of the novel's fifth chapter, continues exploring the consequences of intemperance through Harper's focus on culture versus wealth and writes that the previously lost chapter highlights the "novel's sense of an aristocracy of morals rather than funds" (n.p.). And Andreá Williams reads *Trial and Triumph* to explore how Harper confronts class tensions and anxieties in the Black community. She argues that Harper directs her "narrative energy toward reigning in constantly erupting class discord in the postbellum city she depicts" and that the novel "shows class tensions as less easily resolved, as differently situated Black Americans see their priorities being at odds" (A. Williams 13).

7. On Minnie's adoption by Quaker abolitionists, see Brigitte Fielder, "'Those people must have loved her very dearly': Interracial Adoption and Radical Love in Antislavery Children's Literature," *Early American Studies: An Interdisciplinary Journal* 14, 4 (2016): 775–78.

8. For more on the double proposal plot in women's fiction, see Karen Tracey, *Plots and Proposals: American Women's Fiction, 1850–90* (University of Illinois Press, 2000).

9. In real life, as in Louis's case, there were exceptions in which enslavers would bequeath assets such as monetary wealth and property to those whom they enslaved and were also related to by blood. For more on this topic, see Bernie D. Jones, *Fathers of Conscience: Mixed-Race Inheritance in the Antebellum South* (University of Georgia Press, 2009).

10. See Dale W. Tomich, *Through the Prism of Slavery: Labor, Capital, and World Economy* (Rowman and Littlefield, 2004); Dale Tomich and Michael Zeuske, "Introduction, the Second Slavery: Mass Slavery, World-Economy, and Comparative Microhistories." *Review* 31, 2 (2008): 91–100; and Dale W. Tomich, "The Second Slavery and World Capitalism: A Perspective for Historical Inquiry," *International Review of Social History* 63, 3 (2018): 477–501.

11. For a reading of Harper's work as transnational and bridging hemispheric Black struggle for freedom across the Americas, not through economic meaning-making but in its poetics, see Monique-Adelle Callahan, *Between the Lines: Literary Transnationalism and African American Poetics* (Oxford University Press, 2011).

12. The economic results of these lessons around historicizing inheritance and Black economic possibility are illuminated by Harper's naming choices: Minnie and Louis are both descendants of men named Louis (Louis's great-uncle and Minnie's father), both of whom contributed, by way of their business in the Saint-Domingue slavery economy, to the economic life of *Louis*iana. When young Louis (Minnie's husband) inherits this fortune, a third "Louis" reorganizes the economic life of Louisiana by investing the inheritance in Black development.

13. In real life, as political economist Jessica Gordon Nembhard documents, "Those who were free before the Civil War provided the only economic base the African American community had immediately after emancipation" (43–44).

14. For another exploration of the themes of self-respect and self-interest in Harper's work, see Fielder, "Radical Respectability and African American Women's Reconstruction Fiction."

15. On the history of African American marriage in the nineteenth century, see Hunter, *Bound in Wedlock*.

16. I draw this metaphor from Marlene L. Daut's analysis that "a slave rebellion metaphorically and often literally entailed overthrowing the father-master" (373).

17. For more on Harper's poem, see Frances Smith Foster's introductory note to "Moses," in Harper, *A Brighter Coming Day*, 135–36, 235–36. See also Frances Smith Foster and Valerie L. Ruffin, "Teaching African American Poetry of the Reconstruction Era: Frances E. W. Harper's 'Moses: A Story of the Nile,'" in *Teaching Nineteenth-Century American Poetry*, edited by Paula Bernat Bennett, Karen L. Kilcup, and Philipp Schwieghauser (Modern Language Association of America, 2007), 142–50. For a full analysis of *Moses: A Story of the Nile*, Harper's book that contained both her poem "Moses" and a four-page prose allegory titled "The Mission of the Flowers," see Alice Rutkowski, "Leaving the Good Mother: Frances E. W. Harper, Lydia Maria Child, and the Literary Politics of Reconstruction," *Legacy* 25, 1 (2008): 83–104. Rutkowski's analysis centers Moses's relationship to his two mothers and reads *Moses* in the context of Harper's Reconstruction politics as well as her literary relationship with Lydia Maria Child.

18. On African American practices of national belonging, see also Martha S. Jones, *Birthright Citizens*.

19. Du Bois would later write on the significance of the meaning of money in relation to national identity: "If we give Mr. Roosevelt the right to meddle with the dollar, if we give Herr Hitler the right to expel the Jew, if we give to Mussolini the right to think for Italians, we do this because we know nothing ourselves. We are as a nation ignorant of the function and meaning of money, and we are looking around helplessly to see if anybody else knows" (quoted in Robinson, *Black Marxism* 196).

20. This reading is inspired by scholarship that reads money as icon, explores the social meanings of money, and undermines economic claims about money's neutrality, works such as Martijn Konings's *The Emotional Logic of Capitalism*, Viviana A. Zelizer's *The Social Meaning of Money: Pin Money, Paychecks, Poor Relief, and Other Currencies* (Princeton University Press, 1997), and Christine Desan's *Making Money: Coin, Currency, and the Coming of Capitalism* (Oxford University Press, 2014).

21. Harper in "Our Greatest Want," Frances Smith Foster notes, "contradicts two ideas that she perceives were being unduly privileged among the free black middle class. Harper reminds her readers that while economic independence and educational advancement were important for racial progress, the most important need was for women and men to be committed to the highest ideals of Christian service and sacrifice for the realization of 'human brotherhood'" (Harper, *A Brighter Coming Day* 96).

22. For an account of Harper's own land ownership, see Eric Gardner, "Frances Ellen Watkins Harper's Civil War and Militant Intersectionality," *Mississippi Quarterly* 70–71, 4 (2017–2018), 505–18.

23. For more on this theme, see Koritha Mitchell's discussion of white violence as a response to Black success in the "Introduction" to *From Slave Cabins*, 1–33.

EPILOGUE

1. There are several sources by literary scholars and economic historians that provide more complete histories of the relationship between literature and economics than I am able to offer here. For earlier scholarship in the subfield of literary economic criticism, see, for example, Woodmansee and Osteen, *The New Economic Criticism*; Gregory P. La Blanc, "Commentary: Economic and Literary History: An Economist's Perspective," *New Literary History*, 31, 2 (2000): 355–77; Elizabeth Hewitt, "The Vexed Story of Economic Criticism," *American Literary History*, 21, 3 (2009): 618–32; Donald N. McCloskey, *If You're So Smart: The Narrative of Economic Expertise* (University of Chicago Press, 1990); and Donald N. McCloskey, *The Rhetoric of Economics* (University of Wisconsin Press, 1985). For more recent scholarship, see, for example, Melissa Kennedy, *Narratives of Inequality: Postcolonial Literary Economics* (Palgrave, 2017); Gary Saul Morson and Morton Schapiro, *Cents and Sensibility: What Economics Can Learn from the Humanities* (Princeton University Press, 2017); Matt Seybold and Michelle Chihara, eds., *The Routledge Companion to Literature and Economics* (Routledge, 2018); Çinla Akdere and Christine Baron, eds., *Economics and Literature: A Comparative and Interdisciplinary Approach* (Routledge, 2017); Robert J. Shiller, *Narrative Economics: How Stories Go Viral and Drive Major Economic Events* (Princeton University Press, 2019); Elizabeth Hewitt, *Speculative Fictions: Explaining the Economy in the Early United States* (Oxford University Press, 2020); Joanna Rostek, *Women's Economic Thought in the Romantic Age: Towards a Transdisciplinary Herstory of Economic Thought* (Taylor & Francis, 2021), and Jacques-Henri Coste and Vincent Dussol, eds., *The Fictions of American Capitalism: Working Fictions and the Economic Novel* (Palgrave MacMillan, 2020). For recent web articles, see, for example, Saanya Jain, "The Study of Economics Could Learn a Lot from Science Fiction: From Leaf Currencies to Gift Economies: A Reading List," *Literary Hub*, October 5, 2020, https://lithub.com/the-study-of-economics-could-learn-a-lot-from-science-fiction; and Carolin Benack, "Economists Have a Lot More in Common with Literature, Especially Novels, than Hard Science: Economic Theory Fundamentally Relies on our Understanding of Fiction," *Scroll.in*, October 16, 2020, https://scroll.in/article/975815/economists-have-a-lot-more-in-common-with-literature-especially-novels-than-hard-science.

2. Several literary scholars have previously documented these shared roots. In *The New Economic Criticism*, Woodmansee and Osteen give an overview of the circumstances surrounding the "birth of the twin discourses" of literature and economics and "how the two spheres profoundly conditioned one another" over time (5–6). Indeed, one might consider the connection between the literary and the economic as natural, given both fields' "engagement with the problematic of representation" (Poovey 5). More recently, Matt Seybold and Michelle Chihara, editors of *The Routledge Companion to Literature and Economics*, acknowledge the homologies of economics and literature in order to move beyond them and to offer literary scholarship that engages intentionally with the history of economics, economic thought, and methods of economic analysis. Economists have also documented the relationship between literature and economics. The best-known example is perhaps Nobel Prize–winning economist Robert J. Shiller who, in his book *Narrative Economics* (Princeton University Press, 2019) traces the relationship between the stories we tell ourselves and economic events.

3. Economists Claudia Goldin and Lawrence F. Katz have written on how institutions shaped academic disciplines in the late nineteenth century. For more, see Claudia Goldin and Lawrence F. Katz. "The Shaping of Higher Education: The Formative Years in the United States, 1890 to 1940," *Journal of Economic Perspectives* 13, 1 (1999): 37–62.

4. It was in the late nineteenth century, literary scholars, economic historians, and theorists agree, that economics took its most decisive turn away from its roots in the humanities. Historian of economic thought Phillip Mirowski explains, "The progenitors of neoclassical economic theory boldly copied the reigning physical theories in the 1870s.... They copied their models mostly term for term and symbol for symbol, and [they] said so" (3). In other words, economic methodologies moved closer to the physical sciences, and economists repurposed physics for their own field. What was called "energy" in the field of physics was called "utility" in the field of economics (4). This move was perhaps the field's most decisive turn away from its roots in the humanities. I am referring here to the economic concept of "marginal utility," introduced by economists William Stanley Jevons, Léon Walras, and Carl Menger. The concept of marginal utility reevaluated the meaning of "value" by shifting the basis of a commodity's value away from labor theory (its cost of production) and toward marginal utility and subjective value (its value to the consumer) (Backhouse 292). To summarize briefly, the concept held that the "value of a commodity was no longer explained in terms of its cost of production (possibly reducible to the labour required to produce it) but in terms of its value to the consumer" (292). It revolutionized economics by breaking from classical economics and pointing economics deliberately in the direction of mathematics and physics and by changing the logics on which the theory of value rested, thus laying the foundation on which modern economic theory is built (292).

5. Helen Stuart Campbell, Caroline Healey Dall, Charlotte Perkins Gilman, and Virginia Penny are four of the over one hundred women with entries in Robert W. Dimand, Mary Ann Dimand, and Evelyn L. Forget, eds., *A Biographical Dictionary of Women Economists* (Edward Elgar, 2000).

6. For more on women lecturers as businesswomen, see Susan M. Yohn, "Crippled Capitalists: The Inscription of Economic Dependence and the Challenge of Female Entrepreneurship in Nineteenth-Century America," *Feminist Economics* 12, 1–2 (2006): 85–109; Angela G. Ray, "What Hath She Wrought? Woman's Rights and the Nineteenth-Century Lyceum," *Rhetoric and Public Affairs* 9, 2 (2006): 183–213; Lynn M. Alexander, "Unsexed by Labor: Middle-Class Women and the Need to Work," *American Transcendental Quarterly: Nineteenth-Century American Literature and Culture* 22, 4 (2008): 593–610; and Lisa Tetrault, "The Incorporation of American Feminism: Suffragists and the Postbellum Lyceum," The *Journal of American History* 96, 4 (2010): 1027–56.

7. See William Dean Howells, "Editor's Study," *Harper's New Monthly* 74 (1887): 482–86.

8. The "Statement of Significance" section of the "National Register of Historical Places Inventory–Nomination Form" for Valley Fall Mills helps gauge the operational size of Chace's mills. According to the record, the average 1860s textile mill in Central Falls, Rhode Island, employed 106 workers. In comparison, Chace's Valley Falls Mill employed 280 men and women and consumed 800,000 pounds of raw cotton in the production of yarns and fabric (4–6).

9. I was directed to this quote in Virginia senator Robert M. T. Hunter's 1850 speech by Matt Karp's blog post "Slavery, Abolition, and 'Socialism' in the U.S. Congress."

10. The literature produced on the relationship between slavery, racial capitalism, and the COVID-19 pandemic has been explosive. For a small sampling of this literature, see, for example, Jennifer Abbasi, "Taking a Closer Look at COVID-19, Health Inequities, and Racism," *Journal of the American Medical Association* 324, 5 (2020): 427–29; Jim Downs, "How the Origins of Epidemiology Are Linked to the Transatlantic Slave Trade," *Time*, September 2, 2021, https://time.com/6094376/transatlantic-slave-trade-disease-outbreaks-epidemiology; Jim Downs, *Maladies of Empire: How Colonialism, Slavery, and War Transformed Medicine* (Harvard University Press, 2021); Leonard E. Egede and Rebekah J Walker, "Structural Racism, Social Risk Factors, and COVID-19—A Dangerous Convergence for Black Americans," *New England Journal of Medicine* 383, 12 (2020): e77(1)–e77(3); Clarence C. Gravlee, "Systemic Racism, Chronic Health Inequities, and COVID-19: A Syndemic in the Making?," *American Journal of Human Biology: The Official Journal of the Human Biology Council* 32, 5 (2020): e23482; Gabriella Onikoro-Arkell, "Confinement and Disease from Slavery to the COVID-19 Pandemic," *Black Perspectives*, May 14, 2020, https://www.aaihs.org/confinement-and-disease-from-slavery-to-the-covid-pandemic; and Whitney N. Laster Pirtle, "Racial Capitalism: A Fundamental Cause of Novel Coronavirus (COVID-19) Pandemic Inequities in the United States," *Health Education and Behavior* 47, 4 (2020): 504–8.

11. Feminist philosophy of economics is a complementary field to this work. Scholars in this field look to literature as part of an intentional effort "to increase the variety of explanations that can count as economics, thus freeing economics from the straitjacket of constrained optimization and formal mathematical modeling" (Barker and Kuiper 3). By moving economics beyond the neoclassical paradigm and its limited set of data sources and by incorporating intersectional accounts of gender, race, and class, they argue, "feminist economics results in better economics, accounts of the economy that are more theoretically robust and empirically accurate" (7).

BIBLIOGRAPHY

Adams, Kate. "Frances E. W. Harper and the 'Quest for a Usable Past.'" *Legacy: A Journal of American Women Writers*, vol. 36, no. 2, 2019, pp. 263–66.
Adams, Katherine. "'This Is Especially Our Crop': Blackness, Value, and the Reconstruction of Cotton." *African American Literature in Transition, 1865–1880*, edited by Eric Gardner, Cambridge UP, 2021, 284–310.
Addison, Daniel Dulany. *Lucy Larcom: Life, Letters, and Diary*. Houghton Mifflin, 1895.
Affleck, Thomas. *Plantation Record and Account Book*. New ed. Weld, n.d. Library of Congress, www.hdl.loc.gov/loc.rbc/rbpe.02501300.
Ahmed, Sara. "A Phenomenology of Whiteness." *Feminist Theory*, vol. 8, no. 2, 2007, 149–68.
———. *Queer Phenomenology: Orientations, Objects, Others*. Duke University Press, 2006.
Alcoff, Linda Martín. *Visible Identities: Race, Gender, and the Self*. Oxford UP, 2006.
Alexander, Sadie Tanner Mossell. *Democracy, Race, and Justice: The Speeches and Writings of Sadie T.M. Alexander*, edited by Nina Banks, Yale UP, 2021.
Alves, Susan. "Lowell's Female Factory Workers, Poetic Voice, and the Periodical." *The Only Efficient Instrument: American Women Writers and the Periodical, 1837–1916*, edited by Aleta Feinsod Cane and Susan Alves, University of Iowa Press, 2001, 149–64.
———. "'My Sisters Toil': Voice in Anti-Slavery Poetry by White Female Factory Workers." *Multiculturalism : Roots and Realities*, edited by C. James Trotman, Indiana UP, 2002, 139–54.
Ammons, Elizabeth. "Freeing the Slaves and Banishing the Blacks: Racism, Empire, and Africa in *Uncle Tom's Cabin*." *Harriet Beecher Stowe's Uncle Tom's Cabin: A Casebook*, edited by Elizabeth Ammons, Oxford UP, 2007, 227–46.
Andrews, William L. *Slavery and Class in the American South: A Generation of Slave Narrative Testimony, 1840–1865*. Oxford UP, 2019.
Ashworth, John. *Slavery, Capitalism and Politics in the Antebellum Republic, Vol. 2: The Coming of the Civil War, 1850–1861*. Cambridge UP, 2007.
Backhouse, Roger E. "Marginal Revolution." *The New Palgrave Dictionary of Economics*, 3rd ed., edited by Steven N. Durlauf and Lawrence Blume, Palgrave Macmillan, 2008, 292–94.
Banks, Nina. "Black Women in the United States and Unpaid Collective Work: Theorizing the Community as a Site of Production." *Review of Black Political Economy*, vol. 47, no. 4, December 2020, pp. 343–62.
Baptist, Edward E. *The Half Has Never Been Told: Slavery and the Making of American Capitalism*. Basic Books, 2014.
Baradaran, Mehrsa. *The Color of Money: Black Banks and the Racial Wealth Gap*. Belknap Press of Harvard UP, 2017.

Barker, Drucilla K., and Edith Kuiper, eds. *Toward a Feminist Philosophy of Economics*. Routledge, 2003.

Bartky, Sandra Lee. "Toward a Phenomenology of Feminist Consciousness." *Social Theory and Practice*, vol. 3, no. 4, 1975, pp. 425–39.

Baucom, Ian. *Specters of the Atlantic: Finance Capital, Slavery, and the Philosophy of History*. Duke UP, 2005.

Baym, Nina. *Woman's Fiction: A Guide to Novels by and about Women in America, 1820–1870*. Cornell UP, 1978.

Beckert, Sven. *Empire of Cotton: A Global History*. Vintage Books, 2014.

Beckert, Sven, and Christine Desan, eds. *American Capitalism: New Histories*. Columbia UP, 2018.

Beckert, Sven, and Seth Rockman, eds. *Slavery's Capitalism: A New History of American Economic Development*. University of Pennsylvania Press, 2016.

Bell, Derrick A., Jr. "Brown v. Board of Education and the Interest-Convergence Dilemma." *Harvard Law Review*, vol. 93, no. 3, January 1980, pp. 518–33.

Bender, Thomas, ed. *The Antislavery Debate: Capitalism and Abolitionism as a Problem in Historical Interpretation*. University of California Press, 1992.

Beniger, James R. *The Control Revolution: Technological and Economic Origins of the Information Society*. Harvard UP, 1986.

Berlant, Lauren. "Poor Eliza." *American Literature*, vol. 70, no. 3, September 1998, pp. 635–68.

Berry, Daina Ramey. *The Price for Their Pound of Flesh: The Value of the Enslaved, from Womb to Grave, in the Building of a Nation*. Beacon Press, 2017.

———. "The Ubiquitous Nature of Slave Capital." *After Piketty: The Agenda for Economics and Inequality*, edited by Heather Boushey, J. Bradford DeLong, and Marshall Steinbaum, Harvard UP, 2017, 126–49.

———. "'We'm Fus' Rate Bargain': Value, Labor, and Price in a Georgia Slave Community." *The Chattel Principle: Internal Slave Trades in the Americas*, edited by Walter Johnson, Yale UP, 2004, 55–71.

Boyd, Melba Joyce. *Discarded Legacy: Politics and Poetics in the Life of Frances E. W. Harper, 1825–1911*. Wayne State UP, 1994.

Brophy, Alfred L. "'Over and Above . . . there broods a portentous shadow,—the shadow of law': Harriet Beecher Stowe's Critique of Slave Law in Uncle Tom's Cabin." *Journal of Law and Religion*, vol. 12, no. 2, 1995–1996, pp. 457–506.

———. *Reparations: Pro and Con*. Oxford UP, 2006.

Brown, Elsa Barkley. "'What Has Happened Here': The Politics of Difference in Women's History and Feminist Politics." *Feminist Studies*, vol. 18, no. 2, 1992, pp. 295–312.

Brown, Gillian. *Domestic Individualism: Imagining Self in Nineteenth-Century America*. University of California Press, 1990.

———. "Getting in the Kitchen with Dinah: Domestic Politics in Uncle Tom's Cabin." *American Quarterly*, vol. 36, no. 4, 1984, pp. 503–23.

Bryant, Christopher J. "Without Representation, No Taxation: Free Blacks, Taxes, and Tax Exemptions Between the Revolutionary and Civil Wars." *Michigan Journal of Race and Law*, vol. 21, no. 1, 2015, pp. 91–124.

Bryant, Mr. "A Southern Cotton Mill." *Friends' Review: A Religious, Literary, and Miscellaneous Journal*, May 19, 1849. Facsimile in *Mill Girls in Nineteenth-Century Print*, American Antiquarian Society, www.americanantiquarian.org/millgirls/items/show/37.

Burnett, Katharine A. *Cavaliers and Economists: Global Capitalism and the Development of Southern Literature, 1820–1860*. Louisiana State UP, 2019.

Byrd, Brandon R. "Black Republicans, Black Republic: African-Americans, Haiti, and the Promise of Reconstruction." *Slavery and Abolition: A Journal of Slave and Post-Slave Studies*, vol. 36, no. 4, 2015, pp. 545–67.

Camfield, Gregg. "The Moral Aesthetics of Sentimentality: A Missing Key to *Uncle Tom's Cabin*." *Nineteenth Century Literature*, vol. 43, no. 3, 1988, pp. 319–45.

Camp, Stephanie M. H. *Closer to Freedom: Enslaved Women and Everyday Resistance in the Plantation South*. University of North Carolina Press, 2004.

———. "The Pleasures of Resistance: Enslaved Women and Body Politics in the Plantation South, 1830–1861." *New Studies in the History of American Slavery*, edited by Edward E. Baptist and Stephanie M. H. Camp, University of Georgia Press, 2006, 87–124.

Carby, Hazel V. *Reconstructing Womanhood: The Emergence of the Afro-American Woman Novelist*. Oxford UP, 1987.

Castronovo, Russ. "Deconstructing Reconstruction." *American Literary History*, vol. 30, no. 3, 2018, pp. 616–26.

Ceccarelli, Leah. "Polysemy: Multiple Meanings in Rhetorical Criticism." *Quarterly Journal of Speech*, vol. 84, no. 4, 1998, pp. 395–415.

Chace, Elizabeth Buffum. *Anti-Slavery Reminiscences*. Freeman & Son, 1891.

Chace, Elizabeth Buffum, and Lucy Buffum Lovell. *Two Quaker Sisters: From the Original Diaries of Elizabeth Buffum Chace and Lucy Buffum Lovell*. Liveright, 1937.

Chakkalakal, Tess. *Novel Bondage: Slavery, Marriage, and Freedom in Nineteenth-Century America*. University of Illinois Press, 2011.

Child, Lydia Maria. *An Appeal in Favor of That Class of Americans Called Africans* [1833], edited by Carolyn Karcher, University of Massachusetts Press, 1996.

Chused, Richard H. "Married Women's Property Law: 1800–1850." *Georgetown Law Journal*, vol. 71, no. 5, 1983, pp. 1359–1425.

Clegg, John. "A Theory of Capitalist Slavery." *Journal of Historical Sociology*, vol. 33, no. 1, March 2020, pp. 74–98.

Cole, Jean Lee. "Information Wanted: *The Curse of Caste*, *Minnie's Sacrifice*, and the *Christian Recorder*." *African American Review*, vol. 40, no. 4, 2006, pp. 731–42.

Collins, Jennie. "New England Factories." *Revolution* (New York City), January 13, 1870, 19–20. Facsimile in *Mill Girls in Nineteenth-Century Print*, American Antiquarian Society, www.americanantiquarian.org/millgirls/items/show/80.

Collins, Patricia Hill. *Black Feminist Thought: Knowledge, Consciousness, and the Politics of Empowerment*. 2nd ed., Routledge, 2000.

Cook, Sylvia Jenkins. *Clothed in Meaning: Literature, Labor, and Cotton in Nineteenth-Century America*. University of Michigan Press, 2020.

———. *Working Women, Literary Ladies: The Industrial Revolution and Female Aspiration*. Oxford UP, 2008.

Cooper, D. J. "On the Intellectual Roots of Critical Accounting: A Personal Appreciation of Tony Lowe (1928–2014)." *Critical Perspectives on Accounting*, vol. 25, nos. 4–5, 2014, pp. 287–92.

Cope, Virginia. "'I Verily Believed Myself to Be a Free Woman': Harriet Jacobs's Journey into Capitalism." *African American Review*, vol. 38, no. 1, 2004, pp. 5–20.

Crusto, Mitchell F. "Blackness as Property: Sex, Race, Status, and Wealth." *Stanford Journal of Civil Rights and Civil Liberties*, vol. 1, no. 1, 2005, pp. 51–170.

Daut, Marlene L. *Tropics of Haiti: Race and the Literary History of the Haitian Revolution in the Atlantic World, 1789–1865*. Liverpool UP, 2015.

Davis, Adrienne D. "'Don't Let Nobody Bother Yo' Principle': The Sexual Economy of American Slavery." *Sister Circle: Black Women and Work*, edited by Sharon Harley, Rutgers UP, 2002, 103–27.

Davis, Rebecca Harding. *Bits of Gossip*. Houghton Mifflin, 1904.

———. *Rebecca Harding Davis's Stories of the Civil War Era: Selected Writings from the Borderlands*, edited by Sharon Harris and Robin Cadwallader, University of Georgia Press, 2010.

———. *Waiting for the Verdict* [1868]. Gregg Press, 1968.

Densmore, Christopher. "Understanding and Using Early Nineteenth Century Account Books." *Archival Issues*, vol. 25, nos. 1–2, 2000, pp. 77–89.

Diran, Ingrid. "Scenes of Speculation: Harriet Jacobs and the Biopolitics of Human Capital." *American Quarterly*, vol. 71, no. 3, 2019, pp. 697–718.

Dobson, James E. "Lucy Larcom and the Time of the Temporal Collapse." *Legacy: A Journal of American Women Writers*, vol. 33, no. 1, 2016, pp. 82–102.

Donnelly, Andrew. "Stowe's Slavery and Stowe's Capitalism: Forced Reproductive Labor in *Uncle Tom's Cabin*." *Women's Studies*, vol. 51, no. 6, 2022, pp. 647–60.

Douglas, Ann. *The Feminization of American Culture*. Noonday Press/Farrar, Straus and Giroux, 1998.

Douglass, Frederick. "Lecture on Slavery." *Frederick Douglass: Selected Speeches and Writings*, edited by Philip S Foner, Lawrence Hill Books, 1999, 164–70.

———. *Narrative of the Life of Frederick Douglass, an American Slave, Written by Himself* [1845], edited by William L. Andrews, W. W. Norton, 1997.

Dreyfus, Hubert. "Intelligence without Representation—Merleau-Ponty's Critique of Mental Representation the Relevance of Phenomenology to Scientific Explanation." *Phenomenology and the Cognitive Sciences*, vol. 1, no. 4, 2002, pp. 367–83.

Du Bois, W. E. B. *Black Reconstruction in America, 1860–1880* [1935], edited by Henry Louis Gates, Jr., Oxford UP, 2007.

Dudden, Faye E. *Fighting Chance: The Struggle over Woman Suffrage and Black Suffrage in Reconstruction America*. Oxford UP, 2011.

Edwards, Richard. *Contested Terrain: The Transformation of the Workplace in the Twentieth Century*. Basic Books, 1979.

Einhorn, Robin L. *American Taxation, American Slavery*. University of Chicago Press, 2006.

Ernest, John. "From Mysteries to Histories: Cultural Pedagogy in Frances E. W. Harper's *Iola Leroy*." *American Literature*, vol. 64, no. 3, 1992, pp. 497–518.

———. *Resistance and Reformation in Nineteenth-Century African-American Literature: Brown, Wilson, Jacobs, Delany, Douglass, and Harper*. UP of Mississippi, 1995.
Farrow, Anne, Joel Lang, and Jenifer Frank. *Complicity: How the North Promoted, Prolonged, and Profited from Slavery*. Foreword by Evelyn Brooks Higginbotham. Ballantine, 2005.
Federal Writers' Project: Slave Narrative Project, vol. 16, Texas, Part 4, Sanco-Young. Manuscript/Mixed Material. Library of Congress, www.loc.gov/item/mesn164.
Fessenbecker, Patrick, and Bryan Yazell. "Literature, Economics, and a Turn to Content." *Minnesota Review*, vol. 2021, no. 96, 2021, pp. 69–81.
Fick, Carolyn E. *The Making of Haiti: The Saint Domingue Revolution from Below*. University of Tennessee Press, 1990.
Fielder, Brigitte. "The Literature of Racial Uplift and White Feminist Failure." *Gender in American Literature and Culture*, edited by Jean M. Lutes and Jennifer Travis, Cambridge UP, 2021, 188–203.
———. "Radical Respectability and African American Women's Reconstruction Fiction." *African American Literature in Transition, 1865–1880*, edited by Eric Gardner, Cambridge UP, 2021, 187–210.
———. *Relative Races: Genealogies of Interracial Kinship in Nineteenth-Century America*. Duke UP, 2020.
Finley, Alexandra J. *An Intimate Economy: Enslaved Women, Work, and America's Domestic Slave Trade*. University of North Carolina Press, 2020.
Fleischman, Richard K. and Thomas N. Tyson. "Accounting in Service to Racism; Monetizing Slave Property in the Antebellum South." *Critical Perspectives on Accounting*, vol. 15, no. 3, 2004, pp. 376–99.
Fogel, Robert William., and Stanley L. Engerman. *Time on the Cross: The Economics of American Negro Slavery*. Little, Brown, 1974.
Foner, Eric. *Reconstruction: America's Unfinished Revolution, 1863–1877*. Harper & Row, 1988.
Ford, Sarah Gilbreath. *Haunted Property: Slavery and the Gothic*. UP of Mississippi, 2020.
Foreman, P. Gabrielle. *Activist Sentiments: Reading Black Women in the Nineteenth Century*. University of Illinois Press, 2009.
Foster, Frances Smith. "Gender, Genre, and Vulgar Secularism: The Case of Frances Ellen Watkins Harper and the AME Press." *Recovered Writers/Recovered Texts: Race, Class, and Gender in Black Women's Literature*, edited by Dolan Hubbard, University of Tennessee Press, 1997, 46–59.
———. "Introduction." *A Brighter Coming Day: A Frances Ellen Watkins Harper Reader*, edited by Foster, Feminist Press, 1990, 3–40.
———. "Introduction." *Minnie's Sacrifice, Sowing and Reaping, and Trial and Triumph: Three Rediscovered Novels*, edited by Foster, Beacon Press, 1994, xi–xxxvii.
———, ed. *Love and Marriage in Early African America*. UP of New England, 2008.
———. *'Til Death or Distance Do Us Part: Love and Marriage in African America*. Oxford UP, 2010.
———. *Written by Herself: Literary Production by African American Women, 1746–1892*. Indiana UP, 1993.

Francis, Jere. "After Virtue? Accounting as a Moral and Discursive Practice." *Accounting, Auditing, and Accountability Journal*, vol. 3, no. 3, 1990, pp. 5–17.

Gallagher, Noelle. "The Bagging Factory and the Breakfast Factory: Industrial Labor and Sentimentality in Harriet Beecher Stowe's *Uncle Tom's Cabin*." *Nineteenth-Century Contexts*, vol. 27, no. 2, 2005, pp. 167–87.

Gallagher, Shaun, and Dan Zahavi. "Phenomenological Approaches to Self-Consciousness." *Stanford Encyclopedia of Philosophy Archive*, Spring 2021 ed., www.plato.stanford.edu/archives/spr2021/entries/self-consciousness-phenomenological.

Gardner, Eric. "African American Literary Reconstructions and the 'Propaganda of History.'" *American Literary History*, vol. 30, no. 3, 2018, pp. 429–49.

———. *Black Print Unbound: The "Christian Recorder," African American Literature, and Periodical Culture*. Oxford UP, 2015.

———. "Frances Ellen Watkins Harper's Civil War and Militant Intersectionality." *Mississippi Quarterly*, vol. 70–71, no. 4, 2017–2018, pp. 505–18.

———. "Frances Ellen Watkins Harper's 'National Salvation': A Rediscovered Lecture on Reconstruction." *Commonplace: The Journal of Early American Life*, vol. 17, no. 4, 2017, www.commonplace.online/article/vol-17-no-4-gardner.

———. "The Return of Frances Ellen Watkins Harper." *ESQ: A Journal of Nineteenth-Century American Literature and Culture*, vol. 66, no. 4, 2020, pp. 591–643.

———. "Sowing and Reaping: A 'New' Chapter from Frances Ellen Watkins Harper's Second Novel." *Commonplace: The Journal of Early American Life*, vol. 13, no. 1, 2012, www.commonplace.online/article/sowing-reapinga-new-chapter-frances-ellen-watkins-harpers-second-novel.

———. *Unexpected Places: Relocating Nineteenth-Century African American Literature*. UP of Mississippi, 2009.

Genovese, Eugene D. *Roll, Jordan, Roll: The World the Slaves Made*. Vintage Books, 1976.

Glickman, Lawrence B. "'Buy for the Sake of the Slave': Abolitionism and the Origins of American Consumer Activism." *American Quarterly*, vol. 56, no. 4, 2004, pp. 889–912.

Glymph, Thavolia. *Out of the House of Bondage: The Transformation of the Plantation Household*. Cambridge UP, 2008.

Goddu, Teresa. *Selling Antislavery: Abolition and Mass Media in Antebellum America*. University of Pennsylvania Press, 2020.

Goldin, Claudia. *Urban Slavery in the American South, 1820–1860: A Quantitative History*. University of Chicago Press, 1976.

Goodman, Paul. *Of One Blood: Abolitionism and the Origins of Racial Equality*. University of California Press, 1998.

Greeson, Jennifer Rae. "The Prehistory of Possessive Individualism." *PMLA: Publications of the Modern Language Association of America*, vol. 127, no. 4, 2012, pp. 918–24.

Griffin, Farah Jasmine. "*Minnie's Sacrifice*: Frances Ellen Watkins Harper's Narrative of Citizenship." *The Cambridge Companion to Nineteenth-Century American Women's Writing*, edited by Dale M. Bauer and Philip Gould, Cambridge UP, 2001, 308–19.

Hager, Christopher, and Cody Marrs. "Against 1865: Reperiodizing the Nineteenth Century." *J19: The Journal of Nineteenth-Century Americanists*, vol. 1, no. 2, 2013, pp. 259–84.

Halpern, Faye. *Sentimental Readers: The Rise, Fall, and Revival of a Disparaged Rhetoric*. University of Iowa Press, 2013.

———. "Word Become Flesh: Literacy, Anti-Literacy, and Illiteracy in *Uncle Tom's Cabin*." *Legacy*, vol. 34, no. 2, 2017, pp. 253–77.

Hammond, James Henry. "Speech of Hon. James H. Hammond, of South Carolina, on the Admission of Kansas, under the Lecompton Constitution: Delivered in the Senate of the United States, March 4, 1858. American Antiquarian Society, www.americanantiquarian.org/Manuscripts/cottonisking.html.

Harmon, Alexandra, Colleen O'Neill, and Paul C. Rosier. "Interwoven Economic Histories: American Indians in a Capitalist America." *Journal of American History*, vol. 98, no. 3, 2011, pp. 698–722.

Harper, Frances Ellen Watkins. "Affairs in South Carolina" [1867]. *A Brighter Coming Day*, 124–25.

———. "Aunt Chloe" [1872]. *A Brighter Coming Day*, 196–208.

———. *A Brighter Coming Day: A Frances Ellen Watkins Harper Reader*, edited by Frances Smith Foster, Feminist Press, 1990.

———. "Enlightened Motherhood" [1892]. *A Brighter Coming Day*, 285–92.

———. "Free Labor" [1857]. *A Brighter Coming Day*, 81.

———. *Iola Leroy; Or, Shadows Uplifted* [1892], edited by Koritha Mitchell. Broadview Press, 2018.

———. "Land and Labor." *Christian Recorder*, November 19, 1870, 1.

———. *Minnie's Sacrifice* [1869]. *Three Rediscovered Novels by Frances E. W. Harper*, edited by Frances Smith Foster, Beacon Press, 1994, 1–92.

———. "Moses" [1869]. *A Brighter Coming Day*, 138–66.

———. "National Salvation" [1867], edited by Eric Gardner, *Commonplace: The Journal of Early American Life*, vol. 17, no. 4, 2017, www.commonplace.online/article/vol-17-no-4-gardner.

———. "Our Greatest Want" [1859]. *A Brighter Coming Day*, 102–4.

———. "Our People." *Christian Recorder*, October 29, 1870, 2.

———. "The Two Offers" [1859]. *A Brighter Coming Day*, 105–14.

———. "We Are All Bound Up Together" [1866]. *A Brighter Coming Day*, 217–19.

———. "Woman's Political Future." *The World's Congress of Representative Women*, edited by May Wright Sewall, Rand, McNally, 1894, 433–36.

Harris, Cheryl I. "Finding Sojourner's Truth: Race, Gender, and the Institution of Property." *Cardozo Law Review*, vol. 18, no. 2, November 1996, pp. 309–410.

———. "Whiteness as Property." *Harvard Law Review*, vol. 106, no. 8, 1993, pp. 1707–91.

Harris, Sharon M. *Rebecca Harding Davis: A Life among Writers*. West Virginia UP, 2018.

———. *Rebecca Harding Davis and American Realism*. University of Pennsylvania Press, 1991.

Hartigan-O'Connor, Ellen. "Gender's Value in the History of Capitalism." *Journal of the Early Republic*, vol. 36, no. 4, 2016, pp. 613–35.

Hartman, Saidiya V. *Scenes of Subjection: Terror, Slavery, and Self-Making in Nineteenth-Century America*. Oxford UP, 1997.

Haskell, Thomas. "Capitalism and the Origins of the Humanitarian Sensibility, Part 1." *The An-*

tislavery Debate: Capitalism and Abolitionism as a Problem in Historical Interpretation, edited by Thomas Bender, University of California Press, 1992, 107–35.

———. "Capitalism and the Origins of the Humanitarian Sensibility, Part 2." *The Antislavery Debate: Capitalism and Abolitionism as a Problem in Historical Interpretation*, edited by Thomas Bender, University of California Press, 1992, 136–60.

Haslam, Jim, and Prem Sikka. *Pioneers of Critical Accounting: A Celebration of the Life of Tony Lowe*. Palgrave Macmillan, 2016.

Heier, Jan Richard. "Accounting for the Business of Suffering: A Study of the Antebellum Richmond, Virginia, Slave Trade." *Abacus: A Journal of Accounting, Finance and Business Studies*, vol. 46, no. 1, 2010, pp. 60–82.

———. "A Content Comparison of Antebellum Plantation Records and Thomas Affleck's Accounting Principles." *Accounting Historians Journal*, vol. 15, no. 2, 1988, pp. 131–50.

Helmreich, Paul C. "Lucy Larcom at Wheaton." *New England Quarterly*, vol. 63, no. 1, 1990, pp. 109–20.

Henry, Paget, and George Danns. "W. E. B. Du Bois, Racial Capitalism and Black Economic Development in the United States." *CLR James Journal*, vol. 26, nos. 1–2, 2020, pp. 267–91.

Historic Beverly. "Set at Liberty: Stories of the Enslaved in a New England Town." Online exhibit, www.express.adobe.com/page/eLxVbaIbhFbIE.

hooks, bell. *Feminism Is for Everybody: Passionate Politics*. Pluto Press, 2000.

Hunter, Tera W. *Bound in Wedlock: Slave and Free Black Marriage in the Nineteenth Century*. Harvard UP, 2017.

Husband, J. *Antislavery Discourse and Nineteenth-Century American Literature: Incendiary Pictures*. Palgrave Macmillan, 2010.

Huston, James L. "Abolitionists, Political Economists, and Capitalism." *Journal of the Early Republic*, vol. 20, no. 3, 2000, pp. 487–521.

———. *Calculating the Value of the Union: Slavery, Property Rights, and the Economic Causes of the Civil War*. University of North Carolina Press, 2003.

———. "Property Rights in Slavery and the Coming of the Civil War." *Journal of Southern History*, vol. 65, no. 2, 1999, pp. 249–86.

———. "Slavery, Capitalism, and the Interpretations of the Antebellum United States: The Problem of Definition." *Civil War History*, vol. 65, no. 2, 2019, pp. 119–56.

Hyman, Louis, and Edward E. Baptist. *American Capitalism: A Reader*. Simon & Schuster, 2014.

"Ida Bean Doll." *American Girl Wiki*, www.americangirl.fandom.com/wiki/Ida_Bean_Doll.

Illouz, Eva. *Cold Intimacies: The Making of Emotional Capitalism*. Polity Press, 2007.

Jackson, Cassandra. *Barriers between Us: Interracial Sex in Nineteenth-Century American Literature*. Indiana UP, 2004.

———. "'I Will Gladly Share with Them My Richer Heritage': Schoolteachers in Frances E. W. Harper's *Iola Leroy* and Charles Chesnutt's *Mandy Oxendine*. "*African American Review*, vol. 37, no. 4, 2003, pp. 553–68.

Jacobs, Harriet A. *Incidents in the Life of a Slave Girl* [1861], edited by R. J. Ellis. Oxford UP, 2015.

Jacobs, John S. "A True Tale of Slavery." *The Leisure Hour: A Family Journal of Instruction and Recreation*, nos. 476–479, 1861. *Documenting the American South*, www.docsouth.unc.edu/neh/jjacobs/jjacobs.html.

Johnson, Walter, ed. *The Chattel Principle: Internal Slave Trades in the Americas*. Yale UP, 2004.

———. *River of Dark Dreams: Slavery and Empire in the Cotton Kingdom*. Belknap Press of Harvard UP, 2013.

———. *Soul by Soul: Life inside the Antebellum Slave Market*. Harvard UP, 1999.

Johnson, Walter, and Robin D. G. Kelly, eds. Race Capitalism Justice. *Boston Review*, MIT Press, 2017.

Jones, Jacqueline. *Labor of Love, Labor of Sorrow: Black Women, Work, and the Family, from Slavery to the Present*. Basic Books, 1985.

———. "'My Mother Was Much of a Woman': Black Women, Work, and the Family under Slavery." *Feminist Studies*, vol. 8, no. 2, 1982, pp. 235–69.

Jones, Martha S. *All Bound up Together: The Woman Question in African American Public Culture, 1830–1900*. University of North Carolina Press, 2007.

———. *Birthright Citizens: A History of Race and Rights in Antebellum America*. Cambridge UP, 2018.

Jones-Rogers, Stephanie. *They Were Her Property: White Women as Slave Owners in the American South*. Yale UP, 2019.

Karcher, Carolyn L. *The First Woman in the Republic: A Cultural Biography of Lydia Maria Child*. Duke UP, 1994.

Karp, Matt. "Slavery, Abolition, and 'Socialism' in the U.S. Congress." *The Junto: A Group Blog on Early American History*, May 13, 2014, www.earlyamericanists.com/2014/05/13/slavery-abolition-and-socialism-in-the-u-s-congress.

Käufer, Stephan, and Anthony Chemero. *Phenomenology: An Introduction*. Polity Press, 2015.

Keckley, Elizabeth. *Behind the Scenes: Thirty Years a Slave, and Four Years in the White House* [1868], edited by Frances Smith Foster, University of Illinois Press, 2002.

Kelley, Robin D. G. "Foreword: Why *Black Marxism*, Why Now?" *Black Marxism, The Making of the Black Radical Tradition*, by Cedric J. Robinson, rev. and updated 3rd ed., University of North Carolina Press, 2020, xi–xxxiii.

Kennedy, Randall. *Interracial Intimacies: Sex, Marriage, Identity, and Adoption*. Vintage Books, 2004.

Kilcup, Karen L. *Nineteenth-Century Women Writers: An Anthology*. Blackwell, 1997.

———. "'Something of a Sentimental Sweet Singer': Robert Frost, Lucy Larcom, and 'Swinging Birches.'" *Roads Not Taken: Rereading Robert Frost*, edited by Earl J. Wilcox and Jonathan N. Barron, University of Missouri Press, 2000, 11–31.

King, Wilma. *Stolen Childhood : Slave Youth in Nineteenth-Century America*. Indiana UP, 1995.

Klein, Rachel Naomi. "Harriet Beecher Stowe and the Domestication of Free Labor Ideology." *Legacy*, vol. 18 no. 2, 2001, pp. 135–52.

Knowles, Katie. "Patches of Resistance on the Badges of Enslavement: Enslaved Southerners, Negro Cloth, and Fashionability in the Cotton South." *Clothing and Fashion in Southern History*, edited by Ted Ownby and Becca Walton, University Press of Mississippi, 2020, 3–31.

Konings, Martijn. *The Emotional Logic of Capitalism: What Progressives Have Missed*. Stanford UP, 2015.

Korobkin, Laura H. "Appropriating Law in Harriet Beecher Stowe's *Dred*." *Nineteenth-Century Literature*, vol. 62, no. 3, 2007, pp. 380–406.

———. "'Something within the Silent Black Man Answered No!'; Or, Is Bartleby Uncle Tom on Wall Street?" *ESQ: A Journal of Nineteenth-Century American Literature and Culture*, vol. 65, no. 4, 2019, pp. 562–601.

Kort, Amy. "Lucy Larcom's Double-Exposure: Strategic Obscurity in *A New England Girlhood*." *American Literary Realism, 1870–1910*, vol. 31, no. 1, 1998, pp. 25–40.

Kuiper, Edith. "Women Economic Writers in the History of Economic Thought (1700–1914)." *Routledge History of Economic Thought*, September 1, 2017.

La Blanc, Gregory P. "Commentary: Economic and Literary History: An Economist's Perspective." *New Literary History*, vol. 31, no. 2, 2000, pp. 355–77.

Larcom, Lucy. *An Idyl of Work*. James Osgood, 1875.

———. *A New England Girlhood: Outlined from Memory*. Houghton Mifflin, 1889.

———. *The Poetical Works*. Houghton Mifflin, 1885.

———. "Weaving." *Poems*, Fields, Osgood, 1868, 134–37.

Laski, Gregory. "Reconstructing Revenge: Race and Justice after the Civil War." *American Literature*, vol. 91, no. 4, 2019, pp. 751–81.

Lauter, Paul. *Canons and Contexts*. Oxford UP, 1991.

Lehman, Cheryl R. "Think Different: Accounting as a Systems Theorist—Gender, Race and Class." *Pioneers of Critical Accounting: A Celebration of the Life of Tony Lowe*, edited by Jim Haslam and Prem Sikka, Palgrave Macmillan, 2016, 163–77.

Levecq, Christine. *Slavery and Sentiment: The Politics of Feeling in Black Atlantic Antislavery Writing, 1770–1850*. Durham: University of New Hampshire Press, 2008.

Levinson, Sanford. "Slavery and the Phenomenology of Torture." *Social Research*, vol. 74, no. 1, 2007, pp. 149–68.

Lewis, Jennifer. "'Careful Living': Frederick Douglass's Phenomenology of Embodied Experience." *Textual Practice*, vol. 33, no. 10, 2019, pp. 1657–1672.

———. "'From the Slave's Point of View': Toward a Phenomenology of Witnessing in Frederick Douglass' 1845 *Narrative*." *ESQ: A Journal of Nineteenth-Century American Literature and Culture*, vol. 65, no. 2, 2019, pp. 257–91.

Lewis, Jessica. "'Poetry Experienced': Lucy Larcom's Poetic Dwelling in *A New England Girlhood*." *Legacy*, vol. 18, no. 2, 2001, pp. 182–92.

Lewis, Leslie W. "Biracial Promise and the New South in *Minnie's Sacrifice*: A Protocol for Reading *The Curse of Caste; or The Slave Bride*." *African American Review*, vol. 40, no. 4, 2006, pp. 755–67.

Lewis, Vashti. "The Near-White Female in Frances Ellen Harper's *Iola Leroy*." *Phylon*, vol. 45, no. 4, 1984, pp. 314–22.

Li, Stephanie. "Motherhood as Resistance in Harriet Jacobs's *Incidents in the Life of a Slave Girl*." *Legacy*, vol. 23, no. 1, 2006, pp. 14–29.
Lockard, Joe. "Lucy Larcom and the Poetics of Child Labour." *English Studies in Canada*, vol. 38, nos. 3–4, 2012, pp. 139–60.
Locke, John. *Two Treatises of Government* [1690], edited by Peter Laslett, 3rd ed, Cambridge UP, 1988.
Loeffelholz, Mary. "'A Strange Medley-Book': Lucy Larcom's *An Idyl of Work*." *New England Quarterly*, vol. 80, no. 1, 2007, pp. 5–34.
Lovell, Thomas B. "By Dint of Labor and Economy: Harriet Jacobs, Harriet Wilson, and the Salutary View of Wage Labor." *Arizona Quarterly: A Journal of American Literature, Culture, and Theory*, vol. 52, no. 3, 1996, pp. 1–32.
Madden, Kirsten K., Janet A. Seiz, and Michèle Pujol. *A Bibliography of Female Economic Thought up to 1940*. Routledge, 2004.
Marable, Manning. *How Capitalism Underdeveloped Black America: Problems in Race, Political Economy, and Society*. South End Press, 1983.
Marchalonis, Shirley. "Lucy Larcom (1824–1893)." *Legacy*, vol. 5, no. 1, 1988, pp. 45–52.
———. *The Worlds of Lucy Larcom, 1824–1893*. University of Georgia Press, 1989.
Marchalonis, Shirley, et al. "Lucy Larcom." *American Women Prose Writers, 1870–1920*, edited by Sharon M. Harris, et al., Dictionary of Literary Biography, vol. 221, Gale, 2000, pp. 246–52.
Marrs, Cody. *Nineteenth-Century American Literature and the Long Civil War*. Cambridge UP, 2015.
———. "Three Theses on Reconstruction." *American Literary History*, vol. 30, no. 3, 2018, pp. 407–28.
Marsh, John. "'We Are Not Slaves': The Shadow of Slavery in Nineteenth-Century Poetry and Song." *A History of American Working-Class Literature*, edited by Nicholas Cole and Paul Lauter, Cambridge University Press, 2017, 110–29.
Marx, Karl. *Capital: A Critique of Political Economy*, vol. 1 [1867]. Translated by Ben Fowkes. Penguin, 1990.
McKittrick, Katherine. *Demonic Grounds: Black Women and the Cartographies of Struggle*. University of Minnesota Press, 2006.
Merish, Lori. *Archives of Labor: Working-Class Women and Literary Culture in the Antebellum United States*. Duke UP, 2017.
———. *Sentimental Materialism: Gender, Commodity Culture, and Nineteenth-Century American Literature*. Duke UP, 2000.
Merleau-Ponty, Maurice. *Phenomenology of Perception*. Routledge, 1962.
Merleau-Ponty, Maurice, Alphonso Lingis, and Claude Lefort. *The Visible and the Invisible: Followed by Working Notes*. Northwestern UP, 1968.
Merrick, Beverly G. "Lucy Larcom." *The American Renaissance in New England: Fourth Series*, edited by Wesley T. Mott, Dictionary of Literary Biography, vol. 243, Gale, 2001, 233–39.
Mills, Charles W. *The Racial Contract*. Cornell UP, 1997.
"*Minnie's Sacrifice* Is the Title." *Christian Recorder*, March 13, 1869, 1.

Mirowski, Phillip. *More Heat Than Light: Economics as Social Physics, Physics as Nature's Economics*. Cambridge UP, 1989.

Mitchell, Koritha. *From Slave Cabins to the White House: Homemade Citizenship in African American Culture*. University of Illinois Press, 2020.

———. "Introduction." *Iola Leroy; Or, Shadows Uplifted*, edited by Mitchell, Broadview Press, 2018, 13–50.

Modell, Sven. "Critical Realist Accounting Research: In Search of Its Emancipatory Potential." *Critical Perspectives on Accounting*, vol. 42, 2017, pp. 20–35.

Morgan, Jennifer L. *Laboring Women: Reproduction and Gender in New World Slavery*. University of Pennsylvania Press, 2004.

Morgan, Philip D. "The Ownership of Property by Slaves in the Mid-Nineteenth-Century Low Country." *Journal of Southern History*, vol. 49, no. 3, 1983, pp. 399–420.

Neary, Janet. *Fugitive Testimony: On the Visual Logic of Slave Narratives*. Fordham UP, 2017.

Nembhard, Jessica Gordon. *Collective Courage: A History of African American Cooperative Economic Thought and Practice*. Pennsylvania State UP, 2014.

"North and South." *Voice of Industry*, vol. 1, no. 35, February 13, 1846, p. 2, www.industrialrevolution.org/original-issues/1846/1846-02-13.pdf.

Northup, Solomon. *Twelve Years a Slave* [1853], edited by Sue Eakin and Joseph Logsdon, Louisiana State UP, 2014.

O'Brien, Colleen C. *Race, Romance, and Rebellion: Literatures of the Americas in the Nineteenth Century*. University of Virginia Press, 2013.

———. "'The White Women All Go for Sex': Frances Harper on Suffrage, Citizenship, and the Reconstruction South." *African American Review*, vol. 43, no. 4, 2009, pp. 605–20.

O'Donovan, Susan Eva. *Becoming Free in the Cotton South*. Harvard University Press, 2007.

Ortiz, Paul. *An African American and Latinx History of the United States*. Beacon Press, 2018.

Painter, Nell Irvin. "Soul Murder and Slavery: Toward a Fully Loaded Cost Accounting." *Southern History across the Color Line*, 2nd ed., University of North Carolina Press, 2021, 13–36.

Pelletier, Kevin. *Apocalyptic Sentimentalism : Love and Fear in U.S. Antebellum Literature*. University of Georgia Press, 2015.

Penningroth, Dylan C. *The Claims of Kinfolk: African American Property and Community in the Nineteenth-Century South*. University of North Carolina Press, 2003.

———. "My People, My People: The Dynamics of Community in Southern Slavery." *New Studies in the History of American Slavery*, edited by Edward E. Baptist and Stephanie M. H. Camp, University of Georgia Press, 2006, 166–78.

Peterson, Carla L. "Capitalism, Black (Under)Development, and the Production of the African-American Novel in the 1850s." *American Literary History*, vol. 4, no. 4, 1992, pp. 559–83.

———. *"Doers of the Word": African-American Women Speakers and Writers in the North (1830–1880)*. Oxford UP, 1995.

———. "Reconstructing the Nation: Frances Harper, Charlotte Forten, and the Racial Politics of Periodical Publication." *Proceedings of the American Antiquarian Society*, vol. 107, no. 2, 1997, pp. 301–34.

Petty, Leslie. "The Political Is Personal: The Feminist Lesson of Henry James's *The Bostonians.*" *Women's Studies: An Inter-Disciplinary Journal*, vol. 34, no. 5, 2005, pp. 377–403.

Poovey, Mary. *Genres of the Credit Economy: Mediating Value in Eighteenth- and Nineteenth-Century Britain*. University of Chicago Press, 2008.

Potter, Eliza, and Xiomara Santamarina, ed. *A Hairdresser's Experience in High Life* [1859]. University of North Carolina Press, 2009.

Pratt, Lloyd. *Archives of American Time: Literature and Modernity in the Nineteenth Century*. University of Pennsylvania Press, 2010.

Putzi, Jennifer. "Poets of the Loom, Spinners of Verse: Working-Class Women's Poetry and *The Lowell Offering.*" *A History of Nineteenth-Century American Women's Poetry*, edited by Jennifer Putzi and Alexandra Socarides, Cambridge UP, 2016, 155–69.

Reynolds, David S. *Mightier than the Sword: Uncle Tom's Cabin and the Battle for America*. W. W. Norton, 2011.

Reynolds, Virginia. "Slaves to Fashion, Not Society: Elizabeth Keckly and Washington, D.C.'s African American Dressmakers, 1860–1870." *Washington History*, vol. 26, no. 2, 2014, pp. 4–17.

Ritzenberg, Aaron. *The Sentimental Touch: The Language of Feeling in the Age of Managerialism*. Fordham UP, 2013.

Robinson, Cedric J. *An Anthropology of Marxism*. 2nd ed., University of North Carolina Press, 2019.

———. *Black Marxism: The Making of the Black Radical Tradition*. Rev. and updated 3rd ed., University of North Carolina Press, 2020.

Robbins, Sarah. *Managing Literacy, Mothering America: Women's Narratives on Reading and Writing in the Nineteenth Century*. University of Pittsburgh Press, 2004.

Rockman, Seth. "Negro Cloth: Mastering the Market for Slave Clothing in Antebellum America." *American Capitalism: New Histories*, edited by Sven Beckert and Christine Desan, Columbia UP, 2018, 170–94.

Roediger, David R. *The Wages of Whiteness: Race and the Making of the American Working Class*. Verso, 2007.

Rosenthal, Caitlin. "Abolition as Market Regulation." *Boston Review*, Winter 2017, pp. 39–144.

———. *Accounting for Slavery: Masters and Management*. Harvard UP, 2018.

———. "Slavery's Scientific Management: Masters and Managers." *Slavery's Capitalism: A New History of American Economic Development*, edited by Sven Beckert and Seth Rockman, University of Pennsylvania Press, 2016, 62–86.

Rosenthal, Debra J. *Performatively Speaking: Speech and Action in Antebellum American Literature*. University of Virginia Press, 2015.

Rostek, Joanna. *Women's Economic Thought in the Romantic Age: Towards a Transdisciplinary Herstory of Economic Thought*. Routledge, 2021.

Samuels, Shirley. "Introduction." *The Culture of Sentiment: Race, Gender, and Sentimentality in Nineteenth-Century America*, edited by Samuels, Oxford UP, 1992, 3–8.

———, ed. *The Culture of Sentiment : Race, Gender, and Sentimentality in Nineteenth-Century America*. Oxford UP, 1992.

Sánchez-Eppler, Karen. "Bodily Bonds: The Intersecting Rhetorics of Feminism and Abolition." *Representations*, no. 24, 1988, pp. 28–59.

Santamarina, Xiomara. *Belabored Professions: Narratives of African American Working Womanhood*. University of North Carolina Press, 2005.

———. "'So you can see, color makes no difference': Race, Slavery and Abolition in *A Hairdresser's Experience in High Life*." *Legacy*, vol. 24, no. 2, 2007, pp. 171–86.

Schermerhorn, Calvin. *Money over Mastery, Family over Freedom: Slavery in the Antebellum Upper South*. Johns Hopkins UP, 2011.

Schuller, Kyla. *The Biopolitics of Feeling: Race, Sex, and Science in the Nineteenth Century*. Duke UP, 2018.

Schweninger, Loren. *Black Property Owners in the South, 1790–1915*. University of Illinois Press, 1990.

Seybold, Matt, and Michelle Chihara, eds. *The Routledge Companion to Literature and Economics*. Routledge, 2019.

Seiz, Janet. "Feminism and the History of Economic Thought." *History of Political Economy*, vol. 25, no. 1, 1993, pp. 185–201.

Senchyne, Jonathan. *The Intimacy of Paper in Early and Nineteenth-Century American Literature*. University of Massachusetts Press, 2019.

Shepard, Grace F., and Lucy Larcom. "Letters of Lucy Larcom to the Whittiers." *New England Quarterly*, vol. 3, no. 3, 1930, pp. 501–18.

Simons, Robert. "The Role of Management Control Systems in Creating Competitive Advantage: New Perspectives." *Accounting, Organizations, and Society*, vol. 15, nos. 1–2, 1990, pp. 127–43.

Sinha, Manisha. "Reviving the Black Radical Tradition." *Boston Review*, Winter 2017, pp. 66–71.

Smallwood, Stephanie. "What Slavery Tells Us about Marx." *Boston Review*, Winter 2017, 78–82.

Smith, Adam. *An Inquiry into the Nature and Causes of the Wealth of Nations* [1776]. Harriman House, 2010.

———. *The Theory of Moral Sentiments* [1759]. Penguin Books, 2009.

Smith, Mark M. "Time, Slavery and Plantation Capitalism in the Ante-Bellum American South." *Past and Present*, vol. 150, no. 1, 1996, pp. 142–68.

Smith, Robin Rudy. "Creating a 'Democratic Neighborhood' through Poetic Exchange: Lucy Larcom's *An Idyl of Work*." *Legacy: A Journal of American Women Writers*, vol. 34, no. 2, 2017, pp. 301–20.

Snorton, C. Riley. *Black on Both Sides: A Racial History of Trans Identity*. University of Minnesota Press, 2017.

Spires, Derrick R. *The Practice of Citizenship: Black Politics and Print Culture in the Early United States*. University of Pennsylvania Press, 2019.

Stampp, Kenneth M. *The Peculiar Institution: Slavery in the Ante-bellum South*. Knopf, 1956.

Stancliff, Michael. *Frances Ellen Watkins Harper: African American Reform Rhetoric and the Rise of a Modern Nation State*. Routledge, 2011.

Stanley, Amy Dru. *From Bondage to Contract: Wage Labor, Marriage, and the Market in the Age of Slave Emancipation*. Cambridge UP, 1998.

———. "Histories of Capitalism and Sex Difference." *Journal of the Early Republic*, vol. 36, no. 2, 2016, pp. 343–50.

———. "Slave Breeding and Free Love: An Antebellum Argument over Slavery, Capitalism, and Personhood." *Capitalism Takes Command: The Social Transformation of Nineteenth-Century America*, edited by Michael Zakim and Gary J. Kornblith, University of Chicago Press, 2012, 119–44.

Stansell, Christine. *City of Women: Sex and Class in New York, 1789–1860*. Knopf, 1986.

Steckel, Richard H. "Women, Work, and Health Under Plantation Slavery in the United States." *More Than Chattel: Black Women and Slavery in the Americas*, edited by David Barry Gaspar and Darlene Clark Hine, Indiana UP, 1996, 43–60.

Stevens, Elizabeth C. *Elizabeth Buffum Chace and Lillie Chace Wyman: A Century of Abolitionist, Suffragist, and Workers' Rights Activism*. McFarland, 2003.

Stevenson, Ana. *The Woman as Slave in Nineteenth-Century American Social Movements*. Palgrave Macmillan, 2019.

Stowe, Harriet Beecher. "The Chimney-Corner for 1866, Being a Family-Talk on Reconstruction." *Atlantic Monthly*, January 1866, pp. 88–100.

———. *A Key to Uncle Tom's Cabin Presenting the Original Facts and Documents upon which the Story Is Founded*. John P. Jewett & Co., 1853. *Slavery and Anti-Slavery: A Transnational Archive*.

———. *Uncle Tom's Cabin* [1852], edited by Jean Fagan Yellin, Oxford UP, 1998.

Sumner, Charles. *His Complete Works*, vol. 2. Norwood Press, 1900.

"There Must Be Something Wrong." *Voice of Industry*, vol. 2, no. 31, February 12, 1847, 1, www.industrialrevolution.org/original-issues/1847/1847-02-12.pdf

Thomas, Brook. *The Literature of Reconstruction: Not in Plain Black and White*. Johns Hopkins UP, 2017.

———. "Reconstruction Matters in the Revival of Civil War Literature." *American Literary Realism*, vol. 52, no. 1, 2019, pp. 23–46.

Tomich, Dale. "The Second Slavery and World Capitalism: A Perspective for Historical Inquiry." *International Review of Social History*, vol. 63 no. 3, 2018, pp. 477–501.

———. *Through the Prism of Slavery: Labor, Capital, and World Economy*. Rowman & Littlefield, 2004.

Tompkins, Jane. *Sensational Designs: The Cultural Work of American Fiction, 1790–1860*. Oxford UP, 1985.

Truth, Sojourner, and Olive Gilbert. *The Narrative of Sojourner Truth* [1850], edited by Margaret Washington. Vintage Books, 1993.

Tyson, Thomas N., Richard K. Fleischman, and David Oldroyd. "Theoretical Perspectives on Accounting for Labor on Slave Plantations of the USA and British West Indies." *Accounting, Auditing and Accountability Journal*, vol. 17, no. 5, 2004, pp. 758–78.

United States Department of the Interior, National Park Service, Rhode Island. *National Register of Historic Place Inventory-Nomination Form: Valley Falls Mills*. Rhode Island Historical Preservation Commission, 1977.

Usner, Daniel H., Jr. "American Indians on the Cotton Frontier: Changing Economic Relations with Citizens and Slaves in the Mississippi Territory." *Journal of American History*, vol. 72, 1985, pp. 297–317.

W., Sarah. "The Slave's Revenge." *Voice of Industry*, vol. 2, no. 49, June 18, 1847, p. 1, www.industrialrevolution.org/original-issues/1847/1847-06-18.pdf.

Warhol, Robyn R. "'Reader, Can You Imagine? No, You Cannot': The Narratee as Other in Harriet Jacobs's Text." *Narrative*, vol. 3, no. 1, 1995, pp. 57–72.

Warren, Calvin L. *Ontological Terror: Blackness, Nihilism, and Emancipation*. Duke UP, 2018.

Weimer, David. "Individual, Institution, and Society: Religion and Political Economy in Harriet Beecher Stowe." *J19: The Journal of Nineteenth-Century Americanists*, vol. 4, no. 2, 2016, pp. 249–76.

Weinstein, Cindy. *Family, Kinship, and Sympathy in Nineteenth-Century American Literature*. Cambridge UP, 2004.

———. "Introduction." *The Cambridge Companion to Harriet Beecher Stowe*, edited by Weinstein, Cambridge UP, 2004, pp. 1–14.

Weiss, Gail. "The Normal, the Natural, and the Normative: A Merleau-Pontian Legacy to Feminist Theory, Critical Race Theory, and Disability Studies." *Continental Philosophy Review*, vol. 48, no. 1, 2015, pp. 77–93.

Weld, Theodore Dwight, and Sarah Moore Grimké and Angelina Emily Grimké. *American Slavery as It Is: Testimony of a Thousand Witnesses*. American Anti-Slavery Society, 1839, www.docsouth.unc.edu/neh/weld/weld.html.

Welter, Barbara. "The Cult of True Womanhood: 1820–1860." *American Quarterly*, vol. 18, no. 2, 1966, pp. 151–74.

Whitehead, Celia B. "Another Chapter of *The Bostonians*" [1887]. *Treacherous Texts: An Anthology of U.S. Suffrage Literature, 1846–1946*, edited by Mary Chapman and Angela Mills, Rutgers UP, 2011, pp. 100–107.

———. "Are England and America Doing God's Will?" *Public*, no. 197, January 11, 1902, pp. 637–38.

———. "How Will a Free Society Come, and How Will It Operate?" *Free Society: A Periodical of Anarchist Work, Thought and Literature and the Alliance of the Rockies*, vol. 9, no. 6, February 9, 1902, pp. 13–15.

———. "Pessimism." *North American Review*, vol. 208, no. 756, 1918, pp. 798–99.

Wilder, Craig Steven. *Ebony and Ivy: Race, Slavery, and the Troubled History of America's Universities*. Bloomsbury Press, 2013.

Willard, Frances, and Mary Ashton Livermore, eds. *A Woman of the Century: Fourteen Hundred-Seventy Biographical Sketches Accompanied by Portraits of Leading American Women in All Walks of Life*. Moulton, 1893.

———. "Mrs. Lillie B. Chace Wyman." *American Women: Fifteen Hundred Biographies with over 1,400 Portraits: A Comprehensive Encyclopedia of the Lives and Achievements of American Women during the Nineteenth Century*, Mast, Crowell, and Kirkpatrick, 1897, 806–7.

Williams, Andreá N. *Dividing Lines: Class Anxiety and Postbellum Black Fiction.* University of Michigan Press, 2013.
Williams, Eric. *Capitalism and Slavery* [1944]. University of North Carolina Press, 1994.
Woodmansee, Martha, and Mark Osteen, eds. *The New Economic Criticism: Studies at the Intersection of Literature and Economics.* Routledge, 1999.
Wyman, Lillie Buffum Chace. "And Joe." *Poverty Grass,* Houghton, Mifflin, 1886, pp. 204–56.
Yancy, George. *Black Bodies, White Gazes: The Continuing Significance of Race.* Rowman & Littlefield, 2008.
———. *Look, a White! Philosophical Essays on Whiteness.* Temple UP, 2012.
Yates, JoAnne. *Control through Communication: The Rise of System in American Management.* Johns Hopkins UP, 1989.
Yellin, Jean Fagan. *Harriet Jacobs: A Life.* Basic Civitas Books, 2004.
Young, Iris Marion. *On Female Body Experience: "Throwing Like a Girl" and Other Essays.* Oxford UP, 2005.

INDEX

Note: An 'n' or 'f' following a page number indicates an endnote or figure, respectively.

abolition (emancipation): freedom; reparations; *individual women writers*; accounting and, 48–49, 54–55, 125; Black economic base and, 177n13; debt and, 125; freedom *versus*, 110, 113–14; gradual *versus* immediate, 4, 45, 48–49; inheritance and, 127; labor and, 143–44, 155; personhood and, 129; property and, 115; sailing/sailors and, 173n7; slavery's capitalism and, 158, 159; of slave trade, 123. *See also* anti/proslavery positions (racial politics)

abolitionism/activism: ante/postbellum, 156; Black, 4, 133, 138, 177n13; capitalism and, 34–35, 167n12, 168n18; Chace/Wyman and, 156; individual women writers overviews, 1, 2, 3–4, 6, 8, 156, 157–58; morality/capitalist economics and, 167n12, 168n14; narratives and, 10–11; North/South and, 75–76, 161n2; postbellum, 117–18, 155; property knowledge and, 112; slavery's capitalism and, 1, 14, 22, 24–25, 34; socialism and, 5, 157, 181n9; Weld and the Grimkés and, 7; working class and, 34–35, 76, 143, 156, 167n12, 170n8. *See also* abolition (emancipation); anti/proslavery; positions (racial politics)

accounting and bookkeeping as control: abolition (emancipation) and, 48–49, 51, 54–55, 125; abolitionism and, 167n12, 168n14; accounting controls defined, 24, 27–31, 166n7; *American Slavery as It Is* and, 7–8, 37; cotton market/mills and, 61–62, 66, 94; critical studies, 17; education and, 166n9; enslaved people's skills at, 48; global contexts and, 61; human indeterminacy and, 29, 32, 166n7; inheritance and, 28, 36, 53, 138, 140; Jacobs and, 8, 53; Larcom and, 66, 169n7; law and, 167n10; managerial hierarchy and, 36–45, 166n9; morality *versus* economics and, 165n2; negro cloth and, 94; North/South labor control compared, 24–25, 26, 28–29, 45–46, 61–62; oppressive/liberatory effects of, 166n8; scholarship and, 165n2, 167n10; white womanhood and, 50–51, 52. *See also* credit/debt/loans/mortgages; ledgers; managerial hierarchy and overseers; morality *versus* economics; "pocketbooks"; shadow accounts; Stowe, Harriet Beecher

activism and activist literary networks. *See* abolitionism/activism; anti/proslavery positions (racial politics)

Adams, Katherine, 145

advertisements for fugitives, 53–54, 96, 97f

Affleck, Thomas: *Cotton Plantation Record and Account Book*, 27–28, 30f, 44–45

African Methodist Episcopal Church (AME), 118

agents of slavery (slave traders/catchers), 11, 21, 36, 38–39, 40, 41, 44, 59, 99, 148

agriculture, 5, 62, 144–145. *See also* labor, enslaved and formerly enslaved

Ahmed, Sarah, 88–89, 100–1, 106

Alcoff, Linda Martín, 17, 80–81, 171nn15

Alexander, Sadie, 9

Alliance of the Rockies (monthly newspaper), 157

Alves, Susan: "Lowell's Female Factory Workers," 169n5; "My Sisters Toil," 170, 170n8, 171n16, 172n21

American Anti-Slavery Society, 6, 167n12

American Girl dolls, 174n14

Ammons, Elizabeth, 168nn15,18

Andrews, William L., 176n5

ante/postbellum compared: abolitionist literature, 156; Black class, 177n6; Chace/Wyman compared, 156; inheritance, 121–22; property, 108; slavery's capitalism, 12, 149, 170n9; "tragic mulatta" trope, 176n5. *See also* Civil War; Moses and Pharoah; North/South compared

Anteus, 144

anti/proslavery positions (racial politics): capitalism and, 31–35, 164n12, 168n18; *Minnie's Sacrifice* and, 120; overviews, 15; *Uncle Tom's Cabin* and, 15, 18, 23–26, 35–36, 45–56; "Weaving" and, 79, 82; women's labor and, 76. *See also* abolition (emancipation); abolitionism/activism; morality *versus* economics; racialization/racism

anti-slavery poetry, 62, 119, 140, 170n8, 172n21

Appeal. See Child, Lydia Maria

arithmetic textbooks, 167n9

auction block/slave markets, 37–38, 41, 135

Banks, Nina, 136

Baym, Nina, 132

Beckert, Sven, 2, 161n2; "The Market, Utility, and Slavery in Southern Legal Thought," *Slavery's Capitalism: A New History of American Economic Development*, 165n1

Bell, Derrick, 176n4

Bentley, H. C.: *Bibliography of Works on Accounting by American Authors*, 167n9

Berkshire Hathaway, 156

Berry, Daina Ramey, 11, 165n2; "'We'm Fus' Rate Bargain': Value, Labor, and Price in a Georgia Slave Community," 46

Beverly (MA)/Historic Beverly, 72, 73–74

Black citizenship, economic, 14–17, 19, 118–19, 138–47, 177n13

Black communities and relationships: abolitionism and, 4; accounting and, 29, 31, 37–38; Black economic citizenship and, 119; children's play and, 106; COVID-19 pandemic and, 158; economic citizenship and, 138, 142–43, 146–47; freedom and, 134, 143; inheritance and, 116, 124, 125, 127, 128; landownership and, 144, 145–46; money and, 140; New England and, 72–73; politics, 140–45; property and, 86–87, 121–22; Quakers and, 134; shared property knowledge and, 86–87, 114–16. *See also* Black citizenship, economic; Black uplift/development; families; Harper, Frances Ellen Watkins

Black intellectual history, 9

Black labor power, 143–45

Black love, 130–31

Black Marxism, 17

Black politics. *See* Black communities and relationships

Black professional and business class, 125

Black Radical Tradition, 176n4

Black uplift/development, 119, 120, 125, 128, 130–31, 139, 147–48, 178n23. *See also* landownership

blood, 47, 60, 64, 65, 69, 77, 79, 101, 121, 126, 133, 170, 177n9

bodies and sensations: Black, 82; disjuncture and, 171n17; economic theory/discourse and, 17; enslaved people and, 104–5; *Incidents* and, 17, 19, 87–89, 91, 98–102; intentional arc and, 171nn13–14; labor power as commodity and, 166n7; Merleau-Ponty and, 59, 169n4; race and gender and, 169n4; space and, 88; subjectivity and, 171n11, 172n20; "Weaving" and, 17, 18, 57, 58–59, 67, 70–72, 75, 81, 83, 101, 169n4, 171n12; of white, working-class women, 18, 171n12; white "mill girls" and, 18. *See also* clothing; gender/sexuality; space

bookkeeping. *See* accounting and bookkeeping as control

Boydston, Jeanne: *Home and Work: Housework, Wages, and the Ideology of Labor in the Early Republic*, 10

Brazil, 123

British antislavery movement, 161n2

Brophy, Alfred L., 165n1

Brown, Elsa Barkley, 164n13; "'What Has Happened Here': The Politics of Difference in Women's History and Feminist Politics," 164n13

Brown, Henry Box, 8

Brown, William Wells: *The Black Man: His Antecedents, His Genius, and His Achievements* (W. W. Brown), 124, 156

Bryant, Christopher J., 111–12

Bryant, Mr.: "A Southern Cotton Mill" (1849), 93

Buffet, Warren, 156

Burnett, Katharine A.: *Cavaliers and Economists: Global Capitalism and the Development of Southern Literature, 1820–1860*, 15, 164n12, 165n16

Byrd, Brandon, 124

Camfield, Gregg: "The Moral Aesthetics of Sentimentality," 166n5

Camp, Stephanie M. H.: "The Pleasures of Resistance: Enslaved Women and Body Politics in the Plantation South, 1830–1861," 94–95, 96

Campbell, Helen Stuart, 180n5

capitalism (economics): abolitionism and, 167n12, 168n14; agricultural and mercantile compared, 5; anti/proslavery positions and, 31–35, 164n12, 168n18; definitions, 9–10, 14; economics as fiction, 14, 15, 149–50; everydayness and, 16–17; historicizing, 123; literature and, 11–16, 179nn1–2, 180nn3–4, 181n11; "racial," 9, 25, 53–54, 118–19, 138, 158; women's historians of, 10–11, 164n14. *See also* accounting and bookkeeping as control; class; cotton market; debt/credit/loans/mortgages; economic theory/discourse; gender/sexuality; knowledge; morality *versus* economics; property; racialization/racism; slavery's capitalism; women writers; *individual women writers*

Chace, Elizabeth Buffum, 156–57

Chace, Samuel, 156

Chandler, Elizabeth Margaret, 161n2

Chihara, Michelle: *The Routledge Companion to Literature and Economics*, 179n2

Child, Lydia Maria: overviews, 3–8, 13–14; abolition (emancipation) and, 3–8; abolitionism/activism, 3–5; British antislavery movement and, 161n2; economic discourse, 17–18, 155–56, 161n1; Harper and, 178n17; scholarship and, 5; slavery's capitalism and, 161n2; socialism and, 5, 157

children: abolitionist, 156; accounting and, 42; ante/postbellum inheritance and, 121–22; Aunt Chloe Fleet and, 135; Black uplift and, 148; inherited property, meaning of, 112–13, 131–32, 173n5; D. Larcom and, 72; *Uncle Tom's Cabin* and, 42, 45, 50–52. *See also* inheritance; toys

Chinese immigrants, 16

Christianity, 43, 47, 178n21

Christian Recorder (AME church periodical), 118, 120, 124, 143, 145, 175n1

citizenship. *See* Black citizenship, economic

Civil War: abolitionists and, 156; Black voices on, 118; Haitian Revolution compared, 124; *Incidents* and, 109; Larcom and, 168n1; *Minnie's Sacrifice* and, 121, 133; Northern capitalism and, 155; slavery's capitalism and, 78. *See also* ante/postbellum compared

class: Black labor power and, 143; Black professional/business, 125; domesticity and, 90; economic citizenship and, 146; feminist economics and, 181n11; gender and, 158–59; landownership and, 145; lower/higher, 32; postbellum Black, 177n6; property and, 107; *Uncle Tom's Cabin* and, 42; "Weaving" and, 69, 76, 81–82. *See also* Black uplift/development;

Harper, Frances Ellen Watkins; middle class; money and wealth; upper class/elites; working class. *See also* Black uplift/development; Harper, Frances Ellen Watkins; middle class; money and wealth; upper class/elites; working class

Clegg, John, 167n11

Clifton, Lucille, 81

cloth/fabric/textiles: freedom and, 94–95, 96–97, 103; ideas and, 175n18; *Incidents* and, 85–86, 87, 89–99, 102–3, 105, 108–9, 112, 114; Merleau-Ponty and, 70, 172nn19–20; "poisoned," 76. *See also* clothing; cotton; negro cloth

clothing: accounting and, 23; enslaved people and, 94, 173n6; enslaved/waged labor compared, 169n2; freedom and, 94–95, 96–97; fugitives and, 97f, *Incidents* and, 85–86, 87, 89, 90, 93–99, 102–3, 105, 108–9, 112, 114; *Minnie's Sacrifice* and, 139; North/South laborers and, 74–75; racialization and, 98–99, 109, 110; scholarship on, 164n12; slavery's capitalism and, 139; "Weaving" and, 69, 74, 76–77, 169n2; WPA interview and, 75; writing paper and, 175n18. *See also* cloth/fabric/textiles; fashion; linsey-woolsey; negro cloth; seamstresses and sewing

Cocheco Company, 76

Collins, Jennie, 76

colonization, 49

Colored National Labor Union (CNLU), 143

commodification, 166n7, 167n11, 169n2, 180n4

community (collective) economic practices. *See* Black communities and relationships

consumption (consumerism), 40, 168n2, 180n4

contracts, 10, 167n12

control. *See* accounting and bookkeeping as control; managerial hierarchy and overseers

Cook, Sylvia Jenkins, 63, 175n18; *Clothed in Meaning*, 94, 164n12, 94, 164n12; "The Working Woman's Bard," 170n9

Cooper, D. J.: "On the Intellectual Roots of Critical Accounting," 166n8

Cott, Nancy F.: *The Bonds of Womanhood*, 10

cotton: gender/sexuality and, 18, 19, 58, 74, 78, 175n16; racialized and sexualized, 19; whiteness and, 59, 173n5. *See also* cloth/fabric/textiles; clothing; cotton mills; Larcom, Lucy; seamstresses and sewing

cotton market, 19, 58–62, 63, 70, 71, 74, 75–78, 83–84, 170n9. *See also* accounting and bookkeeping as control; global and transnational

cotton market (*continued*)
    contexts; labor, enslaved/wage compared; Larcom, Lucy
cotton mills, 76, 93, 94, 180n8. *See also* Larcom, Lucy; Lowell mills; Valley Falls Company
COVID-19 pandemic, 158, 181n10
credit/debt/loans/mortgages, 10, 21, 28, 29, 33, 47, 51, 53, 68, 80, 120, 125, 164n12, 165n1. *See also* duties, levies, national debt, taxes
Cuba, 123

Dall, Caroline Healey, 180n5
Daut, Marlene, L., 178n16
Davis, Adrienne D., 11; "Don't Let Nobody Bother Yo' Principle," 10
Davis, David Brion: *The Problem of Slavery in the Age of Revolution 1770–1823*, 9; *The Problem of Slavery in Western Culture*, 9
Davis, Rebecca Harding: *Bits of Gossip*, 154–55; *Waiting for the Verdict*, 154–55
debt/credit/loans/mortgages, 10, 21, 28, 29, 33, 47, 51, 53, 68, 80, 120, 125, 164n12, 165n1. *See also* duties, levies, national debt, taxes
decolonization, 123
Denning, Michael, 171n12
Dessalines, Jean-Jacques, 124
Diran, Ingrid: "Scenes of Speculation: Harriet Jacobs and the Biopolitics of Human Capital," 164n12
disciplinary boundaries, academic, 151
domesticity (homemaking): fiction and, 169n2; Harper and, 131; middle-class consumption and, 168n2; *Minnie's Sacrifice* and, 132, 134; Potter and, 153; property and, 175n17; racialization and, 90, 92; scholarship and, 11, 12, 15; sentimentality and, 166n6, 168n16; slavery's capitalism and, 2–3, 132, 168n16; *Uncle Tom's Cabin* and, 50–53, 132, 168n16, 175n17; white women and, 50–53; *See also* home; Jacobs, Harriet; seamstresses and sewing
Donnelly, Andrew: "Stowe's Slavery and Stowe's Capitalism: Forced Reproductive Labor in *Uncle Tom's Cabin*," 164n12
double proposal plot, 177n8
Douglas, Ann, 25
Douglass, Frederick, 33, 124
Douglass, Sarah, 161n2
Douglass Monthly (periodical), 124
Du Bois, W. E. B., 162n4, 178n19; *Black Reconstruction in America*, 9; *The Philadelphia Negro*, 9

duties, levies, national debt, taxes, 5, 109–10. *See also* debt/credit/loans/mortgages

economics as fiction, 14, 15, 149–50. *See also* literature and economics
economic theory/discourse: academic disciplines and, 180n3; everydayness and, 10–11, 135–36; father-master's logics, 132, 178n16; feminist, 17, 159, 181n11; Keynesian, 9–10; literary analysis and, 20; masculinization of, 5, 151; meaning-making, 14–15, 19, 55, 87–87, 107, 113, 114–16, 119, 124, 132, 138, 150; overviews, 3, 14–15, 17, 19–20, 149–59; women economists, 180n5; women's labor and, 12. *See also* Black communities and relationships; capitalism (economics); Du Bois, W. E. B.; Marx, Karl and Marxism; morality *versus* economics; *individual women writers*
education and schools: Black uplift and, 119; bookkeeping and, 166n9; COVID-19 pandemic and, 181n10; higher education, 180n3; *Minnie's Sacrifice* and, 121, 127, 128, 132, 134–37 passim, 139, 140, 148, 178n21; racial capitalism and, 158; sewing and, 99; slavery's capitalism and, 139; *Uncle Tom's Cabin*, 43, 51; *Waiting for the Verdict* and, 155; "Weaving" and, 62, 80, 118. *See also* knowledge; university system
Edwards, Richard, 166n7
Einhorn, Robin: *American Taxation American Slavery*, 110–11
emancipation. *See* abolition (emancipation)
Engerman, Stanley L., 60; *Time on the Cross: The Economics of American Negro Slavery*, 9
England, 34
England's Industrial Revolution, 8–9
enslaved people: bodies and, 104–5; capitalism and, 8–10; cotton empire and, 164n12; economic citizenship and, 146; economic knowledge and, 105–6; histories of, 4, 9; *Incidents* and, 103–4; industry and, 62; population statistics, 60–61; property and, 172n3; rebellion and, 178n16; West Indian, 8–9. *See also* accounting and bookkeeping as control; enslavers; fugitives; labor, enslaved and formerly enslaved; law; morality *versus* economics; capitalism
enslavers: accounting/bank loans and, 28; capitalists compared, 5; inheritance and, 177n9; *Minnie's Sacrifice* and, 121, 132; property and, 86; Stowe and, 15, 36–45; testimonies of, 7; *Un-*

cle *Tom's Cabin* and, 32–33. *See also* accounting and bookkeeping as control; Grimké, Grimké, and Weld; managerial hierarchy and overseers enslavers, women, 15, 51, 153
"epistemology of ignorance," 89
Ernest, John, 123
Europe, 34
Evans, Lisa: "Framing the Magdalen," 165n3
everydayness (lived experiences) (everyday narratives), 10–12, 18, 40–41, 65–69, 135–36, 154–55, 171n15, 175n17. *See also* bodies and sensations; domesticity (homemaking); Grimké, Grimké, and Weld; historicization; literary form and analysis; subject positions (subjectivity/self)

fabric. *See* cloth/fabric/textiles
factories. *See* cotton market; cotton mills; labor, enslaved/wage compared; Larcom, Lucy
families, 46, 129, 133, 135, 173n10, 174n1, 176n5, 177n7. *See also* Black communities and relationships
Farmers' Alliance and Industrial Union, 157
Farrow, Anne, 60
fashion, 154, 164n12
father-master's economic logics, 132, 178n16
feminist theory, 17, 159, 181n11
Fielder, Brigitte, 133, 173n10, 174n14; "Black Girls, White Girls, American Girls," 175n14; "Radical Respectability and African American Women's Reconstruction Fiction," 177n14; "'Those people must have loved her very dearly,'" 177n7
Fifteenth Amendment (1869), 140–41
Finley, Alexandra J., 11, 99; *An Intimate Economy*, 173n6
Fitzhugh, George, 35
Fleischman Richard K., 28, 167n10
Fogel, Robert William, 60; *Time on the Cross: The Economics of American Negro Slavery*, 9
Foner, Eric: *Reconstruction*, 176n2
Ford, Sarah Gibreath: *Haunted Property*, 175n17
Foreman, P. Gabrielle, 131, 166n6
forgiveness, 134–35
Forten, Sarah, 161n2
Foster, Frances Smith, 117, 118, 126, 135, 175n1, 178nn17,21
Fourier, Charles, 5
Fourteenth Amendment (1868), 17
Francis, Jere, 25
freedom: Black community and, 134, 143; cloth and, 94–95, 96–97, 103; emancipation *versus*, 110, 113–14; gendered, 98; inheritance and, 127–28; landownership and, 144; *Minnie's Sacrifice* and, 119, 125, 127, 131, 136, 177n11; property and, 114–16, 149; as relative (degree of), 108, 112; sewing skills and, 99–100; struggle and, 136. *See also* abolition (emancipation); free labor movement; fugitives
"freedom tax," 111–12
free labor movement, 119. *See also* labor, enslaved/wage compared
free papers, 129
free suffrage movement, 86
fugitives, 53–54, 96–108, 97f, 115. *See also* Underground Railroad
Fugitive Slave Act (1850), 17, 89

Gardner, Eric, 128, 137, 177n6; *Black Print Unbound*, 176n1; "Coloring History and Mixing Race in Levina Urbino's *Sunshine in the Palace and Cottage* and Louise Heaven's *In Bonds*," 176n5; "Frances Ellen Watkins Harper's Civil War and Militant Intersectionality," 178n22; *Unexplained Places*, 118
Garrison, William Lloyd, 156, 170n9
Garrisonians, 4
gender/sexuality: bodies and, 68, 169n4, 171n14; class and, 158–59; consumerism and, 169n2; cotton/cloth and, 18, 19, 58, 74, 78, 175n16; debtand, 120; feminist economics and, 181n11; fugitive practice and, 98–99; *Incidents* and, 172n1; labor, enslaved and formerly enslaved and, 50, 75–76, 89, 105, 196n6; labor and, 10, 152; Larcom and, 73; *Minnie's Sacrifice* and, 138; property and, 19, 88, 92, 105, 107; "reconstruction" and, 137–38; scholarship and, 10; slavery's capitalism and, 3, 159; suffrage and, 141; women writers and, 1–2, 149; working-class women, white, and, 50, 169n5. *See also* bodies and sensations; domesticity (homemaking); enslavers, women; labor, enslaved/wage compared; marriage; women's histories; women's rights; women writers; working-class women, white
Genovese, Eugene D.: *Roll, Jordan, Roll: The World the Slaves Made*, 9
Gilman, Charlotte Perkins, 180n5
global and transnational contexts: cotton market and, 59–61, 62; Harper and, 122–23, 148, 177n11; Potter and, 153; twentieth-century scholarship and, 9, 10–11; *Uncle Tom's Cabin* and, 32; white cognitive dysfunction and, 80;

global and transnational contexts (*continued*) women writers and, 161n2. *See also* imperialism, U.S.; slave trade (human trafficking)
Glymph, Thavolia, 11, 51, 95: *Out of the House of Bondage: The Transformation of the Plantation Household*, 50
Goddu, Teresa A.: *Selling Antislavery: Abolition and Mass Media in Antebellum America*, 7–8, 167n12
Goldin, Claudia: "The Shaping of Higher Education," 180n3; *Urban Slavery in the American South, 1820–1860: A Quantitative History*, 9
Goodman, Paul, 4
Great Migration, 9
Greek Myth, 74, 77, 144
Greek "properties," 173n4
Greeson, Jennifer Rae: "The Prehistory of Possessive Individualism" (2012), 114–15
Griffin, Farah Jasmine, 144
Grimké, A., Grimké, S. M., and Weld, T. D.: *American Slavery as It Is: Testimony of a Thousand Witnesses*, 6–8, 13–14, 17–18, 37

Haiti, 14, 19, 121, 123, 124–25, 148
Halpern, Faye: "Word Become Flesh: Literacy, Anti-literacy, and Illiteracy in *Uncle Tom's Cabin*," 42
Hammond, James H.: "Cotton Is King" Speech, 35
"harmonious order," theory of, 5
Harper, Frances Ellen Watkins: abolition (emancipation) and, 117–18, 123, 125, 127, 143, 146; abolitionism/activism and, 119–20, 147, 176n3, 177nn6,7; Black community, 117–19, 127–39, 142–43, 145–48, 177nn6,13; Black politics, 142–45; Christian service, 178n21; citizenship, economic, 14–17, 19, 118–19, 138–47, 177n13; class, 135, 136, 138, 143–45, 148, 177n6, 178n21; culture *versus* wealth, 177n6; economic value, transformation of, 164n14; Fourteenth Amendment and (1868), 17; globalism/transnationalism and, 122–23, 148, 177n11; historicizing inheritance and, 121, 122–25, 131–32, 134–35, 138, 176n4, 177n12; influences on, 8, 176n4; inheritance, 14–15, 17, 19, 118–19, 122–24; inheritance of knowledge, 144–45; inheritance of money, 124–31, 133, 139–40, 146, 177n9; inheritance of values/ and, 132–37; landownership/labor, 120, 138–39, 142–47, 178n22; money, 142; morality and economics and, 121–138, 177n6; Moses/Pharoah compared, 119–20, 121, 126–27, 178n17; plot of *Minnie's Sacrifice*, 120–21; politics of collective economics, 142–43; Reconstruction and, 37, 124, 132, 137, 140, 176n3; sentimentalism and, 119, 124, 125, 127, 135; suffrage and, 118, 121, 138, 140–42, 147, 148; women writers and, 137–38
Harper, Frances Ellen Watkins other works: American Equal Rights Association speech, 141; Aunt Chloe poems, 135–36, 141; "Enlightened Motherhood," 136–37; "Free Labor," 53, 119, 140; *Iola Leroy*, 120, 130, 131; "Land and Labor," 120, 144, 145, 146; "The Mission of the Flowers," 178n17; "Moses: A Story of the Nile," 120, 126–27, 133–34, 178n17; "Our Greatest Want," 119, 140, 177n21; "Our People," 120, 143; *Sowing and Reaping*, 120, 175n1, 176n6; *Trial and Triumph*, 120, 177n6; "The Two Offers," 119; "We Are All Bound up Together," 120; "Woman's Political Future," 137
Harris, Cheryl I., 129, 154; "Finding Sojourner's Truth," 107–8; "Whiteness as Property," 73–74
Hartigan-O'Connor, Ellen, 11, 164n14
Hartman, Saidiya V., 86, 115: *Scenes of Subjection: Terror, Slavery, and Self-Making in Nineteenth-Century America*, 125
Haskell, Thomas, 167n12
Heaven, Louise: *In Bonds*, 176n5
Heier, Jan Richard, 28
Hercules, 144
historicization, 121, 122–25, 131–32, 134–35, 138, 176n4, 177n12
"histories of the present," 10–11. *See also* 20th and 21st centuries
"histotextuality," 131
home: capitalist accumulation and, 10; Chace and, 156; *Incidents* and, 85, 89, 90–92, 100, 108, 112–13, 174n13; Larcom and, 72; *Minnie's Sacrifice* and, 131, 132, 134, 140, 142, 143, 144, 146; as property, 174n13; *Uncle Tom's Cabin* and, 37, 175n17. *See also* domesticity (homemaking); mortgages/credit/debt/loans
homemaking. *See* domesticity (homemaking); home
hooks, bell, 165n15
humanities, 151
Hume, David, 151
Hungary, regent-president of, 153
Hunter, Robert M. T. (Senator), 181n9

Hunter, Tera, 178n15
Huston, James L., 29, 31, 86, 162, 163, 167n12, 168n14

identity: female whiteness and, 80; fluidity of, 129–30, 131; *Minnie's Sacrifice* and, 121, 129–30, 132; mixed-race, 131, 132; racial historicization and, 121, 125; wealth and, 130–31. *See also* subject positions (subjectivity/self)
ideology, 42
imagination, 56, 150, 151, 165n15
imperialism, U.S., 16, 123, 157. *See also* global and transnational contexts
Incidents in the Life of a Slave Girl. *See* Jacobs, Harriet
Indigenous people, 16
Industrial Revolution, England's, 8–9
industry, 33, 67, 120. *See also* labor, enslaved/wage compared
"Information Wanted" ads, 53–54
inheritance: accounting and, 28, 36, 53, 138, 140; debt and reparations and, 125; of economic discourse and critique, 155–56; freedom and, 127–28; landownership and, 144; law and, 122, 173n8; North/South and, 123–25; as property, 174n13; racialization and, 133, 164n12; real life enslavers and, 177n9; wealth and identity and, 130. *See also* Harper, Frances Ellen Watkins; historicization; money and wealth; property
"intentional arc," 171nn13,14
interest-convergence theory, 176n4

Jacobs, Harriet: abolition (emancipation) and, 89, 108, 110, 113–14, 155; abolitionism/activism and, 86, 108, 112; accounting and, 8, 53; ad for capture of Jacobs, 97; *American Slavery as It Is* and, 8; in the attic, 100–4, 105–6, 112, 114, 175n16; bodies and sensations and, 17, 19, 87–89, 91, 98–102; cloth/fabric/clothing and, 18–19, 85–87, 89–99, 102–3, 106–8, 110, 112, 114; cotton and whiteness and, 173n5; cotton market and, 91–92; debt and inheritance and, 164n12; domesticity and, 89–92, 99, 112–13, 123, 132, 134, 175n17; economic value, transformation of, and, 164n14; enslaved women's economic knowledge and, 105–6; finance, counterlogic of, 164n12; home and, 85, 89, 90–92, 100, 108, 112–13, 174n13; inheritance and, 174n12; labor, enslaved women's, 88, 104–6,

112; money/taxes and, 109–12; objects and, 87–93, 115; objects of freedom in fugitivity, 100–8, 115; objects of freedom in North, 89, 108–15; objects of freedom in South, 89–100, 115; persons as property and, 111, 114–15; phenomenology, 17; properties, ideological, 115, 174n13; property definitions, 19, 86–87, 94, 114–15, 173nn4,5; property knowledge, 14, 18–19, 85–93, 102, 103, 105, 107–8, 112–13, 175n17; property knowledge, shared, 86–87, 114–16; real-life enslaver of, 96; seamstresses, 19, 85, 87, 88, 91–92, 95, 96, 99–100, 102, 104, 105, 106, 114, 116, 174n14; space, 97, 98, 99, 100–4, 106–8, 112–13; *Uncle Tom's Cabin* compared, 175n17; "Weaving" compared, 79, 82, 101–2; whiteness and, 173n5; wider historical frameworks and, 16; women enslavers and, 15
Jacobs, Harriet other works: "Free States," 110
James, C. L. R., 8–9
James, Henrietta: "Another Chapter of *The Bostonians*," 157
James, Henry: *The Bostonians*, 157
Johnson, Jessica Marie, 11
Johnson, Walter: *River of Dark Dreams*, 59–60
Jones, Martha S., 178n18
Jones-Rogers, Stephanie E., 11, 15, 50, 165n2

Kachun, Mitchell A., 176n5
Karcher, Carolyn L., 3, 4, 6
Karp, Matt: "Slavery, Abolition, and Congress," 181n9
Katz, Lawrence F.: "The Shaping of Higher Education," 180n3
Keckley, Elizabeth: *Behind the Scenes*, 53, 54, 153–54, 164n12
Kelley, Robin D. G., 176n4
Keynesian economic theories, 9–10
Kilcup, Karen, 81
King, Wilma, 105, 173n11; *Stolen Childhood: Slave Youth in Nineteenth-century America* (1995), 103
Kingdom of Matthias, 152
knowledge: accounting, 30f, 46, 47, 48, 167n9; agricultural, 144; Aunt Chloe poems and, 135; of books, 134; craft, 99–100; economic, 16–17, 46, 47, 48, 71, 104–5, 112, 133, 136, 140, 141–42, 152; enslaved labor and, 153; inheritance of, 144–45; intentional arc and, 171n13; *Minnie's Sacrifice* and, 136, 137, 147; of nation and the war,

knowledge (*continued*)
133; production of, 151; property, 14, 19, 87, 89, 90, 99–100, 102–3, 105, 107–8, 112–16; of slavery's capitalism, 161n2. *See also* education and schools; everydayness (lived experiences) (everyday narratives); Jacobs, Harriet; subject positions (subjectivity/self)

Ku Klux Klan, 147

labor. *See* labor, enslaved and formerly enslaved; working-class labor, enslaved and formerly enslaved: abolition (emancipation) and, 143–44, 155; accounting and, 48; agricultural knowledge and, 144–45; debt and, 125; gender/sexuality and, 50, 75–76, 89, 105, 169n6; inheritance and, 123, 125; knowledge and, 153; landownership and, 120, 138–39, 142–47; reform efforts and, 117–18; reproductive/sexual, 11, 164n12; thinkers and, 137–38; world of women and, 57–58. *See also* agriculture; domesticity (homemaking); enslaved people

labor, enslaved *versus* wage: *Uncle Tom's Cabin* and, 26–28, 31, 33–35, 49–50, 167n11

labor, enslaved/wage compared: accounting and, 24–25, 26, 28–29, 31–35, 45–46, 49, 55, 61–62; Child and, 5; commodification and, 166n7, 167n11, 169n2; permanence and, 61–62; persons and, 111, 114–15; scholarship and, 10, 12; slavery's capitalism and, 153, 161n2; *Uncle Tom's Cabin* and, 31, 33–34; "Weaving" and, 62, 74–75; whiteness and, 62, 169n5. *See also* accounting and bookkeeping as control; Black labor power; Black uplift/development; domesticity (homemaking); free labor movement; labor, enslaved and formerly enslaved; Larcom, Lucy; morality *versus* economics; North/South compared; racialization/racism; working class

labor, skilled (expertise), 46, 48, 85, 119, 130, 153, 169n6, 172n18. *See also* seamstresses and sewing

labor, writing and (civilizers and the pen), 137–38. *See also* paper

labor reform literature, 156

labor rights, 138. *See also* Black labor power

labor turnover, 61–62

labor unions, 143

landownership, 120, 138–39, 142–47

Larcom, David, 72–73

Larcom, Juno, 72–73

Larcom, Lucy (poem quoted in full 63–65): abolitionism/activism, 17n8, 75, 76, 78, 81–83, 171n18;

Black, enslaved, women laborers, 60–61, 69, 72–73, 75, 78, 80, 83–84, 170n9; bodies/sensations (lived bodies), 17, 18, 57, 58–59, 67, 70–72, 75, 81, 83, 101, 169n4, 171n12; bookkeeping, 169n7; Civil War and, 168n1; cotton/cotton market and, 19, 58–62, 63, 70, 71, 74, 75, 76–77, 78, 83–84, 170n9; economic value, transformation of, 164n14; everyday weaving described, 18, 65–69; family history and, 72; *Incidents* compared, 101–2; Larcom's life history, 72–73, 169n7; nature, 62, 66–68, 79; phenomenology/bodies, 17, 18, 58, 67, 70–72, 82, 83, 169n4, 171n14; space and, 170n10; white, working-class, women, 62, 68, 72, 74, 75–76, 79–83; whiteness and, 72, 77–78; white subjectivity/self, 18, 58–59, 62, 63, 67–68, 70–72, 79–81, 169n5; wider historical frameworks, 16; "world of women," 16, 18, 57–58, 67, 70, 76, 81, 82, 169n3. *See also* labor, enslaved/wage compared

Larcom, Lucy other works: "An Idyl of Work," 68, 170n9; *A New England Girlhood: Outlined from Memory* (Larcom), 66, 72–73; *Poems*, 168n1

Larcom, Phillis, 72; Larcom, Rose, 72; law: accounting and, 167n10; inheritance and, 121–22, 173n8; literary scholarship and, 159; *Minnie's Sacrifice* and, 120;property and, 72–74, 85–87, 91; *Uncle Tom's Cabin* and, 23, 165n1; women enslavers and, 15. *See also* abolition (emancipation); levies, duties, national debt, taxes; loans/credit/debt/mortgages; morality *versus* economics; suffrage

ledgers, 7, 18, 22–45, 30f, 48, 50–51, 139. *See also* accounting and bookkeeping as control; "pocket books"

Leonard, R. S. and Bentley, H. C., *Bibliography of Works on Accounting by American Authors*, 167n9

levies, duties, national debt, taxes, 5, 109–10. *See also* debt/credit/loans/mortgages

Libretti, Tim, 171n12

Lincoln, Mary Todd, 53

linsey-woolsey, 93, 94, 95, 99, 104. *See also* cloth/fabric/textiles; clothing; negro cloth

literary form and analysis, 11–12, 14, 17, 20, 158–59, 164n12. *See also* everydayness (lived experiences) (everyday narratives); imagination; reading practices; scholarship; sentimentalism; "tragic mulatta" trope

literature and economics, 11–16, 179nn1–2,

INDEX

180nn3–4, 181n11. *See also* everydayness (lived experiences) (everyday narratives); women writers

loans/credit/debt/mortgages, 10, 21, 28, 29, 33, 47, 51, 53, 68, 80, 120, 125, 164n12, 165n1. *See also* duties, levies, national debt, taxes

Louisiana, 121, 123, 148, 177n12

Louverture, Toussaint, 124

Lowell (MA), 170, 171n12, 172n20, 172n21

Lowell mills, 59, 60, 62, 75, 77, 169n5, 171n12, 172n21. *See also* cotton mills; Larcom, Lucy

Lowell Offering, The (monthly periodical), 169n5

machines, 170n7, 176n5

managerial hierarchy and overseers, 5, 50–51, 166n7; in *Uncle Tom's Cabin*, 21, 36, 41, 44, 46, 47–48

Marable, Manning: *How Capitalism Underdeveloped Black America: Problem in Race, Political Economy, and Society*, 9

Marchalonis, Shirley, 170nn8,10; *The Worlds of Lucy Larcom, 1824–1893*, 66, 169n7

marginal utility, 180n4

marriage, 119, 121, 129, 130–31, 178n15. *See also* double proposal plot

Married Women's Property Acts (1840s), 86

Marx, Karl and Marxism, 5, 9–10, 17, 35, 139, 167n13. *See also* Black Marxism

materiality (material culture), 16–17, 85, 94, 103, 150, 168n2, 171n12. *See also* bodies and sensations; property; slavery's capitalism

matriliny, 133

McIntosh, Maria J., 15, 165n16

mental activity as labor, 154

Merish, Lori, 168n2, 169n2

Archives of Labor, 171n12

Merleau-Ponty, Maurice: *Phenomenology of Perception*, 58–59, 70, 83, 169n4, 171n13, 172nn19,20. *See also* phenomenology

middle class, 69, 136, 168n2, 169n2. *See also* consumption (consumerism); Harper, Frances Ellen Watkins

millionaires, 155

mills, 152, 156, 164n12. *See also* cotton mills

Mills, Charles W., 79, 80

Minnie's Sacrifice (postbellum Black citizenship). *See* Harper, Frances Ellen Watkins

Mirowski, Phillip, 180n4

Mitchell, Koritha, 130, 131, 176n5; *From Slave Cabins to the White House: Homemade Citizenship in African American Culture*, 92, 178n23

mixed-race identities, 72, 131–32, 144, 176, 177n9

Modell, Sven: "Critical Realist Accounting Research," 166n8

money and wealth: community and, 139, 140, 142; debt/credit and, 120; global economy and, 153; as icon, 139, 178n20; national identity and, 178n19; reparations and, 139; scholarship and, 178n20; sentimentalism and, 119, 124, 125, 127. *See also* accounting and bookkeeping as control; Harper, Frances Ellen Watkins; inheritance; morality *versus* economics; taxes, duties, levies, national debt

Montes, Leonidas: "Das Adam Smith Problem," 165n4

morality *versus* economics: anti/proslavery positions (racial politics);labor, enslaved/wage compared; reparations; abolitionism and, 167n12, 168n14; elite foreign philanthropy and, 153; Harper and, 121–38, 177n6; *Minnie's Sacrifice* and, 142; scholarship and, 165n2; slavery's capitalism and, 165n16; suffrage and, 142; *Uncle Tom's Cabin* and, 31–32, 33–34, 38–45; "Weaving" and, 79. *See also* accounting and bookkeeping as control

Morgan, Jennifer L., 11, 165n2

mortgages/credit/debt/loans, 10, 21, 28, 29, 33, 47, 51, 53, 68, 80, 120, 125, 164n12, 165n1. *See also* duties, levies, national debt, taxes

Moses and Pharoah, 119–20, 121, 126–27, 178n17

motherhood, 38–41, 84, 130, 132–37, 141, 148, 161n2, 178n17

multi-racial families, 176n5

mutual aid, 120, 137, 142–43

narration and narratives. *See* everydayness (lived experiences) (everyday narratives); literature and economics

national debt, duties, levies, taxes, 5, 109–12. *See also* debt/credit/loans/mortgages

nature, 62, 65–68, 79, 101, 105

Neary, Janet: *Fugitive Testimony*, 164n12

negro cloth, 60, 75, 93–95, 96, 104, 173n6

Nembhard, Jessica Gordon, 11, 136–37, 142, 143, 177n13

"Nessus-robe," 77

New England, 33, 72–73, 156. *See also* labor, enslaved/wage compared; Larcom, Lucy; Lowell mills

Newman, Virginia, 95
New Orleans, 14, 19, 41, 121, 123, 124
Norcom, James, 96
Northampton Association of Education and Industry, 152
"North and South" (anonymous), 170n8
North Carolina, 89–90
The Northeast, 19. *See also* New England
Northrup, Solomon: *Twelve Years a Slave*, 104–5
North/South compared, Harriet, Jacobs: abolitionism and, 75–76; accounting and, 49, 79; class and, 69; freedom and, 89; Harper and, 134; immorality and, 45; inheritance and, 123–25; Truth and, 152. *See also* labor, enslaved/wage compared; New England; three-fifths compromise
Nyong'o, Tavia: "Racial Kitsch and Black Performance," 168n17

O'Brien, Colleen, 125, 141
Osteen, Mark: *The New Economic Criticism*, 179n2

Painter, Nell Irvin, 165n2
paper, 109, 112, 175nn16,18
papers, free, 129
partus sequitur ventrem, 122
paternalism, 32–33
Penningroth, Dylan C.: *Claims of Kinfolk*, 109, 173n3
Penny, Virginia, 180n5
perception. *See* bodies and sensations; phenomenology; subject positions (subjectivity/self)
personhood: emancipation and, 129; inherited clothing and, 95;perception and, 59; property and, 21, 28, 33, 86, 87–88, 99, 111, 114–15; "Weaving" and, 74. *See also* subject positions (subjectivity/self); three-fifths compromise
Peterson, Carla L., 119, 125, 127, 177n6; "Reconstructing the Nation," 124
phenomenology, 17, 18, 67, 70–72, 78, 82–83, 88, 116, 151, 169n4. *See also* bodies and sensations; Merleau-Ponty, Maurice
Philadelphia, 5, 9
Phillips, U. B.: "The Economic Cost of Slaveholding in the Cotton Belt," 162n6
Phillips, Wendell, 141
Pierpoint, Jacqueline: "Framing the Magdalen," 165n3
"pocket books," 28, 33, 39, 41–42, 44, 45–46, 53.
See also accounting and bookkeeping as control; ledgers
poetry, anti-slavery, 62, 119, 140, 170n8, 172n21
politics. *See* Black citizenship, economic; Black communities and relationships
possessive individualism, 114–15
Potter, Eliza: *A Hairdresser's Experience in the High Life*, 152–53, 164n12
Pratt, Lloyd: *Archives of American Time*, 173n9
preprinted forms, 28, 33, 61
print culture, 53–54, 175n16, 176n1. *See also* advertisements for fugitives
"proletarian grotesque," 171n12
property: account books and, 28; as characteristic, 173n4; children's souls and, 173n5; definition of, 86–87, 173n4; domestic space and, 112–13; enslaved community and, 172n3; freedom and, 114–16, 149;
gender/sexuality and, 19, 88, 92, 105, 107; ideological, 174n13; knowledge of, 14, 19, 87, 89, 90, 99–100, 102–3, 105, 107–8, 112–16; law and, 72–74, 85–87, 91, 92; personhood and, 21, 28, 33, 86, 87–88, 99, 111, 114–15; racialization and, 88–89, 92, 105, 107; seamstresses as, 99–100; social dimensions of, 86–87; space and, 92, 112–13; *Uncle Tom's Cabin* and, 175n17; weaponized, 90; whiteness and, 73–74, 173n5. *See also* Harper, Frances Ellen Watkins; inheritance; Jacobs, Harriet; landownership
proslavery positions, 164n12. *See also* anti/proslavery positions (racial politics)
Proudhon, Pierre Joseph, 5
Putzi, Jennifer: "Poets of the Loom, Spinners of Verse," 169n3

Quakers, 134, 137, 139, 144, 161n2, 177n7

racialization/racism: bodies and, 169n4; capitalism and, 138, 164n12; clothing and, 98–99, 109, 110; cotton and, 19; COVID-19 pandemic and, 158; domesticity and, 90, 92; economic injustice and, 13; everyday experience and, 171n15; matriliny and, 133; objects and, 88; objects/space and, 88; politics and, 142–43; property and, 88–89, 92, 105, 107; racial capitalism *versus*, 9; "racist canceling out," 172n21; "reconstruction" and, 137–38; slavery's capitalism and, 13; subjective approaches and, 171n15; taxation and, 110; *Uncle Tom's Cabin* and, 25–26, 54–55; "Weav-

INDEX

ing" and, 14, 58–59, 66, 68, 74, 79–80, 82, 83–84; white bodies and, 79–80; women writers and, 149; worlds of women and, 83–84. *See also* anti/proslavery positions (racial politics); Black uplift/development; bodies and sensations; class; slavery's capitalism; whiteness

racial politics. *See* anti/proslavery positions

radical politics, 81–82. *See also* Black Radical Tradition

reading practices, 42–43

realism, 154

Reconstruction: economics and, 145, 176n2; enslaved/white laborers and, 35; *Minnie's Sacrifice* and, 37, 124, 132, 137, 140, 176n3, 178n17; racism/sexism and, 137–38; "shadows of the past" and, 118; women writers and, 154–56. *See also* ante/postbellum compared; Black communities and relationships; Harper, Frances Ellen Watkins

reparations, 2, 118, 121, 125, 130, 139–40, 148, 149, 159

republicanism, 167n12

resource development, 144–45

The Revolution (newspaper), 76

Reynolds, David: *Mightier than the Sword*, 167n13

Rhode Island, 156

Ricardo, David, 151

Robbins, Sarah, 42–43

Robinson, Cedric J.: *Black Marxism: The Making of the Black Radical Tradition*, 9, 176n4

Rockman, Seth, 2, 93, 161n2; "The Market, Utility, and Slavery in Southern Legal Thought," *Slavery's Capitalism: A New History of American Economic Development*, 165n1; "Negro Cloth: Mastering the Market for Slave Clothing in Antebellum America," 93–94

Roediger, David R., 69, 143; *The Wages of Whiteness*, 169n5

Rosenthal, Caitlin, 28–29, 36–37, 61–62; *Accounting for Slavery*, 165n2

Rounmain, Ernest, 124

Ruffin, Valerie L., 178n17

Rutkowski, Alice: "Leaving the Good Mother," 178n17

Saint-Domingue, 19, 121, 122–23, 125, 177n12

Samuels, Shirley, 26

Santamarina, Xiomara, 153; *Belabored Professions*, 164n12

Sara W. (poet): "The Slave's Revenge" (Sarah W.), 170n8

scholarship, 152–153. *See also* economic theory/discourse; "histories of the present"; literary form and analysis; *individual scholars*; overviews, 8–11, 161n3, 163n11; accounting and, 165n2, 167n10; Child and, 5; clothing, 164n12; domesticity, 11, 12, 15; global and transnational contexts, 9, 10–11; labor, enslaved/wage compared, 10, 12; legal policy and, 159; on literature and economics, 11–16, 179nn1–2, 180nn3–4; money, 178n20; morality *versus* economics and, 165n2; 19th century, 159, 164n13; sentimentality/domesticity/market and, 166n6; 20th and 21st century, 2, 4–5, 8, 10, 71, 159; white, working-class literature and, 58; whiteness and, 58–59; women writers and, 164n12

Schuller, Kyla, 138, 166n6

Scottish philosophers, 165n5

seamstresses and sewing, 58, 99–100; *Incidents* and, 19, 85, 87, 88, 91–92, 95, 96, 99–100, 102, 104, 105, 106, 114, 116, 174n14

"Second Slavery," 123

self. *See* identity; personhood; subject positions (subjectivity/self)

Senchyne, Jonathan: *The Intimacy of Paper*, 175n16

sentimentalism: accounting and, 40; actual accounting and, 165n3; domesticity/market and, 166n6, 168n16; Harper and, 119, 124, 125, 127, 135; literary form and analysis, 54–55; money and wealth and, 119, 124, 125, 127;

sentimentalism (*continued*)
overviews, 2, 3, 16–17, 150, 159; racialization, 54–55; Stowe and, 18, 22–26, 33, 35–43, 45, 49–50, 51, 53–56, 166n6

settler colonialism, 16

Seybold, Matt: *The Routledge Companion to Literature and Economics*, 179n2

shadow accounts, 18, 23, 25–26, 29, 31, 33, 36–38, 40, 41, 45, 47–49, 53, 54–55, 66. *See also* Stowe, Harriet Beecher

Shiller, Robert J.: *Narrative Economics*, 179n2

Sigourney, Lydia: "Indian Names," 81

slave markets (auctions), 37–38, 41, 135

slave owners. *See* enslavers

slavery. *See* enslaved people; enslavers; labor, enslaved and formerly enslaved; labor, enslaved/wage compared; slavery's capitalism; slave traders/catchers (agents of slavery)

slavery's capitalism: Civil War and, 78; defined, 2, 9–10, 162nn7,9; historicized, 131–32, 162n9; scholarship and, 8–11; overviews, 149–50, 157–58;Truth and, 152; women writers and, 13–14, 16–17, 137–38, 149–59, 161n2. *See also* abolition (emancipation); ante/postbellum compared; capitalism (economics); class; cotton; gender/sexuality; labor, enslaved and formerly enslaved; morality *versus* economics; property; racialization/racism; scholarship; *individual women writers*

slave trade (human trafficking), 41, 123, 148, 161n2, 181n10

slave traders/catchers (agents of slavery), 11, 21, 36, 38–39, 40, 41, 44, 59, 99, 148

Smallwood, Stephanie E., 165n2

Smith, Adam, 5, 151, 165n5

Snorton, C. Riley: *Black on Both Sides*, 98

Snyder, Mariah: Work Progress Administration interview, 75

socialism, 5, 156–58, 181n9

the South. *See* Louisiana; North/South compared

southern literature, 15, 164n12

space: accounting/ledgers and, 61; accounting/ledgers and, 29, 32; Chace and, 156; cotton market and, 59; *Incidents* and, 97, 98, 99, 100–4, 106–8, 112–13; *Minnie's Sacrifice* and, 138, 140; objects/race and, 88; overviews, 2, 14, 17; property and, 92, 112–13; "Weaving" and, 66, 79, 170n10. *See also* bodies and sensations; domesticity (homemaking)

Spillers, Hortense J., 165n2

spinning, 16, 66, 69, 75, 76, 170n10. *See also* Larcom, Lucy

Spires, Derrick R., 138

Stampp, Kenneth: *The Peculiar Institution: Slavery in the Ante-Bellum South*, 9

Stancliff, Michael, 176n3

Stanley, Amy Dru: *From Bondage to Contract: Wage Labor, Marriage, and the Market in the Age of Slave Emancipation*, 10

Stansell, Christine: *City of Women*, 10

Steckel, Richard H., 169n6

Stewart, Maria, 161n2

Stone, Lucy, 156

Stowe, Calvin, 167n13

Stowe, Harriet Beecher: abolition (emancipation), 9, 45, 48–49, 54–55; abolitionism/activism, 22, 24, 25, 26, 31–32, 34, 35, 36, 45–46; accounting as control, 24–25, 27, 28, 32–45, 47–48, 51, 52, 166nn7,8, 168n16; accounting as fiction, 14, 48, 55–56; anti/proslavery positions (racial politics), 15, 18, 23–26, 35–36, 45–56, 168n18; commodification of labor, 166n7, 167n11; consumerism/domestic fiction, 169n2; culture industry and, 167n12, 169n2; debt and, 21, 33, 47, 51, 165n1; domesticity and, 50–53, 132, 166n6, 168n16, 175n17; economic criticism *versus* theory, 14, 20; economic value, transformation of, 164n14; enslavers, 15, 36–45; forced reproductive labor, 164n12; free/unfree states, 49; historical frameworks, 16; *Incidents* compared, 175n17; influences on, 7–8, 155–56; Larcom on, 172n18; ledgers, 7, 18, 22–45, 30f; *Minnie's Sacrifice* compared, 132; morality *versus* economics, 31–32, 33–34, 38–45; property, 175n17; Scottish philosophers, 165n5; sentimentalism, 18, 22–26, 33, 35–43, 45, 49–50, 51, 53–56, 166n6; shadow accounts, 18, 23–27, 29–31, 33–38, 40–41, 45, 47, 48–49, 53–56

Stowe, Harriet Beecher other works: *A Key to Uncle Tom's Cabin*, 23; "Mayflower," 172n18

subject positions (subjectivity/self): abolition (emancipation) and, 129; bodies and, 171n11, 172n20; clothing and, 94–96; contracts and, 10; freedom and, 113–14; lived body and, 169n4, 171n11,17; Merleau-Ponty and, 169n4; *Minnie's Sacrifice* and, 119; money and, 178n19; narration and, 71; property knowledge and, 115–16; sentimentalism and, 40; slavery's capitalism and, 13, 171n15; "The Slave's Revenge" and, 170n8; "Weaving" and, 18, 58–59, 62, 63, 67–68, 70–72, 79–81; women factory workers and, 169n5. *See also* bodies and sensations; everydayness; identity; knowledge; mental activity as labor; personhood

suffrage, 49, 86, 118, 138, 140–43, 148

Sumner, Charles, 161n2

taxes, duties, levies, national debt, 5, 109–12. *See also* debt/credit/loans/mortgages

textiles. *See* cloth/fabric/textiles

"There Must Be Something Wrong" (anonymous), 170n8

Thistle, Jethro, 72

three-fifths compromise, 110–12

time, 38, 44, 61, 69, 82, 88, 173n9

Tomich, Dale, 123

Tompkins, Jane: *Sensational Designs: The Cultural Work of American Fiction 1790–1860*, 46

toys, 85, 89, 102–3, 105–7, 113, 173n11, 174n14
Tracey, Karen: *Plots and Proposals*, 177n8
"tragic mulatta" trope, 119, 128, 176n5
transnational contexts. *See* global and transnational contexts
Truth, Sojourner: influences on, 7–8; *Narrative of Sojourner Truth*, 152–53, 156, 164n12
Turner, Nat, 90, 92
Tyson, Thomas N., 28, 167n10

Uncle Tom's Cabin. See Stowe, Harriet Beecher
Underground Railroad, 156. *See also* fugitives
Unionist (periodical), 6
university system, 151. *See also* education and schools
upper class/elites, 92, 151, 153. *See also* enslavers; money and wealth
Urakova, Alexandra: "*I* Do Not Want Her, I Am Sure," 168n17
U.S. constitution, 111
utopian community, 152

Valley Falls Company, 156, 180n8
Voice of Industry (paper), 170n8
voting rights (suffrage), 49, 86, 118, 138, 140–43, 148

"Wanted ads," 53–54
Warren, Calvin L: *Ontological Terror: Blackness, Nihilism, and Emancipation*, 113–14
Watson, Henry, 8
wealth. *See* money and wealth
Weaver, Elisha, 118
"Weaving." *See* Larcom, Lucy
Weinberg, Alys Eve, 11
Weld, T. D., Grimké, A., Grimké, S. M.: *American Slavery as It Is: Testimony of a Thousand Witnesses*, 6–8, 13–14, 17–18, 37
West Indian slavery, 8–9
Whitehead, Celia B.: *Free Society: A Periodical of Anarchist Thought, Work, and Literature*, 157
whiteness: antislavery poetry and, 171n16; cotton and, 59, 173n5; fear of wage labor and, 169n5; female identity and, 80; law and, 73–74; *Minnie's Sacrifice* and, 128–31, 133–34; property and

race and, 173n5. *See also under* Larcom, Lucy; white supremacy; white women
white supremacy, 54, 82, 147, 176n5
white women, 50–53. *See also* abolitionism/activism; consumption (consumerism); enslavers, women; working-class women, white; *individual women writers*
Williams, Andreá, 177n6
Williams, Eric: *Capitalism and Slavery*, 8–9
Wilson, Harriet, 164n12
women's histories, 10–11
women's rights, 12, 76, 141. *See also* voting rights (suffrage)
women writers: economic theory/discourse and, 13–16, 149–59; overviews, 1–3, 12, 16–18; slavery's benefits and, 15; slavery's capitalism and, 13–14, 16–17, 137–38, 149–59, 161n2; southern, 164n12; working-class, 2, 78, 170n8, 172n21. *See also* abolitionism/activism; everydayness (lived experiences) (everyday narratives); imagination; literary form and analysis; literature and economics; scholarship; *individual women writers*
Woodmansee, Martha: *The New Economic Criticism*, 179n2
workers' rights, 34
working class: abolitionism and, 34–35, 76, 143, 156, 167n12, 170n8; Black clothing, 98; Harper on, 137; statistics, 76; suffrage and, 141–42; "Weaving" and, 78; women's rights and, 12. *See also* gender/sexuality; labor, enslaved/wage compared; labor, writing and (civilizers and the pen); Larcom, Lucy; racialization/racism; seamstresses and sewing.
working-class women, white, 18, 68–83
working-class women writers, 2, 78, 152–54, 170n8, 172n21
Wright, Gavin: *The Political Economy of the Cotton South: Households, Markets, and Wealth in the Nineteenth Century*, 9
Wyman, Lillie Buffum Chace, 156–57

Yancy, George, 79, 82
Young, Iris Marion, 67, 171n11

www.ingramcontent.com/pod-product-compliance
Lightning Source LLC
Chambersburg PA
CBHW021845230426
43669CB00008B/1093